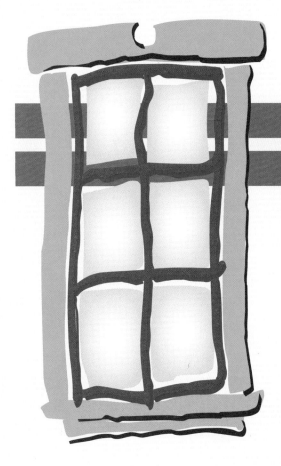

MICROSOFT
ACCESS 97

A TUTORIAL
TO ACCOMPANY
PETER NORTON'S
INTRODUCTION
TO COMPUTERS

GLENCOE
McGraw-Hill

New York, New York   Columbus, Ohio   Woodland Hills, California   Peoria, Illinois

Microsoft Access 97
A Tutorial to Accompany
Peter Norton's Introduction to Computers

Glencoe/McGraw-Hill

A Division of The **McGraw·Hill** Companies

Send all inquiries to:
Glencoe/McGraw-Hill
936 Eastwind Drive
Westerville, OH 43081

ISBN 0-02-804352-9

Development: FSCreations, Inc.
Production: MicroPublishing

Microsoft Office 97 and *Microsoft Access 97* are registered trademarks of Microsoft Corporation.

4 5 6 7 8 9 083 02 01 00 99

C ONTENTS

Preface, ix

LESSON 1
INTRODUCING ACCESS   2

Objectives, 2
Introducing Databases, 3
Launching the Program, 5
  Starting Microsoft Access, 5
Learning Your Way Around Access, 8
  Issuing Commands by Using the Menus, 8
  Contending with Dialog Boxes, 11
  The Toolbars: Command Shortcuts for Mouse Users, 12
Opening a Database, 15
  The Database Window, 16
Objects: The Components of Access, 16
  The Database Table, 16
  Queries: Extracting the Data You Need, 19
  Forms: Viewing, Entering, and Editing Data More Easily, 20
  Reports and Mailing Labels: Generating Printed Output, 22
  Macros and Modules, 23
Printing an Access Report, 23
  Printing a Report, 23
Getting Help When You Need It, 24
  Using the Office Assistant, 24
  Using Contents and Index, 26
  Using ScreenTips, 30
Quitting Access, 31
  Exiting the Program, 32
Lesson Summary and Exercises, 33
  New Terms to Remember, 34
  Matching Exercise, 35
  Completion Exercise, 36
  Short-Answer Questions, 36
  Application Projects, 37

LESSON 2
DESIGNING AND CREATING DATABASES   38

Objectives, 38
Planning Ahead, 39
  Determining the Purpose of the Database, 39
  Determining the Categories of Information You Need, 40
  Determining How Many Tables You Need, 40
  Determining How Tables Will Work Together, 41
Creating a Database, 42
Creating Tables, 44
  Creating a Table with the Table Wizard, 44
  Creating Tables in Table Design View, 50

Selecting Data Types, 52
Picking Field Sizes, 55
Setting Other Field Properties, 56
Choosing a Primary Key, 58
Saving the Table Design, 59
Modifying the Table Design, 60
Adding Captions to Fields, 61
Adding and Removing Fields, 62
Moving a Field, 63
Lesson Summary and Exercises, 65
New Terms to Remember, 66
Matching Exercise, 66
Completion Exercise, 67
Short-Answer Questions, 67
Application Projects, 68

LESSON 3
ADDING AND MAINTAINING DATA IN
DATASHEET VIEW   70

Objectives, 70
Adding Data to a Table, 71
Opening the Table, 71
Adding a Record, 73
Adding Additional Records, 75
Retrieving Data from Another Table, 76
Copying Data from Another Table, 77
Pasting Data into a Table, 78
Copying Data from Another Table, 79
Copying Tables from Another Database, 80
Importing a Table, 80
Editing and Viewing Records in the Datasheet, 81
Moving from Record to Record, 82
Moving from Field to Field, 83
Editing Records, 84
Searching for Records Based on Their Contents, 88
Finding Values in the Table, 88
Replacing Values in the Table, 90
Changing the Datasheet Display, 91
Changing Column Widths, 92
Changing Row Heights, 93
Changing the Order of Fields, 94
Hiding Columns, 95
Freezing Columns, 96
Canceling Changes to the Datasheet Layout, 97
Lesson Summary and Exercises, 98
New Terms to Remember, 99
Matching Exercise, 99
Completion Exercise, 100
Short-Answer Questions, 100
Application Projects, 101

LESSON 4
**RETRIEVING THE DATA YOU NEED: SORTING
AND SELECTING RECORDS**   **104**

Objectives, 104
Sorting and Selecting Data, 105
Using the Sort Commands, 106
    Sorting Your Table, 106
Filtering Your Data, 109
    Using the Filter By Selection Method, 109
    Using the Filter By Form Method, 111
    Using Filter For Input, 116
    Using Advanced Filter/Sort, 117
Designing Basic Queries, 121
    Setting Up a Simple Query, 122
    Modifying and Saving a Query, 125
    Adding and Deleting Fields from Query Design View, 126
    Opening a Saved Query, 128
Querying Multiple Tables, 129
    Building a Multi-Table Query, 129
    Querying for Blank Data, 132
Lesson Summary and Exercises, 134
    New Terms to Remember, 135
    Matching Exercise, 135
    Completion Exercise, 136
    Short-Answer Questions, 136
    Application Projects, 137

LESSON 5
**VIEWING, ENTERING, AND EDITING DATA
WITH FORMS**   **138**

Objectives, 138
When and Why to Use Forms, 139
Creating an AutoForm, 140
    Exploring an AutoForm, 140
Using the Form Wizard, 143
    Creating a Columnar Form with the Form Wizard, 143
    Switching from Form to Datasheet View, 147
    Building a Tabular Form with the Form Wizard, 148
Adding and Editing Data by Use of Forms, 150
    Adding Data Using a Form, 150
    Editing Records Using a Form, 151
Sorting and Selecting Data with Forms, 153
    Sorting Records Through a Form, 153
    Selecting Records Through a Form, 154
Previewing and Printing Forms, 156
    Generating a Printout of a Form, 156
Lesson Summary and Exercises, 158
    New Terms to Remember, 159
    Matching Exercise, 159
    Completion Exercise, 160
    Short-Answer Questions, 160
    Application Projects, 161

LESSON 6
GENERATING REPORTS AND MAILING
LABELS **162**

Objectives, 162
When and Why to Use Reports, 163
Creating an AutoReport, 163
 Exploring an AutoReport, 164
 Viewing Pages in the Report, 166
Using the Report Wizard, 168
 Constructing a Columnar Report with the Report Wizard, 168
 Creating Tabular Reports, 172
Creating Totals in Reports, 176
 Building a Report with Totals, 177
 Adding Totals and Subtotals to the Report, 178
Generating Mailing Labels, 180
 Selecting Mailing Label Forms and Appearance, 180
 Arranging Fields on the Labels, 182
 Sorting Mailing Labels, 183
Printing Reports and Mailing Labels, 184
Lesson Summary and Exercises, 186
 New Terms to Remember, 187
 Matching Exercise, 188
 Completion Exercise, 189
 Short-Answer Questions, 190
 Application Projects, 191

LESSON 7
ADVANCED TOPICS **192**

Objectives, 192
Modifying Forms in Design View, 193
 Sections in Design View, 193
 Working in Design View, 195
 Selecting Form Controls, 199
 Changing Detail Controls in Design View, 201
 Changing the Tab Order, 204
 Modifying the Appearance of the Detail Section, 205
Modifying Reports in Design View, 208
 Viewing a Report in Design View, 208
 Changing the Report Header and Page Footer, 209
 Changing Margins for a Report, 209
 Adjusting Header Widths and Detail Controls, 210
 Resizing Lines in Design View, 212
 Aligning Headings, 213
Working with Multiple Tables, 214
 Identifying Relationships Between Tables, 214
 Understanding Referential Integrity, 216
 Maintaining Referential Integrity, 219
Creating Main Forms and Subforms, 220
Lesson Summary and Exercises, 223
 New Terms to Remember, 224
 Matching Exercise, 224
 Completion Exercise, 225
 Short-Answer Questions, 225
 Application Projects, 226

LESSON 8
EXPLORING HYPERLINKS
AND THE WEB   228

Objectives, 228
Exploring the Web Toolbar, 229
Creating Hyperlinks, 231
    Linking to Another Object, 231
    Linking to Another Database, 236
    Linking to a Web Site, 244
Navigating on the Web, 246
    Visiting a Web Site, 246
    Accessing the Search Page, 247
    Revisiting Favorite Places, 250
Creating Your Own Web Page, 252
Publishing Your Web Page, 256
Lesson Summary and Exercises, 257
    New Terms to Remember, 258
    Matching Exercise, 258
    Completion Exercise, 259
    Short-Answer Questions, 259
    Application Projects, 260

COMMAND SUMMARY   262

GLOSSARY   270

INDEX   274

Microsoft Access 97 Tutorial, one of the instructional tools that complements Peter Norton's *Introduction to Computers,* covers the basic features of Access 97. Glencoe and Peter Norton have teamed up to provide this tutorial and its ancillaries to help you become a knowledgeable, empowered end user. After you complete this tutorial, you will be able to create and modify Access documents and to explore hyperlinks and the World Wide Web.

STRUCTURE AND FORMAT OF THE ACCESS 97 TUTORIAL

Microsoft Access 97 Tutorial covers a range of functions and techniques and provides hands-on opportunities for you to practice and apply your skills. Each lesson in *Microsoft Access 97 Tutorial* includes the following:

- *Contents and Objectives.* The Contents and Objectives provide an overview of the Access features you will learn in the lesson.

- *Explanations of important concepts.* Each section of each lesson begins with a brief explanation of the concept or software feature covered in that lesson. The explanations help you understand "the big picture" as you learn each new Access 97 feature.

- *New terms.* An important part of learning about computers is learning the terminology. Each new term in the tutorial appears in boldface, is defined the first time it is used, and appears in the margin. As you encounter these words, read their definitions carefully. If you encounter the same word later and have forgotten its meaning, you can look up the word in the Glossary.

- *Hands On activities.* Because most of us learn best by doing, each explanation is followed by a hands-on activity that includes step-by-step instructions, which you complete at the computer. Integrated in the steps are notes, tips, and Office Assistant hints to help you learn Access 97.

- *Illustrations.* Many figures point out features on the screen and illustrate what your screen should look like after you complete important steps.

- *Lesson Summary.* At the end of each lesson, a Lesson Summary reviews the major topics covered in the lesson. You can use the Lesson Summary as a study guide.

- *New Terms to Remember.* All the new terms introduced in the lesson are identified. Verify that you can define each term.

- *Review exercises.* At the end of each lesson are three types of objective questions: a Matching Exercise, a Completion Exercise, and Short-Answer Questions. When you complete these exercises, you can verify that you have learned all the concepts and skills that have been covered in the lesson.

- *Application Projects.* The Application Projects provide additional hands-on practice to apply your problem-solving skills and your skills to use Access 97 to create or modify actual Access 97 documents.

■ *Command Summary, Glossary, and Index.* A Command Summary, a Glossary, and an Index appear at the back of the tutorial. The Command Summary reviews both mouse and keyboard techniques for completing Access 97 tasks. Toolbar buttons are included where appropriate. Use the Glossary to look up terms that you don't understand and the Index to find specific information.

■ *Student Data Disk.* Attached to the inside back cover of this tutorial you will find a 3½" disk called the Student Data Disk. This disk contains Access 97 files for you to use as you complete the hands-on activities and the end-of-lesson activities. Before you use the Student Data Disk, make a backup copy immediately. If you run out of storage space as you use your Student Data Disk to complete the activities in this tutorial, save additional files to a blank formatted disk.

After you complete this tutorial, you will be able to create, process, and present information in a variety of ways using Access 97, thus helping you to become a highly productive employee in today's workforce.

ABOUT PETER NORTON

Peter Norton is a pioneering software developer and an author. Norton's Desktop for Windows, Utilities, Backup, AntiVirus and other utility programs are installed worldwide on millions of personal computers. His *Inside the IBM PC* and *DOS Guide* have helped countless individuals understand computers from the inside out.

Glencoe teamed up with Peter Norton to help you better understand the role computers play in your life now and in the future. As you begin to work in your chosen profession, you may use this tutorial now and later as a reference book.

REVIEWERS

Many thanks are due to Jim Johnson, Valencia Community College—West, Orlando, Florida; Sandra Lehmann, Moraine Park Technical College, Fond du Lac, Wisconsin; Patsy Malavite, The University of Akron—Wayne College, Orrville, Ohio; and Larry Manning, Tyler Junior College, Tyler, Texas, who reviewed the manuscript and provided recommendations to improve the tutorial.

MICROSOFT

ACCESS 97

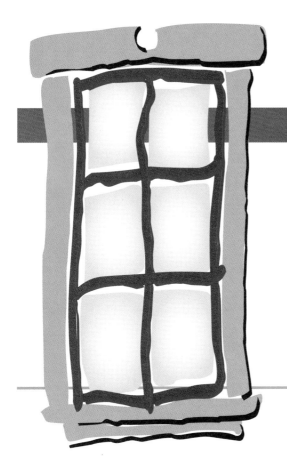

OBJECTIVES

After you complete this lesson, you will be able to do the following:

- *Understand the uses of databases and some basics about how they work.*
- *Start the Access program.*
- *Find your way around Access.*
- *Open a database.*
- *Identify the basic components of an Access database.*
- *Print an Access report.*
- *Get online help from Access when you need it.*
- *Quit Access when you're finished working with it for the day.*

CONTENTS

Introducing Databases

Launching the Program

Learning Your Way Around Access

Opening a Database

Objects: The Components of Access

Printing an Access Report

Getting Help When You Need It

Quitting Access

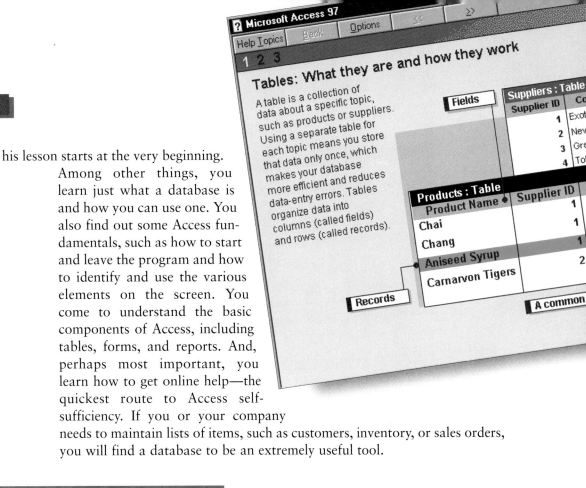

This lesson starts at the very beginning. Among other things, you learn just what a database is and how you can use one. You also find out some Access fundamentals, such as how to start and leave the program and how to identify and use the various elements on the screen. You come to understand the basic components of Access, including tables, forms, and reports. And, perhaps most important, you learn how to get online help—the quickest route to Access self-sufficiency. If you or your company needs to maintain lists of items, such as customers, inventory, or sales orders, you will find a database to be an extremely useful tool.

INTRODUCING DATABASES

database An organized collection of information about similar entities. In Access, database also means a collection of objects—such as reports, forms, tables, and queries—associated with a particular topic.

DBMS (database management system) A system for storing and manipulating the data in a database.

You may have only a hazy idea, or no idea, about what a database is. Quite simply, a **database** is an organized collection of data about similar things—such as employees, customers, or inventory items. You probably use some kind of manual database on a daily basis, whether it's a phone book, your office Rolodex, or a paper filing system.

As you begin to work with databases, you may encounter the term **DBMS**, for **database management system**—a system for storing and manipulating the data in a database.

An electronic database program such as Access lets you do many of the same things you do with manual systems—such as storing, retrieving, and manipulating information. What are the advantages of maintaining a database on a computer? While it's not difficult to set up a database with Access, the job does require some advance planning, and transferring your data from a manual to a computerized system can be a significant chore. The real benefits of electronic databases are threefold: First, they can store massive amounts of data in a very small amount of space. Second, they enable you to manipulate your data with ease, sorting it into the desired order. (You might want to arrange customers alphabetically by last name sometimes, and in order by ZIP Code at other times.) And third, you can quickly extract just the information you need for the task at hand. (For example, you may decide to hunt down all customers whose bills are past due.) Figure 1-1 shows an example of a customer table from a database.

field

BE FRUITFUL CUSTOMER LIST

Last Name	First Name	Address	City	State	ZIP Code
Apfelbaum	Franklin	1777 Lois Ln.	Rock Creek	NC	28333-1234
Bechdel	Alice	7374 Backwoods Rd.	Sebastopol	CA	97777-1111
Criton	Will	1 Oak Place	Providence	RI	02900-2338
Dempster	Anne	25 Forest Knoll	Santa Rosa	CA	99887-2355
Everett	Joan	2234 Hanley Place	Baltimore	MD	21122-5634
Frankel	James	32123 Overlook Ave.	Portland	OR	99876-2389
Guggenheim	Mason	75 Grizzly Peak Blvd.	Orinda	CA	94700-5412
Hatfield	Emma	1314 23rd Ave.	Biddeford	ME	57432-6034

record

FIGURE 1-1

Sample table from a database

tables Receptacles for data organized into a series of columns (fields) and rows (records).

fields Columns in a table that contain categories of data.

records Rows in a table that contain the set of fields for one particular entity.

relational databases Database programs that let you link two or more tables in order to share data between them.

A database is not just any accumulation of data, but a collection of related data stored in a very particular format. (Imagine the difference between a large file drawer haphazardly stuffed with documents in no particular order and a neat file drawer containing labeled file folders—in alphabetical order—full of documents. Which is more useful?) In Access, data is stored in **tables**. Tables organize information into a series of **fields** (columns) that contain categories of data and **records** (rows) that contain the set of fields for one particular entity. The table shown in Figure 1-1 includes fields for each customer's last name, first name, address, city, state, and ZIP Code. In this case, a record consists of all fields that apply to a single customer. For example, the first record includes all the information pertaining to Franklin Apfelbaum; the second record includes all the information about Alice Bechdel; and so forth. (You'll learn how to design tables in the next lesson, and you'll learn how to enter data into tables in Lesson 3.)

Most Access databases will actually contain one or more tables that you can use together when the need arises. If you have more than one general category of information—such as customer addresses and customer orders—it's best to place them in separate tables. While you work, you may require data from multiple tables; for example, you might want to list both customer addresses and orders on an invoice form. You can do this easily in Access, provided that the tables include common fields by which they can be linked.

For example, if both your customer address and order tables include a field that contains customer ID numbers, Access can find each customer's orders by scanning the order table for records with the matching customer ID number. This arrangement saves you from having to store copies of the customer name and address data in several places. It streamlines your database by eliminating the duplication of data and at the same time reduces the risk of data entry error. (If you enter a name only once, you are less likely to make a mistake.) Database programs that let you link, or relate, two tables in this manner are known as **relational databases**. You'll learn more about working with multiple tables in Lessons 2 and 7.

LAUNCHING THE PROGRAM

Before you can begin to know the Access database, you need to start the program, which involves just a few easy steps.

STARTING MICROSOFT ACCESS

In this section, you start Access, bringing it up on the screen so you can acquaint yourself with its features firsthand.

HANDS ON

1. Turn on your computer.

After a moment, you should see the Windows 95 Desktop, similar to the one in Figure 1-2.

Desktop icons

The Start button

FIGURE 1-2
The Microsoft Windows 95 Desktop

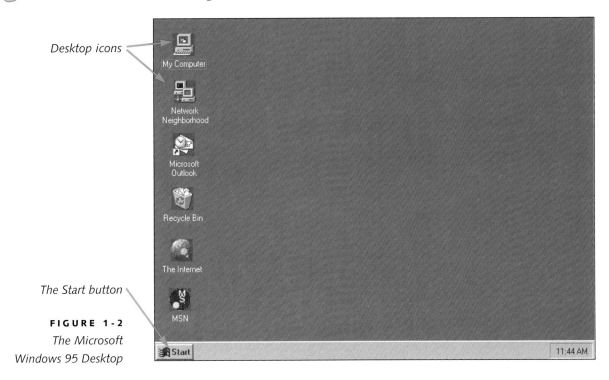

2. Click the Start button on the taskbar.

NOTE

Click *means to move your mouse until the mouse pointer is located over the desired option or item and then press and quickly release the left mouse button.* **Double-click** *means press and quickly release the left mouse button twice in rapid succession.* **Right-click** *means to press and quickly release the right mouse button.*

click A mouse action in which you move the mouse until the mouse pointer is located over the desired option or item and then press and quickly release the left mouse button.

3. Point to Programs.

4. Point to Microsoft Access, as shown in Figure 1-3.

5. Click Microsoft Access.

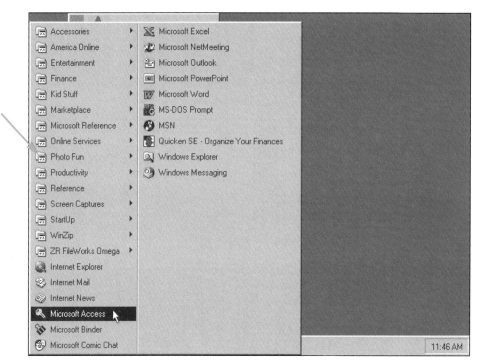

The Programs menu

F I G U R E   1 - 3
*The Windows 95
Programs menu*

N O T E   *If you can't find Microsoft Access on the Programs menu, look for it on the Microsoft Office 97 menu.*

T I P   *Windows 95 and Microsoft Office give several ways to start programs. Your Desktop may have a shortcut icon to launch Microsoft Access or there may be an Office Shortcut Bar on your screen. You may double-click the shortcut icon to start Access, but don't use the Office Shortcut Bar until you are more familiar with the program and the databases on your disk.*

double-click A mouse action in which you press and quickly release the left mouse button twice in rapid succession with the mouse pointer over your selection.

right-click A mouse action in which you press and quickly release the right mouse button.

You'll see an hourglass icon, then the Microsoft Access identifying screen, and finally the Microsoft Access initial dialog box, as shown in Figure 1-4. This dialog box lets you start a new database file or work with an existing one.

6. For the moment, click the Cancel button to remove the dialog box.

You'll see the Microsoft Access startup window, as shown in Figure 1-5.

In the startup window, many features are not yet available because you haven't opened a database. For example, note that if you click the Edit menu, all of the options beneath it are grayed (meaning that they're currently disabled). As you'll soon find out, the available Access options change depending on what you're doing at the moment.

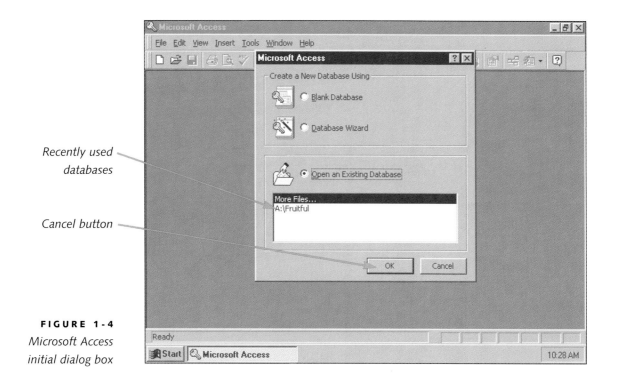

Recently used
databases

Cancel button

FIGURE 1-4
*Microsoft Access
initial dialog box*

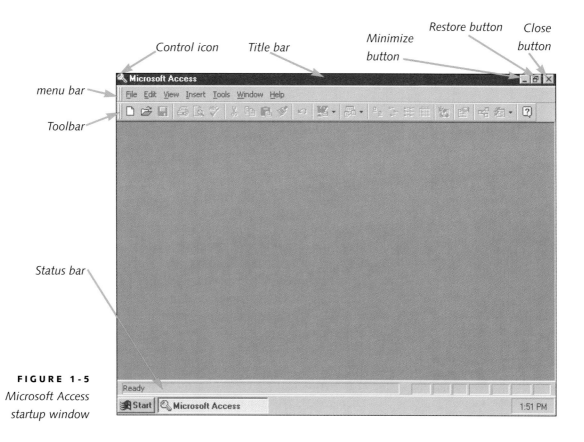

Control icon   Title bar   Minimize   Restore button   Close
                                            button   button

menu bar

Toolbar

Status bar

FIGURE 1-5
*Microsoft Access
startup window*

LEARNING YOUR WAY AROUND ACCESS

In this section, you'll learn how to identify and use the elements of the Access screen. If you've worked with other Windows 95 programs before, many of these items should be familiar to you. Even if you haven't, the Access interface is easy to understand and easy to use. Table 1-1 highlights the main features of the Access screen.

TABLE 1-1: THE ACCESS SCREEN

Title bar	Contains the Control icon, the name of the program, and the Minimize, Maximize, Restore, and Close buttons.
Control icon	Clicking this icon displays a menu which allows you to manipulate the window. Double-clicking this icon closes the window.
Minimize button	Removes the window from the screen. You will know that the program is still running because it appears as a button on the taskbar.
Maximize button	Enlarges the window so that it fills the entire screen.
Restore button	Returns the window to its previous size.
Menu bar	A set of options below the Access title bar that lead to associated pull-down menus.
Database Toolbar	A series of buttons that contain mouse shortcuts for frequently used commands.
Status bar	Provides information concerning what you are currently doing or where you are in the program. Includes the state of each **toggle key**—a key that turns on and off, such as Caps Lock and Num Lock.

toggle key A key that turns on a function when you press it and turns off the function when you press it again. Examples include Num Lock and Caps Lock.

ISSUING COMMANDS BY USING THE MENUS

menu bar Bar below the title bar that lists the names of the available menus.

The Access **menu bar** appears below the title bar. Menus provide one of the main means of issuing commands in Access; there are both keyboard and mouse techniques for issuing menu commands. If you prefer the mouse, you can click the desired menu bar option to display the corresponding pull-down menu. Then, to select an option from the menu that appears, simply click it.

hot key Underlined letter in menu or option names that you use to select that option. Press the hot key in combination with Alt to open a menu; then press the hot key by itself to choose an option within a menu.

It's almost as easy to select menu options with the keyboard. To open a menu, press Alt in combination with the underlined letter (also called the **hot key**) in the menu name. For example, you can press Alt+F to pull down the File menu. Once you've opened a menu, you can choose any option within it just by pressing the hot key in the option name. Both techniques for working with menus will seem easy if you've used any other Windows program.

Even though Access has other convenient shortcuts for executing commands, it's a good idea to have at least a working knowledge of the menu system. Keyboard methods of issuing menu commands are often the most convenient if you're in the middle of typing data. And, it's essential to know these techniques in case your mouse fails to operate one day.

Table 1-2 gives a brief description of the types of options available on the menus.

TABLE 1-2: THE ACCESS MENUS

MENU	DESCRIPTION
File	Allows you to control your databases by opening, saving, and printing them.
Edit	Allows you to rearrange the objects within a database by copying, moving, and deleting them.
View	Allows you to change how the Database window looks on the screen.
Insert	Allows you to insert various objects into a database.
Tools	Allows you to access some of Access' specialized tools such as the spelling checker or database utilities.
Window	Allows you to split your screen into several small windows so that you can view more than one object or Database window at once.
Help	Allows you access to Access' online Help system.

EXPERIMENTING WITH THE MENUS

Here you'll experiment with the available menus to get a feel for how they work.

HANDS ON

1. Click File from the menu bar and take a look at the File menu.

Access displays the File pull-down menu, as shown in Figure 1-6.

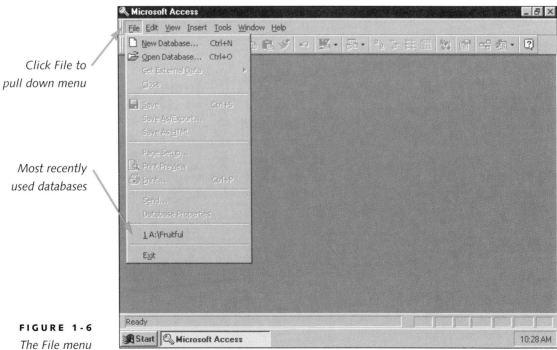

Click File to pull down menu

Most recently used databases

FIGURE 1-6
The File menu

2. Try clicking the Page Setup option.

This produces no effect. Menu options that are grayed are disabled (not available) in the current context.

3. Click the Open Database option.

Access displays the Open dialog box, as shown in Figure 1-7. Choosing any menu option whose name is followed by an ellipsis (three dots) displays a dialog box that asks for further information.

You'll learn more about dialog boxes in a moment.

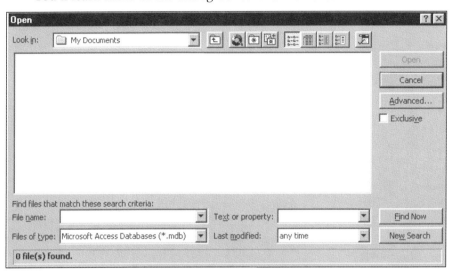

FIGURE 1-7
The Open dialog box

4. For now, press Esc or click the Cancel button.

Access removes the dialog box from the screen without carrying out any action and closes the File menu.

5. Click Tools from the menu bar; then move to the Database Utilities option.

Choosing a menu option that has a small triangle to its right leads to an additional menu.

6. Move back to the File menu.

Notice the key combinations Ctrl+N and Ctrl+O to the right of the New Database and Open Database options at the top of the menu. These are **keyboard shortcuts**—a quick means of using the keyboard to execute commands without going through the menu system.

7. Press Esc twice or click anywhere outside the File menu.

Access removes the File menu from view; you can use either of these techniques to leave a menu without issuing a command.

8. Press Ctrl+O.

Remember, this is the keyboard shortcut for the Open Database command.

keyboard shortcuts A way of using the keyboard to execute a command without going through the menu system. Usually a combination of Ctrl plus one letter keystroke.

Once again, you'll see the Open dialog box that you saw in Figure 1-7. Notice that this time you didn't need to open the File menu or choose an option from within it.

Leave the Open dialog box on the screen so you can refer to it while you learn a bit more about dialog boxes in the upcoming section.

CONTENDING WITH DIALOG BOXES

dialog box A special type of window that requests further information needed before a command can be executed.

As you learned, menu options followed by an ellipsis lead to dialog boxes. A **dialog box** is simply a special type of window that requests further information that Access needs before it can proceed with the command. Dialog boxes like the one shown in Figure 1-7 can include any number of common items with which you may already be acquainted. Table 1-3 lists some of the features common to dialog boxes.

TABLE 1-3: COMMON DIALOG BOX FEATURES

Check boxes	Boxes that you click to select an option. Clicking a box places a ✔ in it. Clicking again removes the ✔ and deselects the option.
Option or radio buttons	Buttons that let you choose one of several options. Clicking one selects the option and deselects the others.
List boxes	Boxes that present a number of selections from which you can choose.
Drop-down list boxes	Boxes that supply a set of options from which you can choose. The options are only visible after you click on the downward-pointing arrow to the right of the box.
Text boxes	Boxes that permit you to type in the desired value.
Command buttons	Buttons that allow you to complete your choices in the dialog box. Most dialog boxes use a command button labeled OK to accept the choices you have made and close the dialog box. A Cancel command button is usually available to close the dialog box without accepting the settings.

ENTERING CHOICES IN A DIALOG BOX

In this exercise, you will work with several of the buttons, boxes, and lists in the Open dialog box.

HANDS ON

1. Click on the downward-pointing arrow to the right of the Look In box.

A drop-down list similar to the one in Figure 1-8 appears. The Look In box lets you choose the disk drive and folder in which your database is stored.

2. Put the Student Data Disk that came with this tutorial into your A: drive.

Click this arrow
to show drop-down list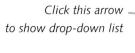

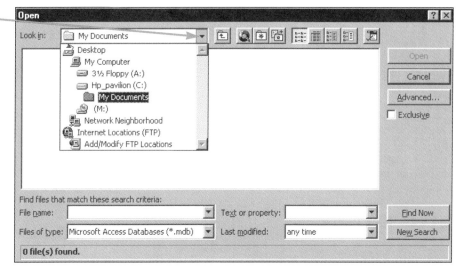

FIGURE 1-8
Look In drop-down list

NOTE

*This tutorial assumes that your Student Data Disk will run from drive A. If your Student Data Disk only fits in Drive B, place it there. You will have to change drive **A** to **B** in this and all other steps in the tutorial.*

3. Click the 3½″ Floppy (A:) option.

A list of the databases stored on the disk in drive A: appears.

4. Click the Up One Level toolbar button just to the right of the Look In box.

The Look In box reads *My Computer* and you should see a list of the available disk drives in the list box.

5. Double-click drive C: icon in the list box.

root folder The main folder in a disk. Every folder and file is located within the root folder.

All of the folders directly under the drive C: root folder appear in the list box. The **root folder** is the main folder on a disk. Within the root folder may be files and other folders—themselves containing files and folders. You can double-click on folders in the list box, use the Look In box, or click the Up One Level toolbar button to find the folder and database file you want to use.

6. Click the Cancel button on the right side of the dialog box.

The screen returns to the previous blank appearance. The Cancel button lets you escape from the dialog box without performing any of the changes you might have selected in the dialog box.

THE TOOLBARS: COMMAND SHORTCUTS FOR MOUSE USERS

toolbar A row of graphical buttons for executing common commands quickly.

Directly underneath the menu bar is Access' **toolbar**, a collection of buttons that function as mouse shortcuts for issuing common commands. Like the available menu options, the available toolbar buttons may change depending on what you're doing at the moment. As you saw in Figure 1-5, most of these buttons are currently grayed, meaning they are unavailable. Access actually offers a number of different toolbars, which it displays—and you'll learn about—as needed.

You may be wondering how you'll remember the purpose of each button. The icons themselves often provide a clue—for instance, the button for opening a file features a picture of an open file folder. If you can't guess the button's purpose from its picture, rest your mouse pointer over the button. Access displays the button name in a small box immediately below the toolbar button; this is called a **ToolTip**. ToolTips are handy reminders when you can't recall the function of a particular toolbar button.

ToolTip The name of a toolbar button displayed immediately below the toolbar when the mouse pointer is placed over the button.

Table 1-4 shows the commands that are available on the Database toolbar.

TABLE 1-4: ACCESS' STANDARD TOOLBAR

TOOLBAR BUTTONS		DESCRIPTION
New Database		Creates a new database.
Open Database		Opens a database you have already created and saved.
Save		Saves the layout, design, structure, or content of a database object.
Print		Prints the selected database object on your printer.
Print Preview		Allows you to preview how the selected database object will look on the printed page.
Spelling		Checks the spelling in your database object.
Cut		Removes the selected item and places it on the Clipboard—a temporary storage place for information used by all Windows applications.
Copy		Copies the selected item and places this copy on the Clipboard.
Paste		Pastes an element from the Clipboard into the active database object.
Format Painter		Copies the formatting of one control to another control.
Undo		Reverses the last action you took that changed your database.

OfficeLinks		Merges Microsoft Access data with data from another Microsoft Office program.
Analyze		Analyzes a table and creates a more efficient table design.
Large Icons		Displays objects in the Database window as large icons.
Small Icons		Displays objects in the Database window as small icons.
List		Displays objects in the Database window as small icons in alphabetical order and shows them organized vertically on the screen.
Details		Displays the name, description, date modified, date created, type, and owner of each database object.
Code		Displays the code behind a selected form or report in the Module window.
Properties		Displays the properties sheet for the selected item.
Relationships		Displays the relationships between tables and queries.
New Object: AutoForm		Creates a new object.
Office Assistant		Displays the Office Assistant—an animated character that can answer your specific questions, offer helpful tips, and provide Help for any Access feature.

USING THE TOOLBAR

With the following steps, you will use a toolbar button to perform a commonly used command.

1. Move your mouse pointer to the New Database button on the far left of the toolbar.

After a second or so, the ToolTip "New Database" appears below the button. As you can see, you can easily find out what a toolbar button does—just position the mouse pointer on the button in question and wait a second!

2. Click the second toolbar button, the Open Database button.

After a few seconds, the Open dialog box appears. You have three ways to open a database: from the File menu's Open Database option, with the Ctrl+O shortcut key, or by clicking the Open Database toolbar button.

3. Click Cancel to close the dialog box.

Once again, you return to your blank Access screen.

OPENING A DATABASE

Most of what you do in Access will involve working with databases. Now you will open a sample database provided on your Student Data Disk.

HANDS ON

1. Click the Open Database button.

   Access displays the Open dialog box, which you saw earlier.

2. Click the drop-down arrow beside the Look In box.

3. Make sure your Student Data Disk is in drive A:.

4. Click the 3½″ Floppy (A:) drive in the drop-down list.

   You'll see the database files in the list box.

5. Double-click **Fruitful.mdb** in the list box.

NOTE   *The .mdb extension may or may not be present depending upon how your computer is set up.*

The Database window for the Fruitful database appears, as shown in Figure 1-9. Also notice that many more menu and toolbar options become available.

NOTE   *The Tables tab in the Database window should be selected. If it is not, click it.*

Tables object tab

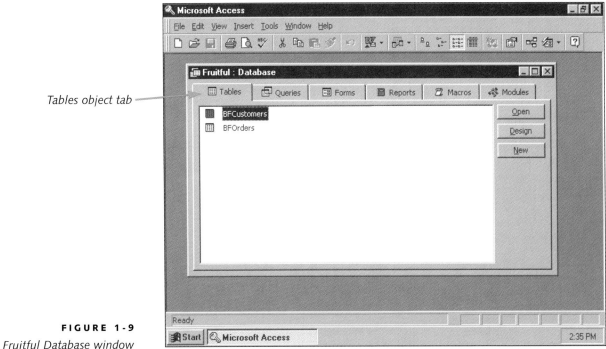

FIGURE 1-9
Fruitful Database window

THE DATABASE WINDOW

Database window A window that lets you gain access to all the objects (tables, forms, reports, queries, and so on) in a particular database.

Object tabs A set of tabs across the top of the Database window that represents the types of objects available in Access.

The **Database window** enables you to gain access to all the tables in your database, as well as to a number of other database objects (or components)—such as forms and reports—that you'll learn about shortly.

The **Object tabs** across the top of the Database window represent the types of objects available in Access. When you click a tab you see an alphabetical list of the objects in question. The Tables object button is selected by default; unless you choose another, you will see a list of the tables in the Fruitful database. Clicking the Reports tab would display any reports in the Fruitful database, and so on.

When you're finished working with a particular database, you can close the Database window by choosing Close from the File menu or by clicking the Close box in the Database window's upper-right corner. For now, leave the Fruitful database open so you can explore the various components of Access in the next section.

BJECTS: THE COMPONENTS OF ACCESS

objects The major components of Access, including tables, queries, forms, reports, macros, and modules.

In Access, the term *database* means not just the raw data stored in tables, but a collection of **objects**. These objects are really nothing mysterious; they're just the various components of Access—the data, reports, requests, actions, and forms that you use to enter, display, print, and find exactly the information you need in the database. An Access database can contain six types of objects—tables, queries, forms, reports, macros, and modules.

THE DATABASE TABLE

You've already learned about one Access object: the table, which is the holding area for all of your data. The table is like a large sheet of paper divided into columns and rows, which contain the information central to the database. A table has two parts—the information itself and the structure of the table. The structure controls the kind of information that can be entered into the table.

VIEWING A TABLE

Perform the following steps to look at the contents of one of the tables in the Fruitful database.

HANDS ON

1. If the **Fruitful** Database window is not already opened, open it.

You should see the Fruitful Database window on the screen, as previously shown in Figure 1-9. Notice that the Tables object tab is selected by default and the names of the two tables in the Fruitful database are displayed under the tab.

2. Click the BFCustomers table to select it, and then click the Open button.

The data in the BFCustomers table appears, arranged in a grid of columns (fields) and rows (records), as shown in Figure 1-10.

3. Click the Maximize button on the right side of the BFCustomers title bar.

You should see a full screen display of the table.

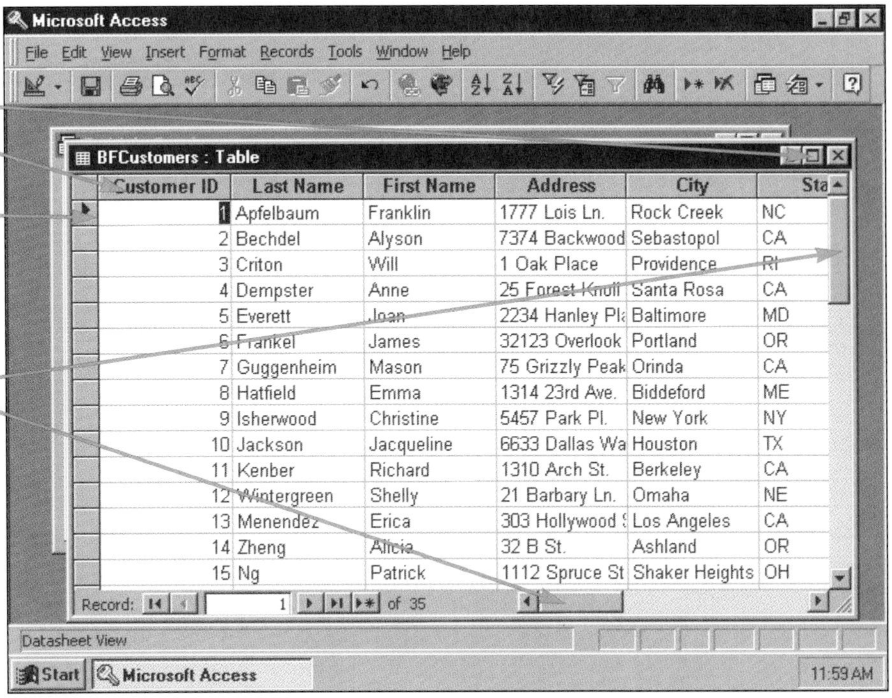
Maximize button
Field
Record
Scroll bars
Microsoft Access
File Edit View Insert Format Records Tools Window Help
BFCustomers : Table
Customer ID Last Name First Name Address City Sta
1 Apfelbaum Franklin 1777 Lois Ln. Rock Creek NC
2 Bechdel Alyson 7374 Backwood Sebastopol CA
3 Criton Will 1 Oak Place Providence RI
4 Dempster Anne 25 Forest Knoll Santa Rosa CA
5 Everett Joan 2234 Hanley Pl Baltimore MD
6 Frankel James 32123 Overlook Portland OR
7 Guggenheim Mason 75 Grizzly Peak Orinda CA
8 Hatfield Emma 1314 23rd Ave. Biddeford ME
9 Isherwood Christine 5457 Park Pl. New York NY
10 Jackson Jacqueline 6633 Dallas Wa Houston TX
11 Kenber Richard 1310 Arch St. Berkeley CA
12 Wintergreen Shelly 21 Barbary Ln. Omaha NE
13 Menendez Erica 303 Hollywood Los Angeles CA
14 Zheng Alicia 32 B St. Ashland OR
15 Ng Patrick 1112 Spruce St Shaker Heights OH
Record: 1 of 35
Datasheet View
Start Microsoft Access
11:59 AM

FIGURE 1-10
The BF Customers table

4. Click and use the **scroll bars** to view portions of the table not visible on the screen.

TIP *Scroll bars appear along the bottom and right side of the window as shown in Figure 1-10. Click the arrows or drag the scroll bars to view other parts of the table.*

scroll bars Shaded bars along the bottom and right side of a window used to view hidden portions of a document.

5. Press Ctrl+End to move to the end of the table.
6. Press Ctrl+Home to move to the beginning of the table.

   Ctrl+Home and Ctrl+End are very useful shortcuts for moving through a long file.

7. Press Tab twice.

   This action selects the word *Franklin*. Pressing Tab moves the insertion point to the next column (field).

8. Press ↓.

   This selects the word *Alyson*. Pressing ↓ moves the insertion point down one record (row) at a time.

TIP *You can also use Shift+Tab or ← to move back one column or ↑ to move up one row.*

9. Type **Alice**

   The word *Alice* replaces the selected word *Alyson*.

10. Click the table's Close button to the right of the menu bar.

N O T E   *Do not click the Access Close button; this will close the Access program.*

Access removes the BFCustomers table from the screen, returning you to the Database window for the Fruitful database.

VIEWING TABLE DESIGN

With the next few steps, you will see the design of the table, rather than its contents. The table's design determines the types of fields it will have.

HANDS ON

1. With the BFCustomers table still selected in the Database window, click the Design button.

You will see the BFCustomers table in what is called **Design view**, as shown in Figure 1-11. As you'll learn in the next lesson, you can set up and modify the layout of a table in Design view.

Design view A view that permits you to set up and modify the structure and appearance of tables, queries, forms, reports, macros, and modules.

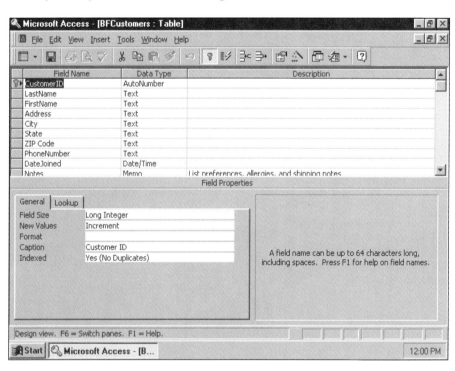

FIGURE 1-11
BFCustomers table in Design view

The Design view is split into two windows. The upper window shows the names and other information about the fields (columns) used in the table. The lower window further defines the properties used for the field currently selected.

2. Press F6.

Your insertion point moves into the lower window.

3. Click the drop-down arrow to the right of the Field Size box.

You will see the options for the size of the field. In the next lesson, you will learn all about these options.

4. Click the File menu and then click Close.

Again, Access closes the table, returning you to the Database window for the Fruitful database.

QUERIES: EXTRACTING THE DATA YOU NEED

query A question to the database, asking for a set of records from one or more tables or other queries that meets specific criteria.

A **query** is just what its name implies: a question to the database, generally asking for a set of records from one or more tables that meets specific criteria. For example, you might ask the database to display all the customers in Hawaii or any customers whose bills are past due. Access responds to such queries by displaying the requested data. Because a query is a stored question, rather than the stored response to a question, the results of the query will remain up to date even if the data in your tables changes. Queries are particularly valuable because they enable you both to view and operate on selected subsets of your data.

VIEWING QUERIES

Queries are stored in the Queries object tab window. These next steps will show you the results of running a query in the Fruitful database.

HANDS ON

1. Click the Queries object tab in the Database window.

You'll see a list of the queries in the Fruitful database.

2. Click the Post 95 Cust query and then click Open.

Access reveals the Post 95 Cust query, as you can see in Figure 1-12. Notice that this query displays selected data from the BFCustomers table you saw earlier. As you may have figured out, the query asks to display the customers who joined after 1995.

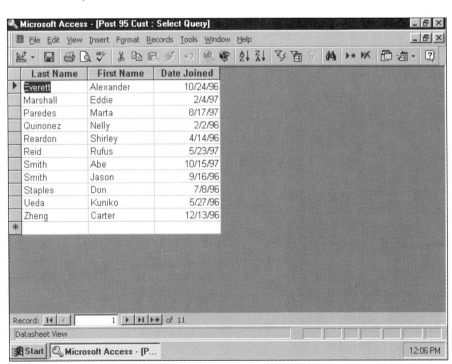

FIGURE 1-12

Display resulting from a query

3. Click the query window's Close button.

Access closes the query, returning you to the Database window.

4. With the Post 95 Cust query still selected, click the Design button.

Access displays the Query Design window. This window lets you choose the fields to be displayed, the order in which they will appear, and the criteria to be used to select records.

5. Click the query window's Close button.

Once again, you move back to the Database window.

FORMS: VIEWING, ENTERING, AND EDITING DATA MORE EASILY

forms Screens that present a custom layout for your data, enabling you to view, edit, and enter the data from your tables.

You can view, enter, and edit data in tables (where data is laid out in series of rows and columns). Often, however, it's more convenient to use custom forms for this purpose. Access **forms** are the electronic equivalent of paper forms; yet, with them you can create a custom layout for your data—determining how the data from your tables is presented. For example, you could create a form that presents a single record at a time for data entry or editing or one that displays only certain fields from a particular table. Forms are especially useful when you want to create a more friendly or visually manageable environment for data entry or when you need to control which data is displayed.

ADDING A RECORD IN THE FORM VIEW

HANDS ON

1. Click the Forms object tab in the Database window.

You'll see a list of the forms in the Fruitful database.

2. Click the BF Cust Names & Addresses form and then click the Open button.

Access reveals the BF Cust Names & Addresses form, as you can see in Figure 1-13. Notice that this form displays the first record from the BFCustomers table you saw earlier.

3. Click the New Record button on the toolbar.

A new blank record is displayed.

4. Press ⎡Tab⎤.

The insertion point moves into the second entry, *Last Name*.

N O T E   *Once you have started typing data in the Last Name field, Access will automatically insert a number in the Customer ID field.*

New Record button

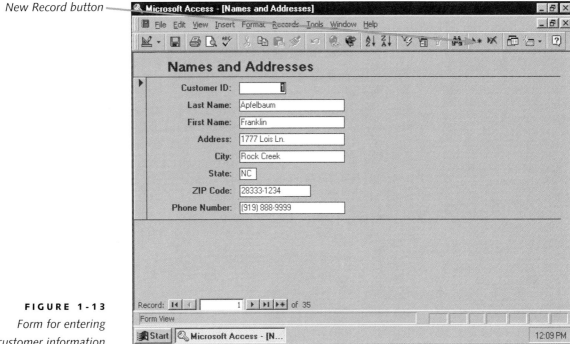

FIGURE 1-13

Form for entering customer information

5. Type each of the following entries into the form, pressing Tab after each item.

Last Name:	Rodriguez
First Name:	Francisco
Address:	6312 Ogden Dr.
City:	Los Angeles
State:	CA
ZIP Code:	900268623
Phone Number:	2139344420

NOTE   *When you enter the ZIP Code and Phone Number, Access fills in the punctuation marks normally used in these items. Also, a new blank form appears when you press Tab after entering data in the last field.*

6. Click the form's Close button.

Access closes the form, returning you to the Database window.

REPORTS AND MAILING LABELS: GENERATING PRINTED OUTPUT

reports Database objects that permit you to produce polished printed output of the data from tables or queries. Some Access reports automatically generate totals and grand totals of the values in particular fields.

mailing labels Sets of names and addresses or other information that you can gather from tables or queries and print for mass mailings and the like.

WYSIWYG On-screen view or preview that closely resembles the final printed output. WYSIWYG is computer jargon for "what you see is what you get."

HANDS ON

Often, you'll want not only a set of data on the screen but also some type of printed output. Access **reports** are printed output of your data. **Mailing labels** are another kind of printed output—they contain just names and addresses, making it easy to send out mass mailings. You can base your reports or mailing labels on data from tables or queries. You can also create reports that show totals and grand totals of the values in a particular field, such as salary or sales. You can print forms, as well as data from tables and queries, but reports enable you to produce presentation-quality output with ease.

PREVIEWING A REPORT ON THE SCREEN

Before you print a database report, you can see what it will look like on the screen. The next few steps display a database report. You will view a **WYSIWYG** ("what you see is what you get") preview that gives you a good idea of what this report will look like when printed.

1. Click the Reports object tab.

Access displays a list of the reports in the Fruitful database.

2. Click the 1997 Orders Tabular report, and then click the Preview button.

In a moment, Access reveals the 1997 Orders Tabular report as shown in Figure 1-14.

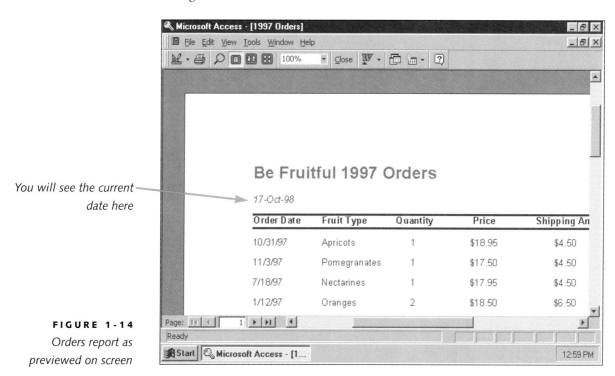

You will see the current date here

FIGURE 1-14
Orders report as previewed on screen

3. Click File and then click Close.

Access closes the report, returning you to the Database window.

MACROS AND MODULES

macro   A set of one or more actions that you can use to automate a task.

action   An instruction or command that you can combine with other instructions in a macro to automate a task.

module   A set of programmed statements that are stored together as a unit; a module is used to automate a task.

A **macro** is an Access object that is made up of a command or series of commands that you can use to automate a task. Each command within a macro is called an **action**. Macros are often created to automate tasks that you repeat frequently. Then, instead of issuing several separate actions manually, you can run the macro and the set of actions will be performed automatically. Macros are designed to save time and effort.

Macros are best used for relatively simple tasks, such as opening forms or running reports. For more complex tasks, a module can be programmed. Modules are sets of programmed statements that are stored together as a unit.

PRINTING AN ACCESS REPORT

The information collected in your database tables is easily viewed on your screen. To share your data with others, however, you usually need to print the report. Before you attempt to print a report object, be sure that your printer is **online**—that is, ready to accept the output from your computer. Generally, this involves two steps: ensuring that the printer has enough paper and checking that the printer is turned on. Check your printer before completing the next exercise. The Ready or Online indicator light should be on. If you have a dot-matrix printer, make sure that the paper is fed through the tractor. If you have a laser or inkjet printer, check that the paper tray is full enough.

online   The status of a printer when it is ready to accept output from your computer.

PRINTING A REPORT

Once you are satisfied that the report looks good on the screen, you are ready to print it on the printer. With the following steps, you will do just that.

1. Check that 1997 Orders Tabular is still selected in the Reports object tab.

2. Click the File menu and choose Print.

The Print dialog box appears, as shown in Figure 1-15.

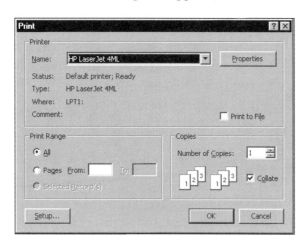

FIGURE 1-15

The Print dialog box

3. Click the OK button.

A printed copy of the 1997 Orders Tabular report will be produced.

NOTE

You can also click the Print toolbar button to produce a printout. When you use the Print toolbar button, the report is printed immediately; that is, the Print dialog box will not appear.

GETTING HELP WHEN YOU NEED IT

No matter how much or how little you know about Access, you're going to need help at some point. Like many programs, Access provides an extensive online Help system. Simply said, Help is an electronic manual that you can open with the press of a key or the click of a mouse button. (If you've used another Windows 95 program, you'll probably have a good grasp of how to get online Help in Access, because Help systems in all Windows 95-based programs are very similar.) Online Help has several advantages over paper manuals: You don't need to remove your fingers from the keyboard or mouse to get assistance and you can choose from several methods of making your way through the Help system, so you can use it as best suits your temperament or needs.

There are three ways you can use the Help system of Access—Office Assistant, Contents and Index, and ScreenTips. You can explore all three and choose your favorite.

USING THE OFFICE ASSISTANT

Office Assistant An animated character that can answer specific questions, offer tips, and provide Help for Access features.

If you've used other Microsoft Office 97 applications, you may have noticed the Office Assistant peeking around the corner of your document. The **Office Assistant** is an animated character that can answer your specific questions, offer helpful tips, and provide Help for any Access feature—often even before you ask. You can activate the Office Assistant by clicking the Office Assistant toolbar button, by selecting Microsoft Access Help from the Help menu, or by pressing F1.

The following steps show you how to ask the Office Assistant for help to print a form:

HANDS ON

1. Click the Office Assistant toolbar button or choose Microsoft Access Help from the Help menu. The **Office Assistant** as shown in Figure 1-16 appears and asks you what you would like to do.

2. In the What Would You Like To Do? box, type **print a form**.

3. Click the Search button.

The Office Assistant will answer with several topics from which you can choose.

4. From the topics available, select the one that describes how to print a form. If you need to view more choices, click the See More option.

The Print a Form Help window appears.

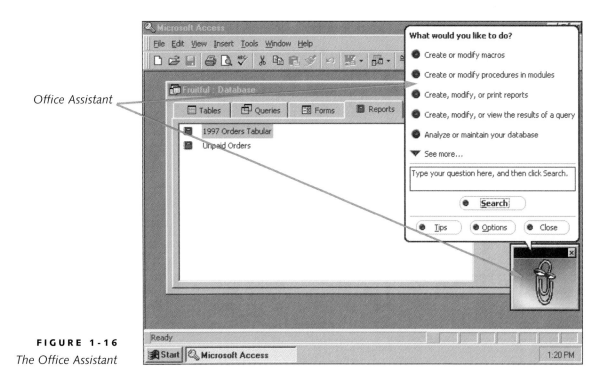

Office Assistant

FIGURE 1-16
The Office Assistant

5. Click the button next to Print a Form From the Database Window. The Help window in Figure 1-17 appears describing how to print a form from the Database window.

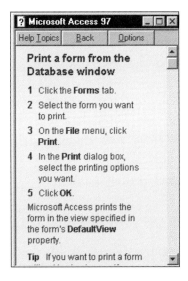

FIGURE 1-17
The Print a Form From the Database Window window

6. Read the information in the Help window. To find out more about the Print toolbar button, scroll to the bottom of the Help window and rest the mouse pointer on the picture of the Print toolbar button. Notice that the pointer changes to the shape of a hand; this change indicates that you may click the object.

7. Click the mouse button to see a description of the toolbar button.

8. Click the definition to remove it from the screen. Then click the Close button to close the Help window.

9. The Office Assistant will appear near the corner of your Database window. Close the Office Assistant by clicking its Close button.

N O T E   *Sometimes a light bulb appears next to the Office Assistant to indicate that a tip is currently available. You may click the light bulb to read the tip that the Office Assistant displays.*

T I P   *If you want more details about using Access' Office Assistant, choose Contents and Index from the Help menu. Then from the Contents tab, choose the Getting Help book and choose the Office Assistant book. You may now explore various topics.*

USING CONTENTS AND INDEX

Contents and Index is an option on the Help menu that allows you to view the Help system's table of contents or find a topic in the index or in the Help database. If you are not sure what the name of a feature is, or if you have no luck finding the needed information with the Office Assistant, you might want to try this method of help.

USING THE CONTENTS TAB

Use the following steps to read about creating tables in Access.

HANDS ON

1. Choose Contents and Index from the Help menu.

2. If it is not already displayed, click the Contents tab.

3. Scroll through the list of help topics, if necessary, until you find the one called Creating, Importing, and Linking Tables. Double-click the book icon in front of Creating, Importing, and Linking Tables. A list of subtopics appears. Those that follow a book icon will contain further subtopics. Those that display a question mark icon will lead you directly to a Help window.

4. Double-click the Creating Tables book so that more subtopics appear.

5. Double-click the Create a Table icon. The Create a Table Help window appears as shown in Figure 1-18.

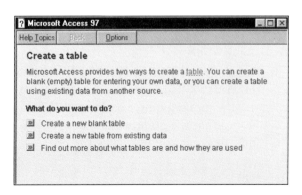

FIGURE 1-18
The Create a Table Help Window

6. Click the underlined word *table* in the first sentence.

A window defining the word appears on the screen. A word or phrase that is colored green and underlined by a broken line is called a **glossary term**. You can click a glossary term whenever you need a definition of the term.

glossary term *An underlined word or phrase in the Help system that shows you the definition of the word or phrase when you click it.*

7. Read the definition and then click it to remove it from the screen.

8. Place your mouse pointer over the jump icon before Find Out More About What Tables Are and How They Are Used.

jump *An icon that enables you to "jump" to another related Help window.*

A **jump** enables you to "jump" to another related Help window. Notice that the mouse pointer changes to the shape of a hand when it is positioned over a jump.

9. Click the Find Out More About What Tables Are and How They Are Used jump icon.

Access displays the Help window, as shown in Figure 1-19. Notice that this window provides a visual guide to important features. You can click any of the following three boxes to show additional information in this window: Fields, Records, and A Common Field Relates Two Tables.

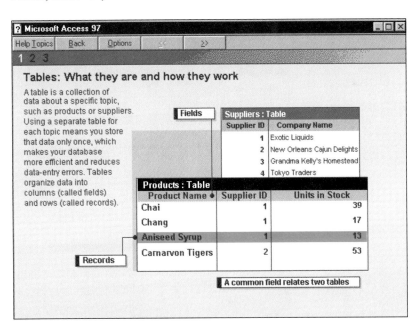

FIGURE 1-19
The Find Out More About What Tables Are and How They Are Used Help window

10. Click the Fields box.

A window pops up describing the fields in the table.

11. Read the text in the pop-up window and then click anywhere on the screen to remove it.

12. Click the 2 near the top-left corner of the window.

Access takes you to the second Help window about tables.

13. Explore this window and then move to the third Help window by clicking the 3 near the top-left corner of the window.

14. When you are finished exploring, click the Help Topics button near the top of the Help window.

Access returns you to the Contents tab of the Help Topics window.

USING THE INDEX TAB

The Index tab can be used when you know the category or topic name you want to find. In the following steps, you'll look for help on shortcut keys for menus.

HANDS ON

1. Click the Index tab of the Help Topics window to display the index.

2. Type the letter **m** in the text box at the top of the Index dialog box.

Access skips straight to "Macintosh PICT files," which is the first keyword beginning with the letter *m*.

3. Now type e.

Access now displays a new set of keywords that begins with the letters *me*.

4. Type **nus** so that the word **menus** appears in the list of keywords.

5. Scroll down until you see the subtopic *shortcut keys* and then click to select it as shown in Figure 1-20.

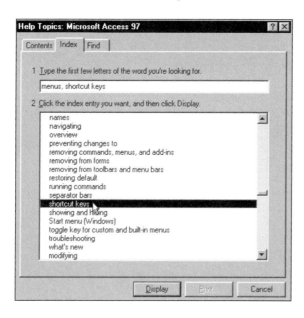

FIGURE 1-20

The Index tab

6. Click the Display button.

The Help window in Figure 1-21 appears.

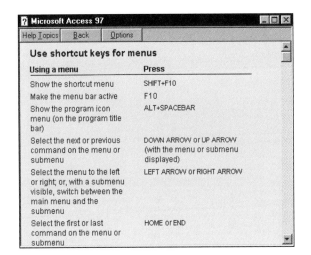

FIGURE 1-21

The Use Shortcut Keys for Menus Help window

7. Read the Help window and then click the Help Topics button to return to the Help Topics window.

USING THE FIND TAB

In these next few steps, you'll use the Find help feature to get assistance with queries.

HANDS ON

1. Click the Find tab near the top of the Help Topics window.

N O T E *The first time that you use the Find tab you may see the Find Setup Wizard dialog box. If so, click on the Minimize Database Size button and then click Next and then Finish to create a list of words and phrases in which you can search.*

After a few moments, you'll see the dialog box, as shown in Figure 1-22. The text box at the top works the same way as the text box in the Index tab. In this case, however, you type in words or phrases that may be in the Help Topics screens, rather than the name of the category.

2. Type **que**

The list box in the middle of the window detects that you want help with a word or phrase that begins with the letters *que*. A series of words and phrases appears that assist you in refining your search. If you click on one of these words or phrases, the list box at the bottom of the screen displays the topics in which your word can be found.

3. Click queries in the list box.

4. Scroll to the bottom of the Click a Topic portion of the dialog box.

5. Click the Work With a Database topic.

6. Click the Display button at the bottom of the dialog box.

The Work with a Database Help window is displayed.

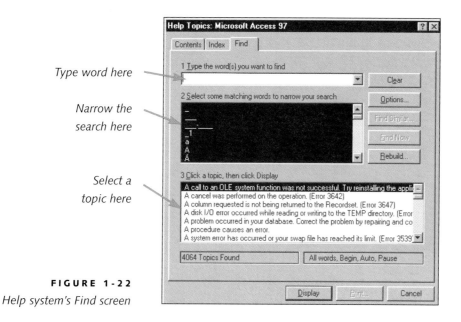

Type word here

Narrow the search here

Select a topic here

FIGURE 1-22

Help system's Find screen

Feel free to explore the jumps from this screen.

7. When you are finished, click the Close button to close the Help window.

T I P *If you want more details about using Access' Help system, choose the Getting Help book from the Contents tab.*

USING SCREENTIPS

ScreenTips Text boxes that appear on the screen showing the name and description of various elements on the Access screen.

ScreenTips show information about different elements on the Access screen. When you select What's This? from the Help menu, the mouse pointer changes in appearance to show a question mark. While this cursor is displayed, you can click almost any element on the screen—a menu command, a toolbar button, a tab in the Database window—to see its name and description.

To read ScreenTips for various elements, follow these steps:

HANDS ON

1. Select What's This? from the Help menu.

The mouse pointer changes in appearance to include a question mark next to the arrow.

2. Move the mouse pointer over the Spelling toolbar button and click the mouse button.

As illustrated in Figure 1-23, the name and description of the Spelling toolbar button will appear.

3. Read the definition and then click anywhere on the screen to remove it.

4. To use the ScreenTips keyboard shortcut, press Shift+F1 on the keyboard.

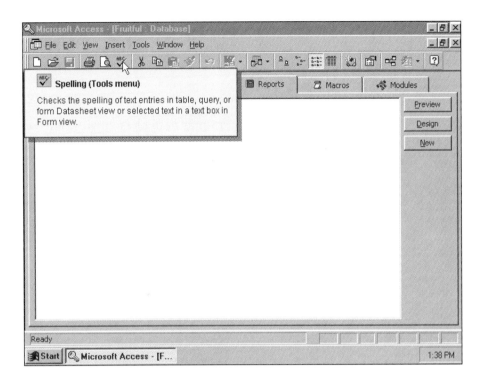

FIGURE 1-23

*Spelling toolbar button
ScreenTip*

5. When the ScreenTips mouse pointer appears, click the Tables tab in the Database window.

A definition of the Tables tab will appear.

6. Read the definition and then click anywhere on the screen to remove it.

7. If time permits, continue to use ScreenTips to explore other parts of the screen.

TIP *If you want more details about using ScreenTips, choose Contents and Index from the Help menu. Then, from the Contents tab, choose the Getting Help book. Then choose and display Ways to Get Assistance While You Work to explore ScreenTips.*

Regardless of the method you use to get help, once you reach a help window, you can display the definitions of words or phrases by clicking on glossary terms. You can also switch from one Help topic to a related one by clicking Back. Lastly, you can return to the list of help topics by selecting Help Topics.

QUITTING ACCESS

When you've finished using Access, do not simply turn off your computer. Instead, you need to exit the program properly. The following are several options for properly quitting the program:

- Click the File menu and then click Exit.

- Double-click the Control icon at the far left end of the Access title bar.

■ Press Alt + F4 .

■ Click the Close button at the far right end of the Access title bar.

EXITING THE PROGRAM

These last steps in the lesson will have you exit the Access program.

HANDS ON

1. Click the Close button of the Database window.

You return to the screen you saw near the beginning of this lesson.

2. Click the Close button on the far right side of the Access title bar.

The program ends and you return to your Windows 95 Desktop.

LESSON SUMMARY AND EXERCISES

After you complete this lesson, you should know how to do the following:

INTRODUCING DATABASES

■ To understand a database management system, you must see data stored in tables, organized into categories called fields, and collected into records—sets of fields for one entity.

LAUNCHING THE PROGRAM

■ To run the Access program, click the Start button, point to the Programs menu, and click Microsoft Access.

LEARNING YOUR WAY AROUND ACCESS

■ To select commands from the menu, either click the menu name and options, or hold down Alt and type the underlined letter.

■ To set dialog box options, enter text into the text box, click the desired check boxes, select an option button, and/or click the necessary items from list boxes and drop-down list boxes, and then click OK.

■ To select commands from the toolbar, click the desired button. Let your mouse pointer rest over the button to display its name.

OPENING A DATABASE

■ To open a database, click the Open Database toolbar button. In the Open dialog box, click the Look In drop-down arrow to locate the drive and folder where the database is stored. Double-click the database name in the list box.

OBJECTS: THE COMPONENTS OF ACCESS

■ To open a database object, click the appropriate tab at the top of the Database window and select the object that you want to use. Then click the Open (or Preview) or Design button. Object tabs are available for tables, queries, forms, reports, macros, and modules.

PRINTING AN ACCESS REPORT

■ To print a report, make sure your printer is online and has enough paper. Then choose File, Print and click OK on the Print dialog box.

GETTING HELP WHEN YOU NEED IT

■ To use the Office Assistant, choose Microsoft Access Help from the Help menu or click the Office Assistant toolbar button. Type the name of the feature with which you need help.

■ To use the Contents feature, choose Contents and Index from the Help menu. Then choose the Contents tab and scroll to find the topic with which you need help.

■ To use the Index feature, choose Contents and Index from the Help menu. Then choose the Index tab. Type letters until you see a suitable keyword; double-click it; and double-click the specific area in which you need help.

■ To use the Find feature, choose Contents and Index from the Help menu. Then choose the Find tab. Type letters until you see a suitable topic. Click the topic to select it and then click a subtopic from the bottom portion of the dialog box. Click the Display button.

■ To display ScreenTips, choose What's This? from the Help menu. Click the screen element with which you need help.

QUITTING ACCESS

■ To quit Access, first close any open databases. Then choose Exit from the File menu; double-click the Control icon; click the Close button; or press Alt + F4 .

NEW TERMS TO REMEMBER

After you complete this lesson, you should know the meaning of the following terms:

action	module
click	Object tabs
database	objects
Database window	Office Assistant
DBMS (database management system)	online
Design view	query
dialog box	records
double-click	relational databases
fields	reports
forms	right-click
glossary term	root folder
hot key	ScreenTips
jump	scroll bars
keyboard shortcuts	tables
macro	toggle key
mailing labels	toolbar
menu bar	ToolTip
	WYSIWYG

MATCHING EXERCISE

Match each of the terms with the definitions on the right:

TERMS	DEFINITIONS
1. DBMS	**a.** Database programs that allow you to link tables
2. query	**b.** One of several mutually exclusive options
3. objects	**c.** Screen display showing things much as they will be printed
4. record	**d.** Items that permit you to move directly to related Help topics
5. field	**e.** A system for storing and manipulating the data in a database
6. relational databases	**f.** One category of information in a table
7. WYSIWYG	**g.** A text box generated by choosing What's This? from the Help menu and clicking a screen element
8. radio button	**h.** Question requesting specific information from the database
9. jumps	**i.** Name for various components of Access
10. ScreenTip	**j.** Group of fields related to a particular entity

COMPLETION EXERCISE

Fill in the missing word or phrase for each of the following:

1. When a menu option is followed by an ellipsis, it leads to a
_____.

2. You can use _____ to automatically perform a set of actions.

3. An Access _____ is a question to the database, usually asking for a specific subset of data.

4. When you want presentation-quality hard copy, you should print a
_____.

5. A _____ is all the fields related to a particular entity.

6. A_____ is a set of programmed statements that are stored together as a unit.

7. In Access, the term _____ means a set of related tables, forms, reports, queries, macros, and modules.

8. A _____ is a single category of information.

9. When you've finished using Access for the day, you should _____ the program.

10. When you click on a grayed toolbar button, _____ happens.

SHORT-ANSWER QUESTIONS

Write a brief answer to each of the following questions:

1. Name the six types of Access objects.

2. Describe mouse and keyboard methods for displaying the Open dialog box without going through the menu system.

3. What is the name of the screen element directly under the Access title bar? Does it ever change?

4. When would you use forms rather than tables for data entry?

5. From within a Database window, how would you open a table in order to change its layout?

6. What is the advantage of printing a report rather than printing a form or a table?

7. Describe the relationship between tables, records, and fields.

8. Name the different types of Help features in Access.

9. Explain the difference between a listing of items in a database and information provided by a query.

10. Describe the types of elements you find in a typical dialog box.

APPLICATION PROJECTS

Perform the following actions to complete these projects:

1. Use the Office Assistant to hunt for information on creating forms with a Wizard. Print the information.

2. Open the **Fruitful** database on your Student Data Disk and open the BFOrders table in Design view. Then use the scroll bar on the right side of the window to view all the field names, data types, and descriptions. (You'll learn more about these table elements—and this window for designing tables—in the next lesson.) On a separate sheet of paper, list all of the field names. Then close the window.

3. Open the BFCustomers table in the **Fruitful** database. Use the scroll bars to browse through the data, noting what data exists and how it is displayed. Notice that you must scroll to the right to see all the fields in the table. Next, close the BFCustomers table, and then open the BFCust Auto Form form. Notice what data you see and how it is displayed. Close the form and then display it in Design view. Close the window.

4. Preview the Unpaid Orders report in the **Fruitful** database. Maximize the window and scroll through the report on the screen. Once you have viewed the report, print it. Close the report window and then close the database.

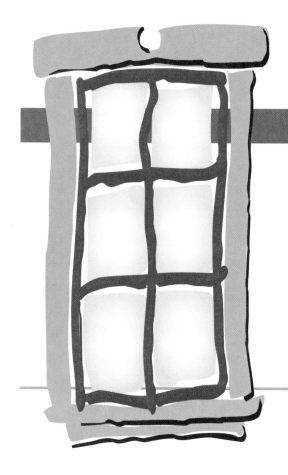

DESIGNING

AND CREATING

DATABASES

OBJECTIVES

After you complete this lesson, you will be able to do the following:

- *Plan your database—determining what data you need to store, how many tables you need, and how those tables should be set up.*

- *Create a database to store your tables.*

- *Create a table with the Table Wizard.*

- *Create a table in Table Design view.*

- *Save your table design.*

- *Modify the design of a table—renaming, adding, removing, and moving fields, among other things.*

CONTENTS

Planning Ahead

Creating a Database

Creating Tables

Saving the Table Design

Modifying the Table Design

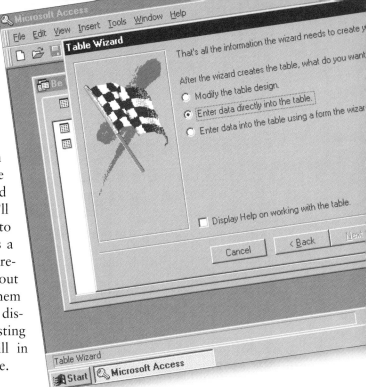

T he most important thing you learn in this chapter is how to plan ahead—how to determine what data items to store and the number of tables you'll need. You then learn how to create a database, as well as a couple of different ways to create tables. Next you find out how to save tables to use them for future work. Last, you discover how to modify existing tables, an indispensable skill in this world of constant change.

PLANNING AHEAD

Proper creation of a database requires careful thought. Unlike documents created with a word processor, changes to a database are more complex than deleting and inserting until the document is just right. You can count on experiencing problems later if you leap too quickly into creating a database without some advance planning. Don't be intimidated, however. This planning process is pretty straightforward. Besides, once you design your database, the tasks you'll perform to actually create an Access database and to build a few tables will be remarkably easy.

Before beginning to build a database, you need to answer several questions:

■ What is the database for and what should it do?

■ What categories of information (or fields) do you need to create in order to achieve the desired results?

■ How should these fields be divided into separate tables?

■ How might these tables relate to each other to use information from two or more of them simultaneously?

DETERMINING THE PURPOSE OF THE DATABASE

It may seem obvious, but the first step in determining how to put together your database is to figure out what it's for. If you have an existing manual database system, investigate that system; review any reports and forms that you'll need to duplicate and note the items of information they must include. Also be sure to talk to people who actually use the database; check up on what they use the system for and what they need. If you're not working with an existing system, think very carefully about what you want the new system to do; jot down the items of information the system should track and sketch out any forms and reports you think you'll need. Throughout the planning process, keep in mind that as you determine what you want out of your database you are learning what data it must contain. For example, if you need to be able to print salary reports according to department, your database must list the department for each employee. Also, consider how you want to sort or extract data: For instance, if you'll want to sort customers by last name, you'll need to include separate fields for a first name and a last name, rather than a single field to contain both names. At this stage in planning, you can make just one large list of all the information you need. In a moment, you'll learn how to break down this information into more manageable chunks.

NOTE   *In the planning stage, you can ask users of the current system to supply you with a "wish list" of things they'd like to be able to do. Keep in mind that you aren't confined to duplicating a current manual system; often you can improve on the existing system while computerizing it.*

DETERMINING THE CATEGORIES OF INFORMATION YOU NEED

The sample application in this tutorial is the database for a fruit-of-the-month club called *Be Fruitful*. Members of this club can choose whether to order the fruit offered for a particular month, and they can also decide how much fruit to order. Some of the information categories needed in this database include:

- The name, address, and phone number of each customer, as well as notes about shipping.

- The date the customer joined the club.

- The types of fruit, their prices, and the units offered (3 pints strawberries, 2 dozen kiwis, and so forth).

- The number of units of fruit each member orders in a month.

- The date an order was placed and when and how the customer paid for it.

DETERMINING HOW MANY TABLES YOU NEED

All but the simplest of databases will contain multiple tables so that Access can use your data more efficiently. In other words, your task is not only to determine what categories of information (or fields) your database should contain but also how that information should be broken down logically into several tables.

The first thing to consider is that each table should contain information on a single subject: In the database for Be Fruitful, for example, you will have one table that contains customer information, a second table that includes information about available fruits, and a third one with order information. You wouldn't include customer names and addresses in the orders table, because these fields describe the customer, not the order. This way of breaking down your database helps you avoid duplication of data. You want to avoid entering the customer's name and address in each order, for example, because this wastes storage space, requires extra typing, and increases the likelihood of data-entry errors. In addition, if you store the customer name and address information in a single customer record rather than in multiple order records, it's much easier to update your data later. It may seem inefficient to divide your data among multiple tables in this way—for example, you may want to use information about both customers and orders in an invoice form—but bear in mind that Access enables you to pull together data from many sources as you create forms and reports.

Tables also should avoid multiple instances of the same field or a similar set of fields. For example, suppose you had a mail-order business and your customers often ordered multiple items at once. To record all of those orders in the orders table, you could have one long record with fields for each item ordered. A better solution would be to have a separate line-items table where each item being ordered is in a separate record.

Finally, as a general rule, do not include fields in your table that will contain data that you can calculate from other fields. For instance, if you have one field for price and one for quantity, you can calculate the total by multiplying these two values together—you don't need to create a separate field for the total.

Figure 2-1 shows a tentative list of fields for the three tables in Be Fruitful's database.

FIGURE 2-1

List of fields for three tables in Be Fruitful's database

BE FRUITFUL FIELDS

BF Customers	BF Fruit	BF Orders
Customer ID	Fruit Type	Customer ID
Contact Last Name	Price	Order Date
Contact First Name	Descriptive Units	Fruit Type
Billing Address		Quantity
City		Price
State or Province		Shipping Amount
ZIP Code		Payment Date
Phone Number		Payment Amount
Date Joined		Payment Type
Notes		Reference
Extra Catalogs		

DETERMINING HOW TABLES WILL WORK TOGETHER

Once you've decided how to divide the database information into multiple tables, you have a corresponding task—to determine how to set up those tables to combine the information they contain into single forms or reports. For instance, if you have separate orders and customers tables, you clearly need a way to pull the data from both tables together to create an invoice that includes corresponding customer and order information.

common field A field that has the same name and data type as a field in one or more other tables. You need to set up common fields in preparation for sharing data between tables. The common field is what lets Access find matching data in different tables.

primary key A field or set of fields that uniquely identifies each record in the table.

For you to be able to use two tables in combination, they must include a **common field**. For example, to ensure that you can relate the fruit-of-the-month club's customers and orders tables, you could include a Customer ID field in both tables. This field would enable Access to match up the order with the customer who placed the order. When determining how to relate tables, you must also consider the concept of primary keys: A **primary key** is a field or set of fields that uniquely identifies each record in the table. Assigning a primary key is particularly important if you need to link data in two tables. In the fruit-of-the-month club's database, for instance, you need a primary key in the customers table—some way to uniquely identify each customer so that you can tell which orders belong to which customers. A Customer ID field can serve this purpose. (You wouldn't want to use the name fields as the primary key, in case you had two customers with the same name.) When you set a primary key, Access sorts records in order according to the values in that key. Because the primary key must uniquely identify each record, Access won't permit you to enter duplicate values in the primary key field(s).

Although there is more to determining how to link your tables, at this stage of the game you'll just include common fields in the tables you need to use together and set some primary keys. In Lesson 4, you'll learn how to create queries that draw on multiple tables; in Lesson 7, you'll learn much more about how to identify the different types of relationships between tables as well as how to establish formal relationships between tables so that Access can enforce certain rules to guarantee that your data makes sense.

OFFICE ASSISTANT

For even more information about planning a database, start the Office Assistant, type **database design**, *click Search, and click the* **About designing a database** *option.*

CREATING A DATABASE

As you may remember from the previous lesson, in Access the term *database* means not just a collection of data, but a set of related tables, forms, reports, queries, and more. Before you begin to create tables in which to store your data, you need to create a database—an easy process that should be all the easier since you've already looked at an existing database in Lesson 1.

Using the following steps, you will create a database to hold your tables, as well as all the related queries, forms, and reports you'll create throughout this tutorial.

HANDS ON

1. Start Access.

Refer to the previous lesson if necessary to jog your memory.

Access brings you to the beginning dialog screen.

TIP   *If Access is already running, choose New Database from the File menu.*

2. Click the Blank Database option and click OK.

You should see the File New Database dialog box, as shown in Figure 2-2. Notice that this dialog box is very similar to the Open Database dialog box you saw in the previous lesson.

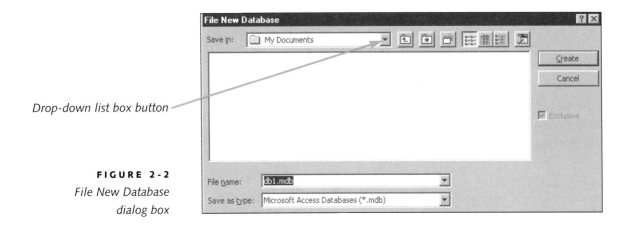

Drop-down list box button

FIGURE 2-2
File New Database dialog box

3. Click the downward-pointing arrow in the Save In drop-down list box.

4. Put your Student Data Disk in drive A:.

You will store all the database objects that you create or modify on your Student Data Disk.

5. Click the 3-1/2 Floppy (A:) drive in the Save In list box.

6. Double-click the **Lessons** folder in the list box.

7. Double-click the first part of the existing file name in the File Name text box.

The suggested name (probably *db1)* is selected.

8. Type **Be Fruitful**

The suggested name is replaced with the name *Be Fruitful.*

NOTE   *Depending upon how your computer is set up, Access may automatically add an extension of .mdb to the file name. The extension identifies the file as an Access database.*

9. Click the Create button.

After a pause, Access displays the Database window for the Be Fruitful database, as shown in Figure 2-3.

In this case, the database is empty. Notice that the Table object tab is selected, but the Database window has no table displayed and the Open and Design buttons are grayed (disabled). You obviously can't open or modify nonexistent tables. If you selected any of the other object tabs, you would see that they also are empty.

FIGURE 2-3

Window for newly created database

CREATING TABLES

Now that you've created a database, the next step is to create some tables so that you can enter your data. You'll be creating the table structure—you'll spell out the fields that the table needs and select various properties for them. In the next lesson, you'll learn how to enter and edit data in the tables you've created. These are the first two essential steps for building a database.

There are two ways to create tables in Access: You can use the Table Wizard, described next, or you can work in Table Design view, described later in this lesson.

CREATING A TABLE WITH THE TABLE WIZARD

Wizard An Access tool that guides you through the process of creating tables, queries, forms, or reports. A Wizard prompts you with questions about the object you are creating and builds the object based on the answers you supply.

During this guided activity, you'll design Be Fruitful's Customers table, which will include the names and addresses of the Be Fruitful customers. When you use a **Wizard**, Access prompts you for the needed information each step of the way. The Table Wizard is a tool provided by Access used specifically to create tables. The Table Wizard gathers information through a series of dialog boxes. At any point in the table-creation process, you can click the Back button to move back one step.

OFFICE ASSISTANT

For a complete list of Wizards available in Access 97, start the Office Assistant and type **Wizards***.*

HANDS ON

1. With the Be Fruitful Database window still open, click the Table object tab (if it isn't already active) and then click the New button.

Access shows you the New Table dialog box, with a list box containing options that include Design View and Table Wizard, as shown in Figure 2-4.

*Choose a method for
creating a new table*

FIGURE 2-4
New Table dialog box

2. Double-click the Table Wizard option.

In a moment, you will see the Table Wizard dialog box, as shown in Figure 2-5. Don't be overwhelmed by the number of options. This is simply a long selection of sample tables—and their accompanying fields—from which you can choose.

*Fields in highlighted
sample table*

*Add selected
field*

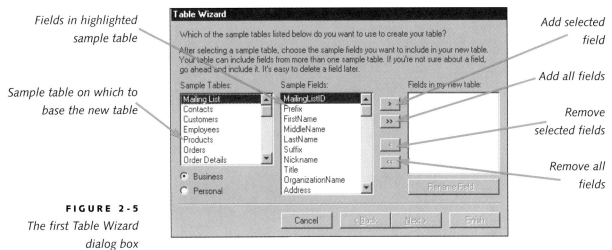

*Sample table on which to
base the new table*

Add all fields

*Remove
selected fields*

*Remove all
fields*

FIGURE 2-5
*The first Table Wizard
dialog box*

3. Click *Customers* in the Sample Tables box. (Scroll down to find it if necessary.)

Notice that the list of field names in the Sample Fields list box changes; this list box now includes sample fields appropriate for a table of customers.

4. Click the CustomerID field name.

5. Click the > button to its right.

This button permits you to add one field at a time to your new table. Access lists the CustomerID field in the Fields In My New Table list box on the right side of the Table Wizard dialog box. Remember, the CustomerID field will be used to link customers and orders.

TIP   *When selecting fields, keep in mind that fields appear in your table in the order that they are listed in the Fields In My New Table list box. You can easily change the order of fields later, as described in "Modifying the Table Design."*

6. Click the ContactFirstName sample field and click the > button.

The ContactFirstName field should appear directly under CustomerID in the Fields In My New Table list box. Notice that Access places the added field below the field that was selected in the Fields In My New Table list box.

Note that the ContactLastName field in the Sample Fields list box is selected.

7. Click the > button.

Access adds the ContactLastName field to the Fields In My New Table list box.

8. Double-click the BillingAddress field in the Sample Fields list box.

Access adds the BillingAddress field to the list on the right; double-clicking one of the sample fields is a shortcut for placing that field name in the Fields In My New Table list box.

9. Add the fields City, StateOrProvince, PostalCode, PhoneNumber, FaxNumber, and Notes, in that order.

N O T E   *You may have to scroll down in the Sample Fields list box to find all of these fields.*

Access lists all the selected fields in the Fields In My New Table list box.

CHANGING FIELDS IN THE FIELD LIST

At times you may decide against including a particular field in your table. Fortunately, this kind of change to the field list is relatively simple to make.

HANDS ON

1. Select FaxNumber in the Fields In My New Table list box.

2. Click the < button.

Access promptly removes the FaxNumber field from the Fields In My New Table list box.

T I P   *You also can click the << button to remove all of the fields at once from the Fields In My New Table list box and the >> button to add all of the fields at once to it.*

You can change field names with ease, too.

3. Select the PostalCode field in the Fields In My New Table box.

4. Click the Rename Field button below the field list box.

The Rename Field dialog box appears with the current field name selected, as shown in Figure 2-6.

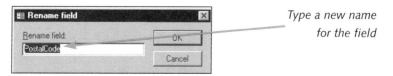

FIGURE 2-6
The Rename Field dialog box

Type a new name for the field

5. Change *PostalCode* to **ZIPCode.**

TIP *If you just type the new text, it will replace the selected text. Alternatively, you could click between the I and C, press [Backspace] to delete the word **Postal,** and type **ZIP.** Keys such as [Delete], [Backspace], [Home], and [End] work the same in text boxes as they do in word processing programs.*

6. Click OK.

The field is renamed in the Fields In My New Table box.

NAMING THE TABLE

You have now selected the desired fields for your table and are ready to choose a name for the table.

HANDS ON

1. Click the Next button near the lower-right corner of the Table Wizard dialog box.

You'll see the Table Wizard dialog box shown in Figure 2-7, which lets you name your table and set the primary key.

Accept this table name or type another

Let Table Wizard choose a primary key

Select your own primary key

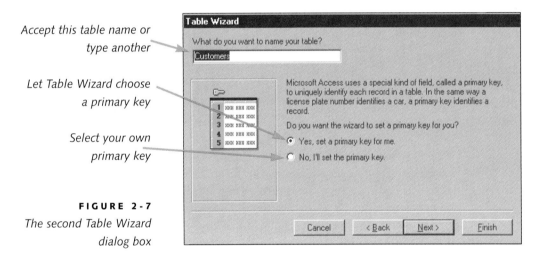

FIGURE 2-7
The second Table Wizard dialog box

Access suggests the name *Customers* for your table—the name of the sample table you selected.

NOTE *Object names such as table and field names can be up to 64 characters long. Access allows any combination of letters, numbers, spaces, and most punctuation characters. Access permits any of the following: period, exclamation mark, accent mark, or brackets. Also, object names cannot begin with a space or an equal sign.*

2. Click to the left of the letter C. (The table name will be deselected and the insertion point will move to the left of the letter C.) Then type **BF**

The entire table name should read *BFCustomers*, indicating that this table will contain information about the customers of the Be Fruitful fruit-of-the-month club.

T I P *Omitting spaces from your object names will make it easier to refer to them later. Also, if you limit the length of the object's name, it will be easier for you to remember and enter it. Don't worry about how the object name appears on the screen or report; you can change these later to more familiar terms.*

3. Click the No, I'll Set The Primary Key option button and then click Next.

Access displays the Table Wizard dialog box shown in Figure 2-8. Remember, a primary key is a field or set of fields that uniquely identifies one record.

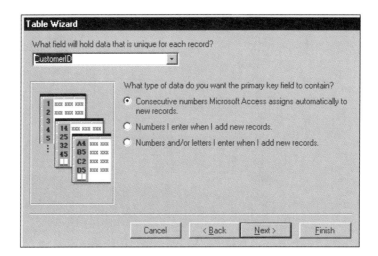

FIGURE 2-8

The third Table Wizard dialog box

Notice that Access suggests the Customer ID field as the primary key field. You could change this by selecting another field from the drop-down list; however, since each customer will have a unique ID number, this field is an appropriate one to set as the primary key.

Also notice that the Consecutive Numbers Microsoft Access Assigns Automatically To New Records option button is selected. When you choose this option, Access automatically provides the Customer ID numbers, ensuring that you don't enter duplicate values in any Customer ID field.

4. Click the Next button to accept the selections.

Access displays the final Table Wizard dialog box—notice the finish-line flag—as shown in Figure 2-9.

5. Choose the Modify the Table Design option button and click the Finish button.

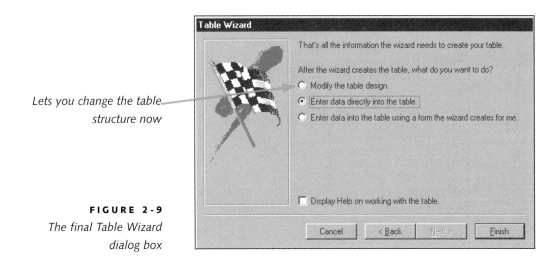

Lets you change the table structure now

FIGURE 2-9
The final Table Wizard dialog box

Access displays the BFCustomers table in Table Design view, as shown in Figure 2-10. (You'll learn how to work in Table Design view in a moment.)

Field names

Primary key indicator

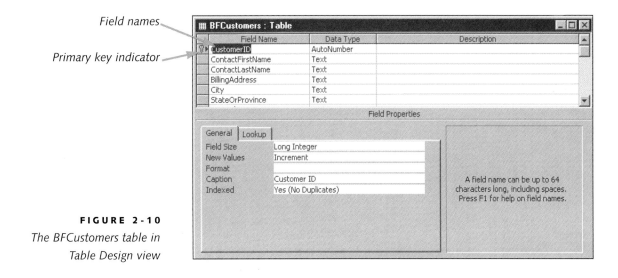

FIGURE 2-10
The BFCustomers table in Table Design view

6. Click the BFCustomers Table's Close button.

Access returns you to the Be Fruitful Database window, which now includes the BFCustomers table.

NOTE   *When you create subsequent tables in a database, the Table Wizard will display an additional dialog box that asks whether the new table is related to any of the existing tables in the database. For now, if you come upon this dialog box, simply indicate that the tables are not related. You'll learn more about how to relate multiple tables in Lesson 7.*

CREATING TABLES IN TABLE DESIGN VIEW

The Table Wizard makes creating a table a straightforward process, but it allows you little flexibility. Fortunately, you can also create tables in Table Design view, which gives you much more control over field characteristics, including their size and the type of data they'll contain.

You can use Table Design view both to create new tables and to modify existing tables—whether you created them in Table Design view or with the Table Wizard.

TOURING THE TABLE DESIGN VIEW

In this guided activity, you'll open a new table in Table Design view, which is slightly more involved to work with than Table Wizard. You'll create a single field in the orders table for Be Fruitful's database to get a feel for the process. After that, you'll learn more about the various aspects of fields before you complete the table.

HANDS ON

1. Make sure the Tables tab in the Be Fruitful Database window is selected.

2. Click the New button.

   Access displays the New Table dialog box as you saw earlier in this lesson.

3. Double-click Design View in the list box.

   Access opens an empty table in Table Design view, as shown in Figure 2-11.

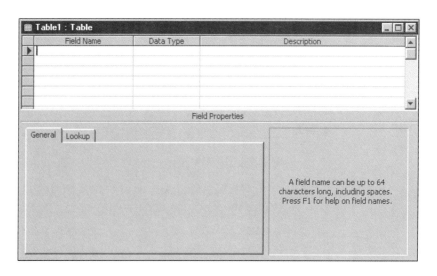

FIGURE 2-11

A new, empty table in Design view

insertion point A vertical line in a text box that lets you see where characters will be inserted when you type them from the keyboard.

Notice that the **insertion point**—the flashing vertical line—is in the Field Name column. Read the information in the lower-right corner of the window, which describes field names.

4. Enter the field name **CustomerID** in the Field Name column.

5. Press Tab to move to the Data Type column.

Access activates the Data Type column, displaying the default data type, which is Text, as well as an arrow that provides you with access to a number of other choices. Notice that the information in the lower-right corner of the window now describes data types.

T I P   *Calculations can be performed more easily if your field names don't include spaces.*

6. Click the downward-pointing arrow in the Data Type column.

Access reveals a drop-down list box displaying the available data types, as shown in Figure 2-12. (You'll learn more about data types in a moment.)

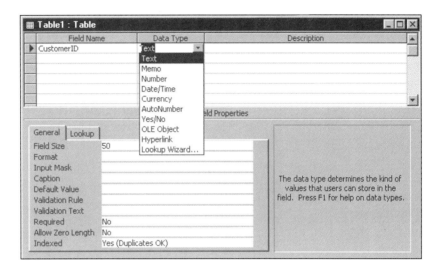

FIGURE 2-12
Data Type drop-down list

7. Click the Number data type.

8. Press Tab.

Your insertion point moves to the Description field. You can enter a description of up to 255 characters for each field. Access displays some information about field descriptions in the lower-right corner of the Table Design window.

9. Type the text **Enter same Customer ID used in BFCustomer table**

10. Press Tab.

Access moves the insertion point down to the next row; now you can enter the specifications for another field.

11. Click the CustomerID field name to move back up to that field.

You can see the Field Properties area in the lower half of the Table Design view window. It lists the field size as well as several other characteristics of the current field, as shown in Figure 2-13. You'll learn more about several of these characteristics shortly, under "Setting Other Field Properties."

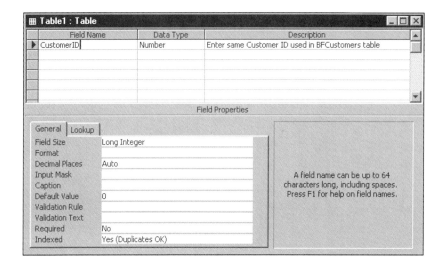

FIGURE 2-13

Field Properties window

12. Press F6 to move down to the Field Properties area of the window; then press F6 again, noting that this moves your insertion point back to the upper portion of the Table Design view window.

You'll enter additional fields a little later, after you learn more of the details about some of the field characteristics you've just encountered.

SELECTING DATA TYPES

data type A designation that determines the type of data that can be entered into a field, such as text, numbers, and dates.

properties The characteristics of a particular field, table, or database.

When you work in Table Design view, you need to decide what data type to use. A **data type** controls the kind of data that can be entered into a field. For example, if you assign the Number data type to a field, you can't enter letters into that field. Most of the choices are fairly intuitive, and only ten data types exist, so you'll learn them quickly. Note that when you choose fields in the Table Wizard, Access automatically assigns them data types. The data type is just one of the properties that fields can have. **Properties** is the term used to describe the characteristics of fields, tables, databases, and so on. Field properties include the field's size and format, as well as limitations on how data can be entered into the field.

- **Text fields** can hold up to 255 characters, including letters, numbers, and punctuation marks. You can use the Text data type for fields that will contain numbers that you won't be using to perform calculations, and you should use the text data type for fields that will contain both numbers and some type of punctuation characters, such as phone numbers or Social Security numbers.

- **Memo fields** can contain up to 64,000 letters, numbers, and punctuation marks. Use this data type when you need to enter longer amounts of text such as free-form comments or fairly lengthy descriptions.

- **Number fields** can only include digits, the decimal point, and the minus (negative) sign. Use this data type for fields that will only contain numbers, and in particular for numbers that you will use to perform calculations—for example, quantity or discount fields. As mentioned, you don't need to use the Number data type for numbers that won't be used in calculations, such as ZIP Codes, and you must not use this data type for numbers that will include punctuation marks, such as phone numbers. (Instead, use the Text data type.) You can actually choose from six different types of Number fields, depending on the type and size of numbers you want to store, as you'll learn in the next section.

■ **Date/Time fields** are for storing dates and times. You could always enter these values in a Text field, but when you use the Date/Time data type, Access prevents you from entering invalid dates or times such as 2/31/98 or 34:35. Other benefits are that Access supplies several different display formats for dates and times and lets you sort dates and times into chronological order. Finally, when you use Date/Time fields, you can perform date arithmetic—subtracting one date from another to determine the number of days between them or adding or subtracting a specified number of days to or from a date to calculate a later or earlier date.

■ **Currency fields** are used to store numeric values, such as salaries or prices, that you want displayed with a currency symbol, a decimal point, and separators (usually commas) every three digits.

■ **AutoNumber fields** store numbers that begin with 1 and that Access increments by 1 automatically as each new record is added to the table. You cannot edit the values in these fields, because they are generated automatically by Access. AutoNumber fields can be used as primary keys because a unique value for each record will be created automatically.

■ **Yes/No fields** can accept only one of two logical values. Usually the responses are shown as either *Yes* or *No*, but they can also be displayed as *True* or *False* or as *On* or *Off*.

■ **OLE Object fields** hold objects, such as Microsoft Word documents, pictures, graphs, and sounds, that have been created in other programs using the OLE protocol.

OFFICE ASSISTANT *The use of OLE object fields is beyond the scope of this book. If you want to learn more about OLE objects, ask the Office Assistant for help.*

■ **Hyperlink fields** allow you to store text or graphics that you can click to link to a file or an Internet site. You'll learn more about hyperlinks in Lesson 8.

■ **Lookup Wizard fields** let you choose values from another table or create a list of values to be used. Choosing this option starts a Wizard to guide you through your choices.

ADDING FIELD NAMES AND TYPES

With the following steps you will add field names and types to the orders table.

HANDS ON

1. Make sure the orders table you began creating is still open in Table Design view and the insertion point is somewhere within the CustomerID field.

2. Click the Maximize button.

The screen is filled with the Design view of the orders table.

3. Click below the field name CustomerID.

The insertion point moves to the second row in the Field Name column.

4. Type **OrderDate** and press ⌊Tab⌋.

Access moves you to the Data Type column, automatically selecting Text as the data type.

5. Click the downward-pointing arrow at the right end of the Data Type drop-down list box.

Access displays the list of available data types.

6. Click Date/Time.

Access closes the drop-down list box and displays Date/Time in the Data Type column to indicate that this data type is selected.

7. Click directly below the OrderDate field.

8. Type **FruitType** as the field name and press ⌊Tab⌋.

Access moves you to the Data Type column, automatically selecting Text as the data type.

9. Leave the data type for the FruitType field as text and enter the following field names and types in the list below:

FIELD NAME	DATA TYPE
Quantity	Number
Price	Currency
ShippingAmount	Currency
PaymentDate	Date/Time
PaymentAmount	Currency
PaymentType	Text
Reference	Text

T I P   *You can select the data type more quickly by typing its first letter while the insertion point is in the Data Type column; for example, press* **n** *to choose number,* **c** *to choose currency, and so on.*

After you have entered the field names and data types, your screen should look like the one in Figure 2-14.

Data types

Field names

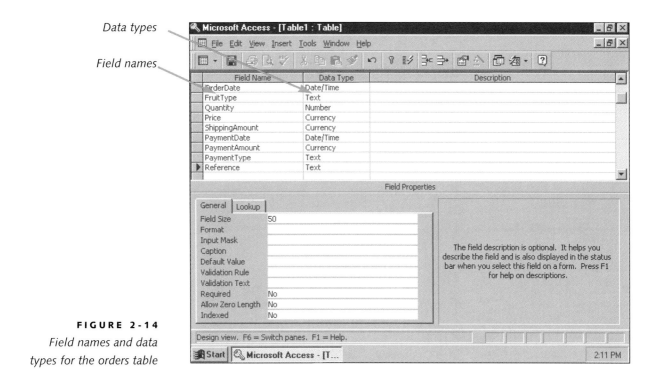

FIGURE 2-14

Field names and data types for the orders table

PICKING FIELD SIZES

For many data types, including Yes/No and Date/Time, Access automatically sets the field size. For Text and Number fields, however, you need to determine the size of the field. As you learned earlier, Text fields can be anywhere from 0 to 255 characters long; you determine the size simply by clicking the Field Size text box in the Field Properties area and entering the desired value. The number you enter determines the maximum number of characters that will fit in the field.

TIP *When you create tables with the Table Wizard or in Table Design view, the default (preset) sizes for Text fields are usually rather high. You'll usually want to decrease the sizes of such fields, using only as many characters as you need. Among other reasons, this helps ensure that correct values are entered. As an example, you would set the field size of a field to hold state abbreviations to two characters. Limiting this field size will prevent users from unintentionally entering three-digit state codes.*

For Number fields, in contrast, you can choose one of the following six number types:

■ The **Byte** number type lets you store whole numbers from 0 to 255. You can't enter fractional values in these fields.

■ The **Integer** number type lets you store whole numbers from -32,768 to 32,767. Again, you can't enter fractional values in this type of field.

■ The **Long Integer** number type lets you store whole numbers from roughly -2.1 billion to 2.1 billion. (Note that AutoNumber fields actually have the Long Integer number type.) Again, you can't enter fractional values in this type of field.

- The **Single** number type lets you store real numbers (fractional values allowed) with seven decimal digits of precision.

- The **Double** number type lets you store real numbers (fractional values allowed) with 15 decimal digits of precision.

- The **Replication ID** number type lets you establish a unique identifier for replication. It is used to identify tables, records, and other objects.

EDITING FIELD SIZES

In the next few steps, you will change some of the default field sizes for the orders table.

HANDS ON

1. Click the FruitType field name.

2. Press F6 .

Access moves you to the Field Size text box under Field Properties. Note the default size for the FruitType field is 50.

3. Type **20**

4. Click the PaymentType field name.

5. Press F6 .

6. Type **15**

7. Click the Reference field name.

8. Press F6 .

9. Type **25**

The field sizes are now smaller, more accurately reflecting the amount of data they will contain.

SETTING OTHER FIELD PROPERTIES

In the Field Properties area at the bottom of the Table Design view window, Access presents various text boxes. The text boxes displayed vary depending on the data type of the selected field. These text boxes enable you to change a range of properties associated with the current field. **Field properties** control the way the field looks and behaves. One such property is field size, as discussed earlier. You can also change other field properties, including the following:

field properties Field settings that control the way a field looks and behaves.

- **Format.** Access provides a number of predefined formats for Number and Date/Time fields, among others. For example, you can choose the Percent format to display numbers as percentages, and you can choose the Medium Date format to display dates in the format *dd-mmm-yy* (as in 19-Jun-98).

- **Decimal places.** If you choose the Number or Currency data type, Access permits you to control the number of decimal places displayed.

■ **Input mask.** If you choose the Text, Number, Date/Time, or Currency data type, Access allows you to create an input mask to ensure that a particular format is applied to the data in that field. For example, you could create an input mask to guarantee that all Social Security numbers would match the format ###-##-#### or that all phone numbers would be in the form (###) ###-####.

■ **Caption.** If you have long field names, you may want to enter captions for certain fields. These captions are used as column headings in tables and as field labels in forms. (You can enter two-word captions such as *First Name* when you have single-word field names such as *ContactFirstName.*) If you leave the caption property blank, the field names themselves are used as labels.

■ **Default value.** Typing a value in the Default Value text box instructs Access to automatically enter that value in this field for new records. For instance, if you have a Yes/No field in which 90 percent of your records contain a Yes response, you can save yourself and others some time by giving the field a default value of Yes. Other examples are default state codes if most of your employees live in a certain state and default quantities if the majority of your customers order the same number of items.

■ **Required.** No is the default for this property. A setting of Yes means that the field must be filled in when you enter a record; that is, Access will not allow you to continue entering data for the next record if you leave the field blank.

OFFICE ASSISTANT   *If you're curious about some of the field properties not mentioned here, highlight them and read the descriptions in the lower-right corner of the screen or consult the Office Assistant.*

CHANGING FIELD PROPERTIES

Now that you've rounded out your knowledge of some of the basic field properties, you're ready to complete Be Fruitful's orders table in Table Design view.

HANDS ON

1. Click the CustomerID field name.

2. Press F6.

The Field Size box should read *Long Integer.*

3. If *Long Integer* does not appear in the Field Size box, display the drop-down list box by clicking the downward-pointing arrow, and choose Long Integer.

Now this field will match up with the CustomerID field in the BFCustomers table, which is an AutoNumber field.

4. Click the Quantity field name.

5. Press F6.

The Field Size is displayed as Long Integer. You can save storage space by making this field smaller.

6. Click the drop-down list arrow beside the Field Size text box.

7. Click Integer.

8. With the Quantity field still selected, double-click the Default Value text box.

The 0 in the box is highlighted.

9. Type **1** to change the 0 to 1.

Now when an order is filled out, Access will assume that the quantity ordered is one unless it is changed.

To find out which field is active, look at the top part of the Table Design view window. An arrow to the left of the field names points to the active field.

10. Click in the Description column of the Reference field.

11. Type **Enter check or credit card number**

The default settings set by Access have been modified now to meet your needs.

CHOOSING A PRIMARY KEY

row selector A small box to the left of a field (in Table Design view) that you can click to select the entire field.

When creating a table with the Table Wizard, you set the primary key in the Table Wizard dialog box. When you create a table in Design view, you must set the primary key yourself. To set the primary key, you first select a field with the row selector. The **row selector** is the small box to the left of a field.

T I P *Clicking the row selector highlights the entire field. You can select multiple adjacent fields by dragging over their row selectors. You can select non-adjacent fields by holding down* Ctrl *and clicking the row selector of each field to be selected.*

SETTING THE PRIMARY KEY

In the orders table, you must choose two fields as the primary key. If you just picked the customer number as the key, you would not be able to distinguish between different orders made by the same customer.

HANDS ON

1. Click the row selector to the left of the CustomerID field.

The entire CustomerID row is highlighted.

2. Press and hold down Shift and click the row selector to the left of FruitType. Then release Shift.

Access highlights the CustomerID, OrderDate, and FruitType fields.

3. Click the Primary Key toolbar button or choose Primary Key from the Edit menu.

Access places small key-shaped icons in the row selectors for the CustomerID, OrderDate, and FruitType fields, as shown in Figure 2-15.

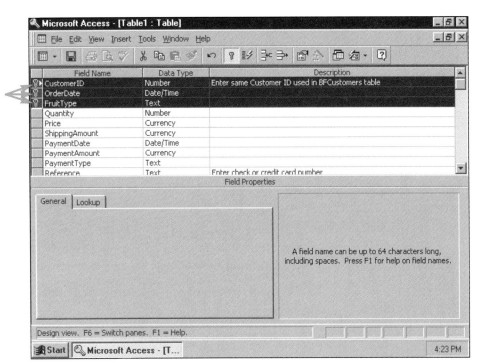

Primary key indicators →

FIGURE 2-15
The Primary Key set for three fields

You've completed the structure for the orders table, but you need to complete one more step; you need to save this table design for future use.

SAVING THE TABLE DESIGN

save To take information from your computer's memory and store it on a more permanent medium—usually a floppy disk or a hard drive.

As you may know, to **save** is the process of taking information from your computer's memory and storing it on a more permanent medium—usually a floppy disk or a hard drive. When you create tables with the Table Wizard, Access automatically saves them, using the table name you supply. When you create or modify tables in Table Design view, in contrast, you need to tell Access to save the table, much as you need to save documents you create with your word processing program. You'll want to save frequently as you work in case of a power outage or other event that can cause you to lose data that hasn't been saved.

N O T E   *When you save a table, it's not placed in a file of its own but instead is stored in the file of the associated database, which may have an **.mdb** extension. For example, both the BFCustomers table you created earlier and the orders table you just created will be stored in the Be Fruitful.mdb file. The same is true of other Access objects—whether they're forms, reports, queries, macros, or modules, they're all stored in the associated database file.*

SAVING THE ORDERS TABLE

Now you'll save Be Fruitful's orders table so you can change its design later if necessary, and, equally important, so you can enter data into it in the next lesson.

HANDS ON

1. Click the Save toolbar button or choose Save from the File menu.

Access displays the Save As dialog box, as shown in Figure 2-16; you will enter a file name for your table in this dialog box.

FIGURE 2-16

The Save As dialog box

2. Type **BFOrders** in the Table Name text box and click OK.

Access returns you to Table Design view, with your table design still visible. Note, however, that the table name *BFOrders* now shows in the title bar. This indicates that the file has been saved.

3. Click the table's Close button to the right of the menu bar.

Access closes the BFOrders table and returns you to the Database window for the Be Fruitful database.

If you attempt to close a table design that includes unsaved changes, Access displays a dialog box asking whether you want to save your changes. You would choose Yes if you want to save the changes, No to discard them, or Cancel to cancel the operation and return to Table Design view.

NOTE   *When you use the Save command to save a table for the first time, Access requests a table name. When you update your table design and save it again, the modified table is simply saved under the same name, so Access has no need to prompt you for a new file name. If for some reason you want to save a copy of the table under a new name, however, you can do so by using the Save As/Export command on the File menu.*

MODIFYING THE TABLE DESIGN

Whether you've created a table with the Table Wizard or in Table Design view, at some point you may need to make changes to the structure of your table. You might need to change field names or data types, to add a field you left out, eliminate a field you no longer need, or in general to reshuffle your fields to better suit your needs or your sense of order. All of these changes can be made in the Table Design view.

WARNING   *You can change the table structure after you've entered data into the table, but proceed with caution if you do. You run the risk of losing or unintentionally modifying your data.*

In this guided activity, you'll modify the BFCustomers table that you created earlier in this lesson. Among other things, you'll add a few new fields, remove a field, and switch the order of two fields. These fundamental skills will serve you well when it's time to refine the design of any table, whether simple or complex.

ADDING CAPTIONS TO FIELDS

captions Words or phrases used to abbreviate or clarify field names. Captions are used as labels in forms and tables.

HANDS ON

In this exercise, you will add a field to the end of the table and create captions for fields. As you learned in the "Setting Other Field Properties" section, **captions** are the words and phrases you type to abbreviate or clarify field names. Captions are used as labels in forms and tables.

1. In the Be Fruitful Database window, click the BFCustomers table and then click the Design button.

You'll see the BFCustomers table in Table Design view, as shown in Figure 2-17.

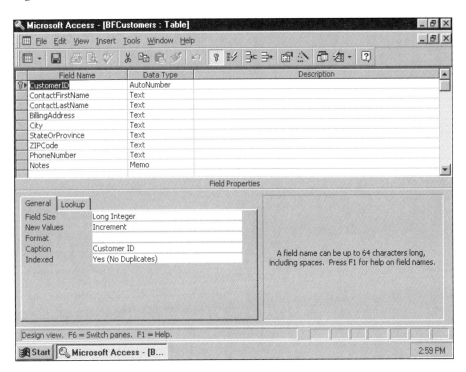

FIGURE 2-17
The BFCustomers table in Design view

2. Click directly below the field name Notes.

3. Type **ExtraCatalogs**

To add a new field at the end of the table structure, you go to the bottom of the display and enter the information for the new field.

4. Press Tab to move to the Data Type column.

5. Type **y** to select Yes/No data type.

6. Press Tab.

7. Type **Offers for holiday specials, exotic fruits, and more**

8. Click in the Caption text box in the Field Properties area.

9. Type **Extra Catalogs**

N O T E *When you create fields with the Table Wizard, captions are automatically assigned to those field names that contain two or more words. For instance, the Table Wizard assigns a caption of Contact First Name to the ContactFirstName field. However, when you create fields in Design view, captions are not automatically created. For consistent spacing within labels (which will appear on reports and forms), add captions to those field names which you create in Design view.*

10. Click anywhere within the ZIPCode field in the top portion of the window.

11. Click the Caption text box.

12. Type **ZIP Code**

During data entry and the display of the table, your fields appear with easier-to-read labels.

ADDING AND REMOVING FIELDS

With the following steps, you will add a new field between existing fields and remove a field. Then you will see how you can "undo" changes to the table when you change your mind or make a mistake.

1. Click anywhere within the row for the Notes field.

2. Click the Insert Rows toolbar button or choose Rows from the Insert menu.

Access adds a blank row above the Notes field and places the insertion point within this row. You use this technique to insert new rows between existing ones rather than after the last row.

3. Type **DateJoined** in the Field Name column.

4. Press ⟨Tab⟩.

5. Choose the Date/Time data type.

6. Type the caption **Date Joined**

7. Click anywhere within the Notes field.

8. Click the Delete Rows toolbar button or choose Delete Rows from the Edit menu.

Access deletes the active row—in this case, the Notes field. Now you realize that you actually need to retain the Notes field.

9. Click the Undo Delete toolbar button or choose Undo Delete from the Edit menu.

Access restores the Notes field.

You can take advantage of the Undo command only if you act quickly enough. Choosing Undo generally undoes your most recent action only, whether you deleted a row, moved a row, typed some text, or chose a new data type. If you've done something else in the interim, however, such as deleting another field or typing some text, you won't be able to undo your earlier action with this command.

MOVING A FIELD

Besides adding and removing fields, you can change the order of the fields in the list—which you'll do in the following steps. Before you finish this lesson, you'll make a few more changes to complete the design of the table.

HANDS ON

1. Click the row selector for the ContactFirstName field.

Access highlights the entire row.

2. Place your mouse pointer directly over the row selector for the selected row and then drag downward.

Access attaches a small grayed rectangle to the bottom of the mouse pointer and also displays a dark horizontal line; the selected field will move to just below the horizontal line if you release the mouse button.

3. Drag downward until the dark horizontal line appears just below the ContactLastName field, as shown in Figure 2-18.

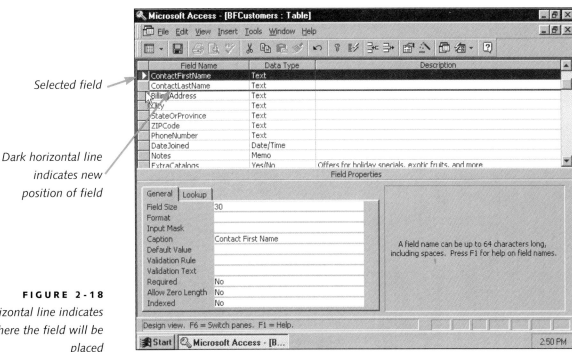

Selected field

Dark horizontal line indicates new position of field

FIGURE 2-18

A horizontal line indicates where the field will be placed

4. Release the mouse button.

Access moves the field to its new location in the table, below the last name field. You even can move several adjacent fields at once by using this method.

FINISHING TOUCHES

Perform these last few steps to improve the appearance and efficiency of the tables.

1. With the BFCustomers Table Design view still open, change the field size of the ContactLastName field to **30**

2. Change the size of the BillingAddress field to **50**

3. Change the size of the City field to **30**

4. Change the size of the StateOrProvince field to **2**

5. Type **List preferences, allergies, and shipping notes** in the Description for the Notes field.

Now that you're through modifying the BFCustomers table, you need to save it again to preserve your changes.

6. Click the Save toolbar button.

Since you named and saved this table earlier, Access saves the updated table without first prompting you for a table name.

7. Close the BFCustomers table.

8. Select the BFOrders table and click the Design button.

9. Create captions for the following fields:

Field	*Caption*
CustomerID	Customer ID
OrderDate	Order Date
FruitType	Fruit Type
ShippingAmount	Shipping Amount
PaymentDate	Payment Date
PaymentAmount	Payment Amount
PaymentType	Payment Type

10. Save the BFOrders table.

11. Close the BFOrders table.

12. Close the Be Fruitful Database window.

13. Exit Access.

LESSON SUMMARY AND EXERCISES

After you complete this lesson, you should know how to do the following:

PLANNING AHEAD

■ Before you create a database, you must determine the purpose of the database, the categories of information you need, how many tables you need, and how the tables will work together.

CREATING A DATABASE

■ Click the Blank Database option on the initial Access dialog box. Choose the drive and folder where the database should be stored, type a name for the database, and click Create.

CREATING TABLES

■ To create a table using the Table Wizard, click the New button in the Tables tab of the Database window. Then choose Table Wizard in the New Table dialog box.

■ To add fields from the sample table, select the field name and click the > button.

■ To rename fields in the field list, click the Rename Field button and type the new name for the field.

■ To create a table in Design view, click the New button in the Tables tab of the Database window and double-click the Design View option.

■ To enter fields in Design view, enter field names, data types, and descriptions in the upper portion of the Table Design view window.

■ To set field properties, enter the field size, input mask, caption, and default value in the Field Properties portion of the Table Design view window.

■ To set the primary key in Design view, click the row selector(s). Then click the Primary Key toolbar button.

SAVING THE TABLE DESIGN

■ To save the table in Design view, click the Save toolbar button and give the table a name.

MODIFYING THE TABLE DESIGN

■ To change a table's design, select the table in the Tables tab of the Database window and click the Design button.

■ To add a field to the end of the table, click the row beneath the last field in the table and enter the name, data type, and other properties for the field.

■ To add a field within the table, click the field below the field to be inserted and click the Insert Rows toolbar button.

- To remove a field from a table, click the field to be removed and click the Delete Rows toolbar button.

- To reverse your most recent action, click the Undo toolbar button.

- To reposition a field in the table, click its row selector and drag the field to its new location.

NEW TERMS TO REMEMBER

After you complete this lesson, you should know the meaning of the following terms:

captions	primary key
common field	properties
data type	row selector
field properties	save
insertion point	Wizard

MATCHING EXERCISE

Match each of the terms with the definitions on the right:

TERMS	DEFINITIONS
1. primary key	**a.** Data type to use for numbers that will be used to perform calculations
2. input mask	**b.** Value that Access enters into field automatically
3. row selector	
4. AutoNumber field	**c.** Feature that enables you to reverse your previous action
5. Date/Time	**d.** Field of same name in two tables that enables you to link those tables together.
6. default value	
7. Undo	**e.** Flashing vertical line that appears in text boxes
8. common field	**f.** Data type that enables you to perform date arithmetic
9. Number	
10. insertion point	**g.** Field property that forces your data into a particular format
	h. Box that you click to highlight an entire field in Design view
	i. Field or fields that uniquely identify each record in a table
	j. Field that Access increments by 1 for each new record

COMPLETION EXERCISE

Fill in the missing word or phrase for each of the following:

1. The _____ guides you through each step of creating a table, prompting you for the needed information.

2. When a field name is long or difficult to identify, a _____ can be used to abbreviate or clarify it.

3. In the top portion of the Table Design view window, you may specify the _____, _____, and _____ for each field.

4. To specify that a field must be filled in, set the _____ property to Yes.

5. The purpose of a(n) _____ is to format your data in a particular way.

6. To make sure your table is not lost due to a power outage, you should _____ your work frequently.

7. A data type that displays numbers with dollar signs is called the _____ type.

8. Text fields can hold up to _____ characters.

9. To reverse your previous action, click the _____ toolbar button.

10. A(n) _____ is an option that controls the kind of information that can be entered into a field.

SHORT-ANSWER QUESTIONS

Write a brief answer to each of the following questions:

1. What must two tables share for you to be able to link them together?

2. List at least two reasons for dividing your data into multiple tables instead of placing it all in one very large table.

3. Mention at least one advantage of creating tables using the Table Wizard; then list at least one disadvantage.

4. Describe at least two reasons why you'd used a Date/Time field rather than a Text field for dates.

5. Which data type would you use for Social Security numbers and why?

6. Explain why you can't enter duplicate values in primary key fields.

7. Under what circumstances would you use a Memo data type rather than a Text data type?

8. List the steps you would perform to add a new field between the DatePurchased and Amount fields in a table.

9. List the steps you would perform to remove the Amount field from a table.

10. How would you make a field called AccountNumber the primary key in a table when in the Design view?

APPLICATION PROJECTS

Perform the following actions to complete these projects:

1. Open the **Be Fruitful** database in the **Lessons** folder of your Student Data Disk. Then create a table with the Table Wizard. Base your new table on the Employees sample table. Add the following fields: EmployeeID, SocialSecurityNumber, LastName, FirstName, MiddleName, Address, City, StateOrProvince, and PostalCode. Retain the suggested table name of *Employees* and let Access create the primary key for you. Indicate that this new table is not related to any of the existing tables in the **Be Fruitful** database. In the final Table Wizard dialog box, choose the Modify the Table Design option button and click Finish to view the newly created table in Table Design view. Notice the primary key. On a separate sheet of paper, state the field which was selected as the primary key and explain why you think Access chose this field as the primary key. When you are finished, close the table. Then select the Employees table in the Database window; click the Edit menu, click Delete, and click Yes to delete the table. Close the **Be Fruitful** database.

2. Create a new database in the **Projects** folder of your Student Data Disk. Name the database **Personal.** Use the Table Wizard to create a table. Base the table on the Tasks sample table. Include the following fields in this order:

   TaskID

   TaskDescription

   StartDate

   EndDate

   Notes

   Name the table **To Dos.** Let Access set the primary key. In the final dialog box, choose the Modify the Table Design button. Use the Design view to add two fields—TaskComplete (a yes/no field) and Priority (an Integer field)—to the end of the list. Create a caption for the TaskComplete field. Review the table structure and write down the data types and field properties for each of the fields. Save and close the table and close the **Personal** database.

3. Create a database called **Music** in your **Projects** folder. Use the Table Wizard to create a table in the **Music** database. Base your table on the Recordings sample table. (Note: you'll have to click the Personal option button to see this sample table.) Add the following fields in this order:

RecordingID

RecordingTitle

RecordingArtistID

MusicCategoryID

RecordingLabel

YearReleased

DatePurchased

Notes

PurchasePrice

Format

Accept the default table name and primary key chosen by Access. In the last dialog box, choose the Modify the Table Design button. Review the table structure and write down the data types and field properties for each of the fields. Close the table.

Create another new table in the **Music** database. This table will include data on recording artists. Do not use the Table Wizard; instead create the table in Design view.

Use the following field names in the order listed along with the associated properties:

Field Name	DataType	Field Properties
RecordingArtistID	AutoNumber	Field Size=Long Integer
		New Values=Increment
		Caption=Artist ID
RecordingArtistName	Text	Field Size=30
		Caption=Artist Name
Notes	Memo	

Choose RecordingArtistID as the primary key. Save the table as **Recording Artists**. Close the table.

Create a third table in the **Music** database. This table will include data on music categories. Create the table in Design view.

Use the following field names in the order listed along with the associated properties:

Field Name	Data Type	Field Properties
MusicCategoryID	AutoNumber	Field Size=Long Integer
		New Values=Increment
		Caption=Artist ID
MusicCategory	Text	Field Size=15
		Caption=Category

Choose MusicCategoryID as the primary key. Save the table as **Music Categories**. Close the table and close the **Music** database.

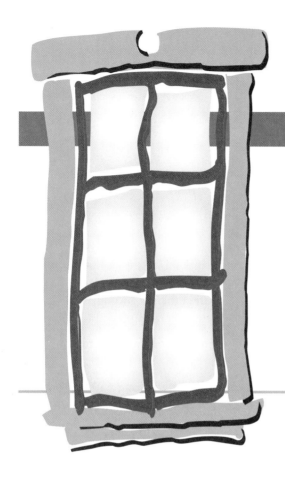

LESSON 3

ADDING AND MAINTAINING DATA IN DATASHEET VIEW

OBJECTIVES

After you complete this lesson, you will be able to do the following:

- *Add data to your tables in Datasheet view.*
- *Copy and paste data from another database.*
- *Navigate through the datasheet.*
- *Select fields, columns, and records.*
- *Edit records.*
- *Delete records.*
- *Undo changes.*
- *Search for and replace particular strings of characters.*
- *Change column widths and row heights in the datasheet.*
- *Rearrange datasheet columns.*
- *Hide and freeze datasheet columns.*

CONTENTS

Adding Data to a Table

Retrieving Data from Another Table

Copying Tables from Another Database

Editing and Viewing Records
  in the Datasheet

Searching for Records Based
  on Their Contents

Changing the Datasheet Display

n this lesson, you'll get to know the datasheet. First, you will discover how to enter data in the Datasheet view; you'll also retrieve additional data from the Student Data Disk provided with this tutorial. Once you have some data on hand, you'll find out several ways of navigating through the datasheet to get to the record you need. You'll also learn how to select fields and records so that you can make changes to them. Then you'll learn how to edit your data—how to modify and replace existing data, delete one or more records, and undo changes when you make that inevitable misstep. Finally, you'll see how to take advantage of the Find and Replace features both to find and to find and change records in a single operation.

Contact Last N	Contact First N	Phone Numbe	Date Joined
			1/15/92
Apfelbaum	Franklin	(919) 888-9999	4/21/92
Bechdel	Alice	(415) 666-5432	6/5/92
Criton	Will	(401) 863-9999	11/15/92
Dempster	Anne	(707) 333-9876	2/5/93
Elias	Joanne	(301) 123-4567	4/27/93
Frankel	James	(503) 882-1499	6/14/93
Guggenheim	Mason	(510) 282-3337	9/4/93
Hatfield	Emma	(207) 223-3445	11/11/93
Isherwood	Christine	(212) 701-8881	12/17/93
Jackson	Jacqueline	(502) 999-2256	1/4/94
Wintergreen	Shelly	(303) 468-9753	3/22/94
Menendez	Erica	(213) 343-3344	5/1/94
Zheng	Alicia	(503) 320-1577	6/29/94
Ng	Patrick	(219) 888-1112	8/29/94
Turlow	Bob	(801) 579-0864	9/5/94
Zheng	James	(503) 220-1928	12/25/94
Marais	Jean-Luc	(617) 333-4444	1/19/94
Savallis	Jordi	(212) 765-4322	

Record: 1 of 35

Datasheet View

ADDING DATA TO A TABLE

In Lesson 2, you spent a great deal of time creating tables. You built table *structures*—choosing the fields that your tables would include and their properties. Now that these structures are in place, you're ready to actually enter data into them. You can add data to your tables by using custom forms, which you'll learn more about in Lesson 5. However, Access also provides the **datasheet**, a layout of rows and columns that permits you to add, edit, and view your data immediately—without distractions or delay. The datasheet's column-and-row format will remind you of a spreadsheet or worksheet if you've ever used one.

datasheet A tabular layout of rows and columns that allows you to add, edit, and view your data immediately.

NOTE *Even if you devise custom forms for data entry, the datasheet remains useful for browsing through a large number of records at once and making minor additions and modifications as you go along.*

OPENING THE TABLE

In this exercise, you'll open the BFCustomers table that you created in the previous lesson.

HANDS ON

1. If necessary, turn on your computer. Then start Access.

2. Insert your Student Data Disk into drive A.

3. When the initial Microsoft Access dialog box appears, look for the file **A:\Lessons\Be Fruitful** in the box that lists recently used files. If it appears, double-click it.

4. If A:\Lessons\Be Fruitful does not appear in the list of files, double-click More Files. Navigate to the **Lessons** folder of your Student Data Disk and double-click **Be Fruitful**.

T I P   *If Access is already running, click the Open Database toolbar button and open the* **Be Fruitful** *file.*

Access displays the Database window for the Be Fruitful database, as shown in Figure 3-1.

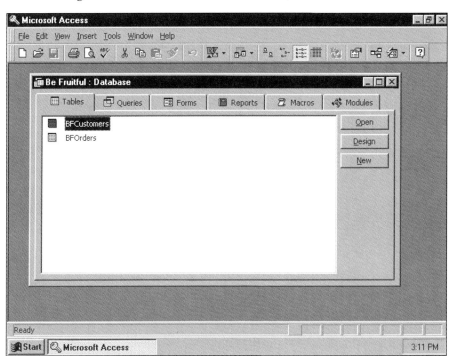

FIGURE 3-1
Tables in the
Be Fruitful database

5. Make sure that the Tables tab is selected in the Database window and select the BFCustomers table.

6. Click the Open button in the Database window.

T I P   *Double-clicking on the table name will also open the table.*

Access opens the BFCustomers table in Datasheet view, as shown in Figure 3-2. You can see some of the field names (or captions) you defined in Lesson 2, but the table is empty; that is, it contains no data. A single blank row appears, waiting for your input.

The triangle to the left of the record indicates the **current record**, sometimes called *the record with the focus*. The box to the left of each record in Datasheet view is called the **record selector**.

current record The record that is active. In Datasheet view, the current record is the row that contains a triangle or pencil icon in the record selector.

record selector The box to the left of a record that you can click to select the entire record.

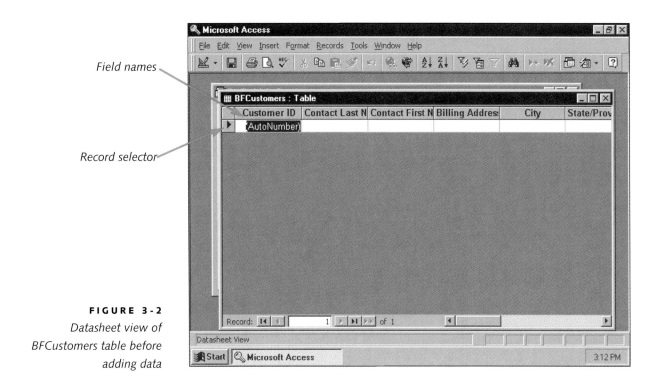

Field names

Record selector

FIGURE 3-2
Datasheet view of BFCustomers table before adding data

ADDING A RECORD

During the next few steps, you'll type in the information for the first record in the table.

HANDS ON

1. Press Tab or click the first blank box under the Contact Last Name field.

Access moves the insertion point into the Contact Last Name field.

TIP *You can press Enter instead of Tab to move to the next field in the datasheet. Use whichever method you find most convenient.*

2. Type **Apfelbaum** and press Tab.

As soon as you start typing, Access automatically enters the value 1 into the Customer ID field for this first customer. When you press Tab, the insertion point moves into the Contact First Name field. Note that Access has created a second blank record with an asterisk (*) in the record selector. An asterisk indicates a new record in which you can type data. The record in which you are typing has a pencil icon in the record selector, as shown in Figure 3-3. The pencil icon indicates that you are currently editing the record and it has not yet been saved.

OFFICE ASSISTANT *For information about symbols that appear in the record selector, type* **record selector** *in the Office Assistant box.*

3. Type **Franklin** and press Tab.

Access moves the insertion point into the Billing Address field.

AutoNumber field automatically assigns the next consecutive number

Pencil icon shows that the record you are editing has not yet been saved

Asterisk indicates a new record

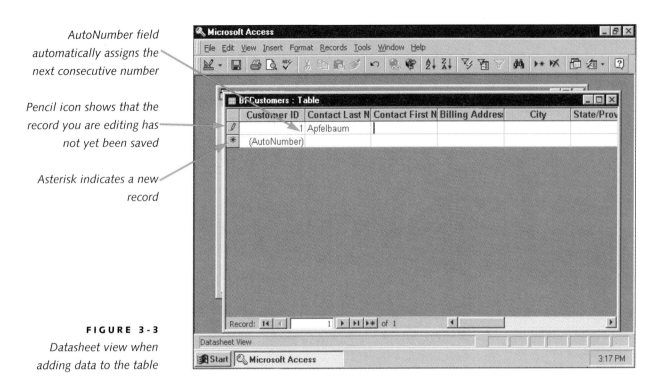

FIGURE 3-3
Datasheet view when adding data to the table

4. Type **1777 Lois Ln.** and press Tab.

5. Type **Rock Creek** and press Tab.

Access scrolls the display so you can see the State/Province field in full. Only a few fields show in Datasheet view at once. Pressing Tab automatically scrolls the display to bring any additional fields into view.

6. Type **NC** in the State/Province field.

7. Press Tab to move to the ZIP Code field (notice that the display scrolls again), enter **28333**, and then enter **1234**

Note that you don't have to enter the hyphen; because of the input mask, Access automatically formats the ZIP Code as 28333-1234.

TIP   *You don't need to enter the punctuation characters in the ZIP Code and Phone Number fields, but it's OK if you do—Access won't enter the extra punctuation marks.*

8. Press Tab to move to the Phone Number field, enter **919**, enter **888**, and finally enter **9999** and press Tab.

Notice that Access once again enters the punctuation for you because of the input mask associated with the Phone Number field.

9. Type **1/15/92** in the Date Joined field and press Tab.

A description of the Notes field appears on the status bar.

NOTE   *If you enter an invalid date, such as 13/15/92 you will see a warning box to inform you of your error. Be cautioned though—if you enter 13/5/92, Access will assume that you intend to enter the 13th day of the 5th month and will translate the date to 5/13/92.*

10. Press Tab to leave the Notes field blank.

You should now see a box in the Extra Catalogs field. Clicking this box puts a check mark in it, meaning *Yes*. Leaving the box blank means *No*. Also, since you entered a description for this field, it appears in the status bar.

11. Press Tab to accept the default value of No.

ADDING ADDITIONAL RECORDS

At this point you are ready to enter several more records in the BFCustomers table.

HANDS ON

1. Press Tab to move to the Contact Last Name field.

2. Type **Bechdel** and press Tab.

As before, Access automatically increments the value in the Customer ID field—this time, entering the value 2—and creates a new blank record at the end of the table.

3. Type **Alice** and press Tab.

4. Type **7374 Backwoods Rd.** and press Tab.

Notice that some of the address scrolled out of view as you typed. When you pressed Tab to move to the next field, only the beginning of the address appeared. Don't worry: It's still all there; it just doesn't fit in the datasheet display. Later in this lesson, you'll learn how to change column widths and row heights so you can see more of your data at once on the screen.

5. Type **Sebastopol** and press Tab.

6. Type **CA** and press Tab.

7. Type **97777-1111** and press Tab.

8. Type **(415) 666-5432** and press Tab. (Remember that you don't have to enter the punctuation for the ZIP Code and Phone Number fields.)

9. Type **4/21/92**

At this point all of the data for the second record has been entered. The remaining fields will be left blank or take on their default value.

10. Click the New Record toolbar button.

Access moves down to the next row to the new blank record into which you can enter data.

T I P *The New Record button moves you to or creates a new record at the bottom of the table. You can use this button to complete your entry of a record. As you saw with the entry of the first record, pressing* Tab *in the last field also moves you to a new blank record.*

Next you'll enter some additional data using the techniques you just learned.

11. Type in the names and addresses listed here.

N O T E   *You can leave all Notes fields blank for the moment, and you can retain the default setting of No for all the Extra Catalog fields.*

Record #3

Contact Last Name	Criton
Contact First Name	Will
Billing Address	1 Oak Pl.
City	Providence
State/Province	RI
ZIP Code	02900-2338
Phone Number	(401) 863-9999
Date Joined	6/5/92

Record #4

Contact Last Name	Dempster
Contact First Name	Anne
Billing Address	25 Forest Knoll
City	Santa Rosa
State/Province	CA
ZIP Code	99887-2355
Phone Number	(707) 333-9876
Date Joined	11/15/92

Record #5

Contact Last Name	Everett
Contact First Name	Joan
Billing Address	2234 Hanley Pl.
City	Baltimore
State/Province	MD
ZIP Code	21122-5634
Phone Number	(301) 123-4567
Date Joined	2/5/93

N O T E   *If you're used to word processing and spreadsheet programs, you may be wondering when to save your data. Access automatically saves your data when you move to a new record. If you want to save before that point, however—perhaps you're entering a long memo field—you can click on the Records menu and then click Save Record or press* Shift+Enter. *Make sure you save your last record by moving to a new record.*

ETRIEVING DATA FROM ANOTHER TABLE

So that you can work with a more realistic amount of material, you'll now retrieve some data from the Student Data Disk. Because you want to add data from another database, you can't just open the other database.

Instead, you'll learn a simple way to do so with fairly standard Windows techniques for cutting and pasting. Keep in mind, however, that this technique enables you to retrieve data only from Access, not from other programs; also, for this technique to work smoothly, you must be gathering data from a table with the same structure as the one into which you're placing the data.

OFFICE ASSISTANT

If you want to retrieve data that was created in a program other than Access, you can either import or link the data so that Access can recognize its format. For further details, consult the Office Assistant.

COPYING DATA FROM ANOTHER TABLE

With the following steps you will retrieve data from your Student Data Disk. To copy the data, you first have to open the table that contains the records you want to add.

HANDS ON

1. Click the File menu and choose Open Database.

2. If the Lessons folder name appears in the Look In box, click the Up One Level button of the Open dialog box. Otherwise, navigate to the root folder of your Student Data Disk.

You will see the Sample database file in the list box.

3. Double-click **Sample** to open the **Sample** database on the Student Data Disk.

NOTE

You don't need to close one database before opening another; Access does this for you.

You should see the Sample Database window. The BFCust, BFFruit, and BFOrd tables appear under the Tables tab.

4. Double-click BFCust to open the BFCust table.

Access displays the BFCust table in Datasheet view, as shown in Figure 3-4.

FIGURE 3-4

Datasheet view of BFCust table

	Customer ID	Last Name	First Name	Address	City	Sta
▶	1	Frankel	James	32123 Overlook	Portland	OR
	2	Guggenheim	Mason	75 Grizzly Peak	Orinda	CA
	3	Hatfield	Emma	1314 23rd Ave.	Biddeford	ME
	4	Isherwood	Christine	5457 Park Pl.	New York	NY
	5	Jackson	Jacqueline	6633 Dallas Wa	Houston	TX
	6	Kenber	Richard	1310 Arch St.	Berkeley	CA
	7	Wintergreen	Shelly	21 Barbary Ln.	Omaha	NE
	8	Menendez	Erica	303 Hollywood {	Los Angeles	CA
	9	Zheng	Alicia	32 B St.	Ashland	OR
	10	Ng	Patrick	1112 Spruce St	Shaker Heights	OH
	11	Turlow	Bob	81 Hacienda Bl	Santa Fe	NM
	12	Zheng	James	15A Vine St.	Ashland	OR
	13	Marais	Jean-Luc	1379 Montgome	Boston	MA
	14	Savallis	Jordi	100 Riverside D	New York	NY
	15	Yates	Lily	999 35th Ave.	Oakland	CA

BFCust : Table

Record: 1 of 30

5. Click the Edit menu and click Select All Records; or press Ctrl+A.

Access highlights all of the records in the table.

6. Click the Copy toolbar button or click the Edit menu and choose Copy.

Although you can't see any change to the screen, Access has copied all of these records to the **Clipboard**, a temporary storage space in your computer's memory.

Clipboard A temporary storage area in your computer's memory.

7. Click the BFCust table's Close button.

Access displays the warning box shown in Figure 3-5.

8. Read the text in the warning box and click Yes to save the data to the Clipboard.

Access closes the BFCust table and returns you to the Sample Database window.

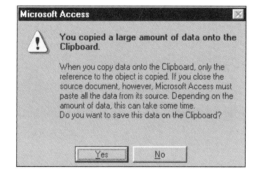

FIGURE 3-5
Warning box displayed when you copy a lot of data

PASTING DATA INTO A TABLE

Now you will paste the data from the Clipboard into your BFCustomers table.

1. Click the Open Database toolbar button.

2. Double-click the **Lessons** folder.

3. Double-click the **Be Fruitful** database.

You return to your Be Fruitful Database window.

4. Double-click the BFCustomers table.

You will see the BFCustomers table with the five records that you entered earlier.

5. Click the Edit menu and choose Paste Append.

The Paste Append option lets you add records to the end of your table. Before it adds the records, however, Access displays the dialog box shown in Figure 3-6. In this box, you can choose Yes to add the records or No to cancel the operation.

FIGURE 3-6

Dialog box that gives you the option to add the records

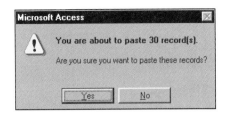

WARNING

You can't use the normal Paste button on the toolbar to paste these records from the Clipboard; you must use the Paste Append command on the Edit menu.

6. Read the text in the dialog box and click Yes.

7. Click anywhere within the table to remove the highlighting. Then click the table's Maximize button.

Your BFCustomers table should resemble the one shown in Figure 3-7. The display at the bottom of the table window indicates that the table now contains 35 records.

Table now contains 35 records

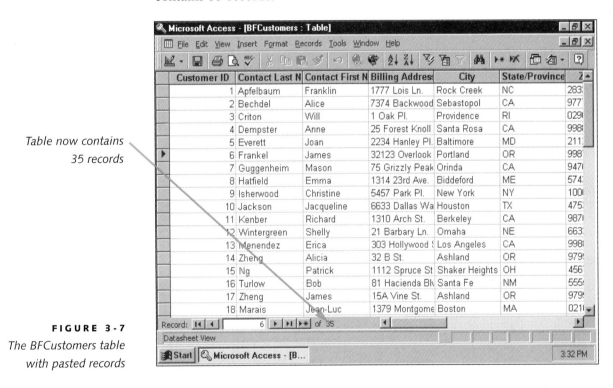

FIGURE 3-7

The BFCustomers table with pasted records

COPYING DATA FROM ANOTHER TABLE

In the next few steps, you will copy the records from a table on the Student Data Disk into your BFOrders table, using the same technique you used in the previous exercise.

HANDS ON

1. Close the BFCustomers table.

2. Open the **Sample** database from the Student Data Disk.

3. Double-click the BFOrd table.

4. Press Ctrl+A to select all records.

5. Click the Copy toolbar button.

6. Close the BFOrd table.

The warning box asks if you want to save the data you copied to the Clipboard.

7. Click Yes.

8. Open the **Be Fruitful** database in your **Lessons** folder.

9. Double-click the BFOrders table. Notice that no data has been entered into the table yet.

10. Click the Edit menu and select Paste Append.

A warning box asks if you want to paste 187 records into the table.

11. Click Yes.

You now have a table with 187 records. Imagine how much time you saved by pasting the data rather than entering each record one at a time!

OFFICE ASSISTANT   *Keep in mind that you can copy and paste between tables with the same structure. If Access identifies a problem, it will create a Paste Error table to hold the data that could not be pasted. For more information on paste errors, ask the Office Assistant.*

COPYING TABLES FROM ANOTHER DATABASE

import The operation in which data from outside of the database is brought into the database.

Another method you can use to add data from another database is to **import**—the process of bringing data from one file into another. In importing, however, you copy an entire table into your database. The new records and the structure of the table you'll import are on your Student Data Disk.

IMPORTING A TABLE

Now you will use Access's Import feature to bring all of the records from a table into your Be Fruitful database.

HANDS ON

1. Click the Close button of the BFOrders table.

The Be Fruitful Database window is on the screen.

2. Click the File menu, move to Get External Data, and then click Import.

The Import dialog box appears, as shown in Figure 3-8.

3. Click the Up One Level button.

4. Double-click the **Sample** database.

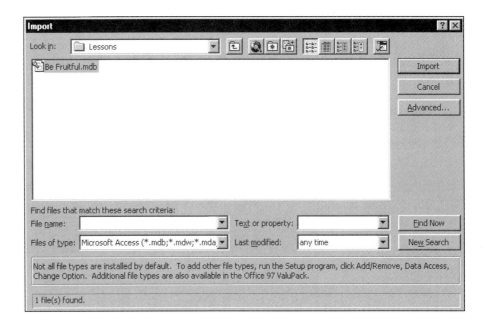

FIGURE 3-8
The Import dialog box

The Import Objects dialog box appears, as shown in Figure 3-9. This dialog box lets you select the objects that you want to copy from the Sample database into the Be Fruitful database.

Tables in Sample database

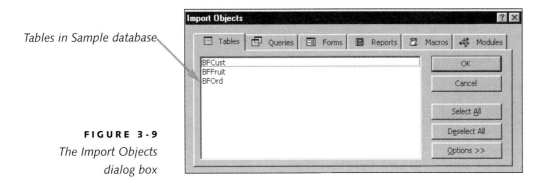

FIGURE 3-9
The Import Objects dialog box

5. Click the Tables tab, if it is not already active.

6. Click BFFruit and then click OK.

After a short pause, the BFFruit table—and all of its records—are copied into the Be Fruitful database. You should see the new table in the Be Fruitful Database window.

E DITING AND VIEWING RECORDS IN THE DATASHEET

Once you've entered a substantial amount of data into your table, you need to know how to move around in the datasheet. When you have only a few records, you can always move the focus to another record just by clicking it. When you have larger amounts of data, you need a few additional strategies to find the records you want and select the fields you want to work on at the moment. You'll learn both keyboard and mouse techniques for navigating through the datasheet while you move through the records that you just entered into the BFCustomers table.

N O T E   *Remember, the record with the focus is simply the one you're editing at the moment. This record usually has a triangle in its record selector, but it would have a pencil if you've made any changes that haven't been saved.*

MOVING FROM RECORD TO RECORD

These next steps illustrate how to maneuver through the records and fields in the BFCustomers table.

1. Open the BFCustomers table.

2. Click the table's Maximize button.

Notice the navigation buttons at the bottom of the window, as shown in Figure 3-10. You use these buttons to make your way from record to record. Note that the text box reads "1" and the gray area to its right reads "of 35." This tells you that the table currently has 35 records and the focus is on the first record. Also notice that the insertion point is in the Customer ID field of the first record.

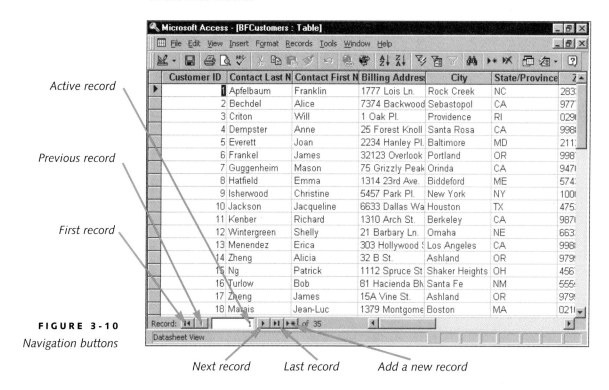

Active record

Previous record

First record

FIGURE 3-10
Navigation buttons

Next record   Last record   Add a new record

3. Click the Last Record button.

Access moves the focus to the last record in the table, placing a triangle in its record selector and highlighting the data in the Customer ID field. The current record is now listed as record 35.

N O T E   *When you use any of the navigation buttons, Access moves the focus to a new record but leaves the same field highlighted. For instance, if the Contact First Name field is selected, clicking the Last Record button moves the focus to the last record in the table and highlights that record's Contact First Name field.*

4. Now click the First Record button.

Access moves the focus to the first record in the table—the record for Franklin Apfelbaum. Once again, the data in the Customer ID field is highlighted.

5. Click the Next Record button twice.

Access moves the focus to the record for Will Criton, the third record.

6. Click the Previous Record button.

The focus moves to the record for Alice Bechdel, the second record.

7. Double-click the current record number (it should be 2) in the text box at the bottom of the screen.

8. Type 3 and press Enter.

The focus moves to the third record—that of Will Criton.

TIP   F5 *is the shortcut key for the GoTo command. Pressing* F5 *selects the current record number so you can type in the number of the record you want to go to.*

There are also easy keyboard techniques for moving from record to record.

9. Try pressing ↓ twice.

The focus moves down two rows, to the record for Joan Everett.

10. Press ↑ three times.

The focus moves up three rows, to Alice Bechdel's record.

MOVING FROM FIELD TO FIELD

So far you've moved from record to record—leaving the same field selected; but, you can also move from field to field. At the moment, you should be in the Customer ID field in the record for Alice Bechdel.

HANDS ON

1. Press Tab.

The highlighting moves over to the Contact Last Name field within the same record.

Pressing Tab moves you to the next field or to the first field of the next record if you're in the last field of the record.

2. Press Shift+Tab.

The highlighting should move back to the Customer ID field.

Pressing Shift+Tab moves you to the previous field or to the last field of the previous record if you're in the first field of the record.

3. Press End.

Pressing End moves you to the last field in the current record.

Access selects the Extra Catalogs field in Alice Bechdel's record.

4. Press Home.

Pressing Home moves you to the first field in the current record.

Access selects the Customer ID field in Alice Bechdel's record.

5. Now press Ctrl+End.

Pressing Ctrl+End moves you to the last field of the last record.

6. Now press Ctrl+Home.

Pressing Ctrl+Home moves you to the first field of the first record.

TIP *If Home, End, Ctrl+Home, and Ctrl+End aren't working as anticipated, first press F2 to highlight the current field, and then try again. As you'll learn in a moment, the F2 key lets you switch between editing and navigating through your data.*

If your table includes more records than will fit on the screen at once, you can also use the vertical or horizontal scroll bars to scroll up and down or to the left or right through your table. However, when you use the scroll bars, the display moves but the focus doesn't change. To switch the focus to a record that you've scrolled into view, click anywhere within it.

EDITING RECORDS

Once you've tracked down the records in which you're interested, you're ready to begin editing. You can easily delete or replace the contents of a particular field, and you can also add to or change the contents of a field. You can delete one or more entire records as well. The Undo feature is useful when you need to reverse your previous action.

EDITING THE BFCUSTOMERS TABLE

Now you'll make a number of changes to the BFCustomers table.

1. The BFCustomers table should still be open. If any records or columns are selected, just click anywhere within the table to remove the highlighting.

2. Press F5, type 5, and press Enter to move to the record for Joan Everett.

3. Press Tab or Shift+Tab until you get to the Contact First Name field for Joan Everett.

Access selects the first name Joan. Note that the entire field is highlighted. **Select** means to choose an item to indicate to Access that you want to operate on that particular item. You now see the field in **reverse video**, with white text against a dark background.

HANDS ON

select To choose an item to indicate to Access that you want to operate on that particular item. Alternatively, select can mean to extract specified subsets of data based on criteria that you define.

reverse video White text against a dark background.

TIP *You can also select fields by double-clicking or by dragging over their contents.*

WARNING *Be careful to notice when a field is selected. If you press Delete when any field is selected, you will delete the contents of the field, and anything you type will replace that content.*

4. Click after the *n* in Joan or press F2.

Notice that the highlighting disappears and is replaced by a blinking insertion point immediately after the *n* in Joan. As you probably know, the insertion point indicates where the text you type will appear, as well as where any deletions will occur.

5. Type **ne** to change the name to Joanne.

6. Press ←.

This action does not move you to the previous field but instead moves the insertion point one character to the left.

7. Press F2 to select the contents of the Contact First Name field.

TIP F2 *is a toggle key. Pressing it once removes the highlighting from a selected field and lets you edit the field's contents. Pressing it again highlights the field's contents.*

8. Press ← again.

This time, pressing ← selects the Contact Last Name field for Joanne Everett's record.

9. Type **Elias**

Access automatically deletes the last name Everett, replacing it with the name Elias.

UNDOING EDITING MISTAKES

When you're making changes to a table, it's quite easy to make changes to the wrong field or wrong record. Fortunately, the Undo feature that you used in the previous lesson works here, too.

HANDS ON

1. Double-click the last name *Guggenheim* in record 7.

2. Press Delete to delete the entire name.

3. Press Esc or click the Undo toolbar button.

Access undoes the change, bringing back the last name you just deleted.

4. Double-click the last name *Hatfield* in record 8.

5. Type **Hernandez**

Access replaces the old last name with the new one.

6. Press Tab to move to the Contact First Name field.

7. Type **Rosa**

8. Press Tab again to move to the Billing Address field.

9. Type **204 Panoramic Way**

10. Press Esc or click the Undo toolbar button.

The address changes from *204 Panoramic Way* back to *1314 23rd Ave.*

11. Press Esc again or click the Undo toolbar button two more times.

Access reverses the rest of the changes to the current record all at once, restoring the name *Emma Hatfield.*

N O T E   *Depending on the last action you performed, the Undo button's name changes. For instance, if you just typed text and want to undo it, the ToolTip for the Undo button reads "Undo Typing." If you want to undo a deletion you just made, the name changes to "Undo Delete."*

UNDOING CHANGES TO A SAVED RECORD

Thus far, you have learned how to undo changes to the current field or undo multiple changes to the current record. When you complete the edits in a record and move to another record, your changes are saved automatically. You might think that the regular Undo keys will not reverse these changes. Fortunately, the Undo option will fix the changes if you catch them in time.

HANDS ON

1. Move the insertion point to the Notes field for record number 4, *Anne Dempster.*

2. Type **Loves kiwis**

3. Press ⟨Tab⟩ to move to the Extra Catalogs field.

4. Press ⟨Spacebar⟩.

The ⟨Spacebar⟩ puts a check mark in this Yes/No field.

5. Press ⟨Tab⟩.

Access automatically saves the changes to Anne Dempster's record when you move to the next record.

6. Click the Edit menu and choose Undo Saved Record.

Access reverses the changes to the Dempster record, even though the record had been saved. This Undo command reverses only the most recent action; if you've done anything else since then, you can't undo the changes to a saved record in this way.

DELETING RECORDS

You can delete entire records from the table. To do so, you must first select the record. With the next steps, you'll remove one of the records from the table.

HANDS ON

1. Click the record selector for Richard Kenber's record (record number 11).

The entire record is selected.

 2. Click the Delete Record toolbar button or press ⟨Delete⟩.

Access displays the warning box shown in Figure 3-11, warning you that you're about to delete a record and giving you a chance to stop the change.

FIGURE 3-11

Warning box telling you that you are about to delete a record

3. Read the text in the box and click Yes.

WARNING

When you delete one or more records, you cannot undo the operation with the Undo command. Your only way out is to cancel the operation when Access displays its warning box.

Access deletes the selected record and moves the subsequent records up to take its place. Note, however, that the values in the Customer ID field have not changed. As you'd expect, customers retain the same ID numbers even if other customers are removed from the database.

NOTE

You can also delete entire fields in Datasheet view by choosing Delete Column from the Edit menu. However, be extremely sure that you want to delete the field and all of its contents before issuing this command. This action cannot be reversed with the Undo command, so if you change your mind you must add the field and retype all of the data in it.

EDITING IN THE ZOOM WINDOW

When you have a lot of text in a field such as a large text or memo field, editing can be difficult. The Zoom window lets you work with these fields much more easily, as you will see during the following steps.

1. Press `Tab` repeatedly until you get to the Notes field for Shelly Wintergreen's record.

2. Press `Shift`+`F2`.

Access opens the Zoom window shown in Figure 3-12; you can use this window to enter longer amounts of text or to edit fields that have a lot of text.

FIGURE 3-12
Zoom window for entering and editing data

3. Type the following text:

Mrs. Wintergreen is an elderly woman. If she is home and you have a moment, try to knock (loudly) on the door and chat for a minute. She is allergic to pomegranates but loves all other fruits we currently offer. OK to leave packages at the back door if she is not home.

4. Click OK.

You return to the Datasheet window, where you see only a tiny amount of the text you just typed.

5. Press and hold down ← to scroll through the text in Mrs. Wintergreen's Notes field.

Notice how much more difficult this is than viewing the text in the Zoom window.

ADDING INFORMATION WITH THE DITTO KEY

ditto key The Ctrl+' key combination, which repeats the value from the same field in the previous record.

Earlier in this lesson, you learned how to add a new record to the table. With the following steps, you learn how to duplicate information from the previous record with the ditto key. The key combination Ctrl+' is known as the **ditto key**; it repeats the value from the same field in the previous record.

HANDS ON

1. With the insertion point still in the Notes field for Shelly Wintergreen, press F2.

Pressing F2 takes you out of the edit mode of the memo field.

2. Press Ctrl+End.

You move to the end of the table. If you had not pressed F2 first, you would have been taken to the end of the text for the memo field you were editing.

3. Press Tab twice to move to the Contact Last Name field of the new blank record automatically generated by Access.

4. Press Ctrl+'. (Hold down Ctrl while pressing the single quote key.)

Access inserts the name Smith into the current field.

5. Press Tab and enter **Cassandra** in the Contact First Name field of your new record.

6. Press Tab and then press Ctrl+' again to duplicate the Billing Address field from the previous record. Continue in this manner, duplicating the City, State/Province, ZIP Code, and Phone Number fields.

7. In the Date Joined field, enter **4/22/98**

8. Press Tab three times to complete the new record.

SEARCHING FOR RECORDS BASED ON THEIR CONTENTS

When you move around in a small table, you usually can find the record you want either by scrolling or by using the navigation buttons and keyboard methods you learned earlier in this lesson. However, as your tables grow larger, it becomes more difficult to track down the records you need by these methods. Luckily, Access provides the Find command, which lets you search for records based on their contents, and the Replace command, which lets you both search for and replace specific values.

FINDING VALUES IN THE TABLE

With these steps, you'll experiment with the Find command to see how it works.

HANDS ON

1. Make sure that the BFCustomers table is still open in Datasheet view. Move to the Contact Last Name field of the first record.

2. Click the Find toolbar button or click the Edit menu and choose Find.

Access displays the Find In Field dialog box, as shown in Figure 3-13. Notice that the dialog box title bar also lists the current field, Contact Last Name. By default Access looks for the specified value in the current field only.

Type text that you want to find

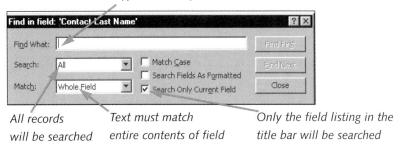

FIGURE 3-13
The Find In Field dialog box

All records will be searched   *Text must match entire contents of field*   *Only the field listing in the title bar will be searched*

3. In the Find What text box, type **Zheng** and click the Find First button.

The name Zheng is highlighted and the record for Alicia Zheng now has the focus. Access leaves the dialog box open—in case you want to continue searching for other records.

N O T E *You click on the Find First button to find the first instance of the text in the table; then you click on the Find Next button to find the next instance of the text after the current record.*

4. Click the Find Next button.

The record for the second customer with the last name of Zheng (James Zheng) is selected.

5. Click the Find Next button again.

The record for Carter Zheng is selected.

6. Click the Find Next button once more.

A dialog box appears telling you that the search item was not found. This message means that no other customers who have the last name of Zheng were found.

7. Click OK to remove the dialog box.

Access returns to the Find in Field dialog box.

8. Double-click the text in the Find What text box and then enter **Joanne**. Then click the Find First button.

Access alerts you that it "finished searching the records" without finding the specified item. This message tells you that no customers with the last name of Joanne were found.

9. Click OK to clear the dialog box.

10. Click the Search Only Current Field check box to deselect it.

11. Click Find First.

This time, Access finds the record that contains the value Joanne—because it's searching through all fields, not just the Contact Last Name field. Note that when you remove the check from the Search Only Current Field check box, the dialog box's name changes to Find, because Access is no longer searching through one particular field.

T I P   *If you want to find text within a field, pull down the Match drop-down list box and select the Any Part of Field option.*

REPLACING VALUES IN THE TABLE

If you repeatedly press Find Next the focus moves to each subsequent record that contains the Find What value. But what if you want not only to find, but also to change those values?

As you'll discover, the Replace command is particularly valuable for changing multiple instances of the same characters. For example, suppose you abbreviated *Boulevard* incorrectly throughout your table—maybe you spelled it *Bvld*. You could correct every instance of the mistake with a few easy steps.

HANDS ON

1. Click Close to close the Find dialog box.

2. Press ⌨Ctrl+⌨Home to move to the top of the table.

3. Click the Edit menu and choose Replace.

You'll see the Replace dialog box, as shown in Figure 3-14.

Type over previous text

FIGURE 3-14
The Replace dialog box

Type the replacement text

Notice that the Find What text box shows the value from your previous Find operation. Also note that the Search Only Current Field is unchecked; this, too, is a carry over from the previous Find operation.

You are about to change all of the abbreviations *Pl.* with the full word *Place*.

4. Click the Match Whole Field check box to deselect it.

This action is necessary because you're looking for characters *within* a field.

5. Double-click the text (Joanne) in the Find What box and type **Pl.** (include the period).

6. Press ⌨Tab.

7. Type **Place** in the Replace With box.

8. Click Find Next.

Access moves the focus to Will Criton's record, the first record containing the string of characters *Pl.*

9. Click the Replace button.

Access replaces *Pl.* with *Place* in Will Criton's record and also moves to the next record that contains the specified string, the record for Joanne Elias.

10. This time, click the Replace All button.

Access displays a warning box telling you that you will not be able to undo the changes made by this operation, as shown in Figure 3-15.

FIGURE 3-15

Warning box telling you that you can't undo the operation

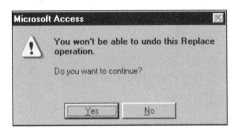

TIP

*The Replace All option can be a great time saver, but keep in mind that Replace is safer than Replace All. If you use Replace and Access stops on a record you don't want to change, you can click the Find Next button to go on to the next instance without changing the current one. If you use Replace All, you don't have the option to stop some occurrences. For instance, if you wanted to replace all occurrences of the word "red" with "blue," Access will not only change occurrences of "red" but also words that contain "red." Words such as "b*red*," "p*red*ator," and "pou*red*" would be affected.*

11. Click Yes.

Access changes the records for both Joanne Elias and Christine Isherwood.

12. Click the Close button on the dialog box.

CHANGING THE DATASHEET DISPLAY

In many cases, the default datasheet layout will adequately meet your needs. At times, however, you might like to customize the datasheet layout. Among other things, you can change column widths and row heights, move columns, hide columns, and freeze columns so that they're always visible on the screen. For example, you might want to reduce the widths of several columns so you can see more columns on the screen at once, or you might want to freeze the Contact Last Name column so you can always tell at a glance whose record you're working on, no matter which field you're in.

NOTE

Changes to the datasheet layout only affect the display of your data in the Datasheet view—they do not affect the table structure.

CHANGING COLUMN WIDTHS

This exercise will give you some practice customizing the datasheet by changing the widths of the columns in the Datasheet display.

HANDS ON

1. You should still be viewing the BFCustomers table in Datasheet view. If not, open the table.

2. Place the mouse pointer over the border between the column selectors (the heading at the top of each column) for the Customer ID and Contact Last Name fields.

The mouse pointer will change into a vertical bar with a horizontal double-headed arrow attached; this pointer indicates that you drag to the left to narrow the column to the left of the pointer, or drag to the right to widen the column to the left.

3. Hold down the mouse button and drag to the left to narrow the Customer ID field until it's only two or three characters wide.

Although the column heading won't show in full, you'll still be able to see the complete Customer ID numbers.

4. Place the mouse pointer over the border between the column selectors for the State/Province and ZIP Code fields, and drag to the left to narrow the State field.

At this point, your Datasheet window might look something like the one shown in Figure 3-16. Notice that you can now see more fields without scrolling.

Field widths narrowed

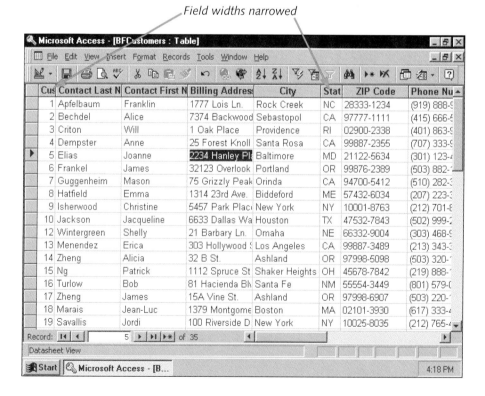

FIGURE 3-16

Changing column widths

TIP   *Although you can't undo column width changes with the Undo command, you can close the table and choose not to accept the changes.*

TIP   *To automatically resize a column so you can see all of the data in the longest record (or the entire field name if it's longer than the data), double-click the right column selector border.*

CHANGING ROW HEIGHTS

Just as you changed the width of the columns, you can also change the height of the rows. You'll do this during the following steps.

HANDS ON

1. Place the mouse pointer over the border between any two record selectors.

The mouse pointer changes into a horizontal bar with a vertical double-headed arrow attached.

2. Drag downward to the horizontal line indicating the next row, and then release the mouse button.

Access increases the row height of all rows in the table to about twice their original size, as shown in Figure 3-17.

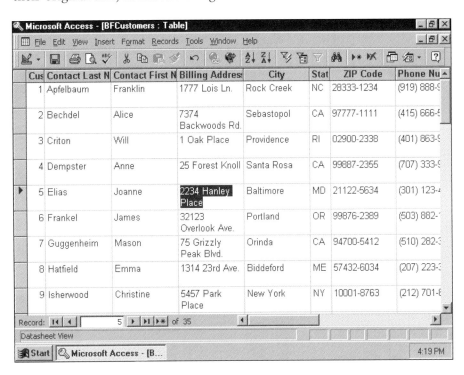

FIGURE 3-17
Changing the height of rows

When you have long fields, increasing the row height lets you see more of the field contents at once. In the Billing Address field, for instance, notice that the longer addresses now wrap to the next line instead of disappearing from view.

NOTE   *When you change a row height, Access changes the height of all rows in the table, not just one (in contrast to when you adjust column widths).*

3. Now return the rows to their original height by placing the mouse pointer over the border between any two record selectors, dragging upward until the black line is at the row's midpoint, and then releasing the mouse button.

CHANGING THE ORDER OF FIELDS

If you reduce column widths and maximize the screen and you still can't see all the fields you want to view, you can move columns to see just the ones you want.

HANDS ON

1. Click the column selector for the Phone Number field.

Access highlights the column to indicate that it's selected.

2. With the mouse pointer still located over the column selector, drag the column to the left, making sure to hold the mouse button down.

Notice that, as you drag, Access displays a heavy vertical line to indicate where the column will go when you release the mouse button.

3. Drag the selected column until the heavy vertical line is just to the right of the Contact First Name field, and then release the mouse button.

Access places the Phone Number column immediately to the right of the Contact First Name column, as shown in Figure 3-18.

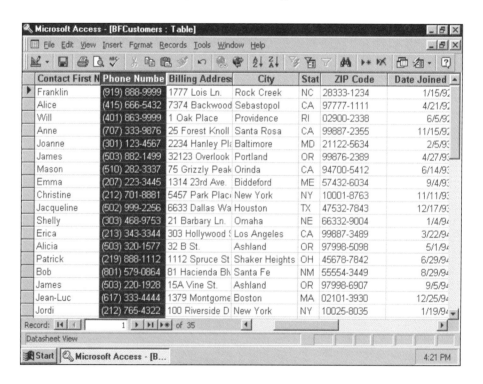

FIGURE 3-18
The order of the fields has been changed

TIP   *You can move several adjacent columns at once by selecting all of them and then dragging on the column selector for one of them.*

HIDING COLUMNS

In some situations, hiding columns may be a better solution than moving them. If you wanted to view names, phone numbers, and date-joined information—but didn't need to see any other data in the table—you could hide all the other columns.

HANDS ON

1. Select the Customer ID field by clicking its column selector.

2. Click the Format menu and choose Hide Columns.

Access removes the Customer ID column from view. You must use the Unhide command to redisplay one or more hidden columns.

TIP *After selecting a column, you can also use a shortcut menu to hide it. Right-click the selected column(s) and choose Hide Columns from the shortcut menu that appears.*

3. Click the Format menu and choose Unhide Columns.

Access displays the Unhide Columns dialog box shown in Figure 3-19.

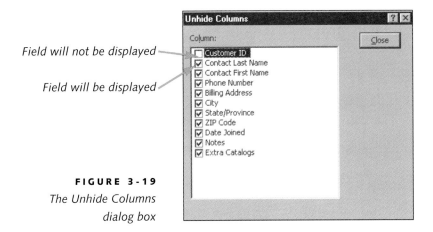

Field will not be displayed

Field will be displayed

FIGURE 3-19
The Unhide Columns dialog box

In the Column box, check marks indicate which fields are displayed. You can hide or unhide columns in this dialog box by clicking in the check box.

4. Click the check box beside the Billing Address field.

Access removes the check mark to the left of the field name and conceals the field in the Datasheet window.

5. Click the check box beside the City field.

Access removes the City field's check mark and conceals the field in the Datasheet window.

6. Hide the Extra Catalogs, Notes, State/Province, and ZIP Code fields.

7. Click the Close button in the Unhide Columns dialog box.

Access returns you to the datasheet, which should show only the Contact Last Name, Contact First Name, Phone Number, and Date Joined fields, as shown in Figure 3-20.

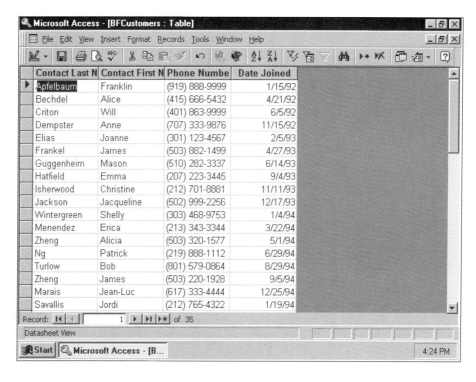

FIGURE 3-20

Hiding columns lets you concentrate on the fields you need to view

8. Click the Format menu and choose Unhide Columns.

9. Click all of the hidden columns so that check marks appear.

10. Click the Close button.

Access brings all the columns back into view.

FREEZING COLUMNS

freeze An option that lets you make columns permanently visible on the screen.

HANDS ON

In some cases, you may want to **freeze** one or more columns so they always remain in view. For example, you may wish to view the fields to the right of the screen without losing the Contact Last Name field.

1. Click the Contact Last Name column selector.

The entire column is highlighted.

2. Click the Format menu and choose Freeze Columns.

Access moves the Contact Last Name column to the left-most column in Datasheet view.

3. Scroll to the right, either by pressing Tab repeatedly or by using the horizontal scroll bar until you see the Date Joined field.

The Contact Last Name field remains visible; it's frozen into place as the left-most column of Datasheet view, as you can see in Figure 3-21.

4. Click the Format menu and choose Unfreeze All Columns.

Access unfreezes all columns. Any formerly frozen columns remain in the left-most position in the datasheet, until scrolling takes them out of view.

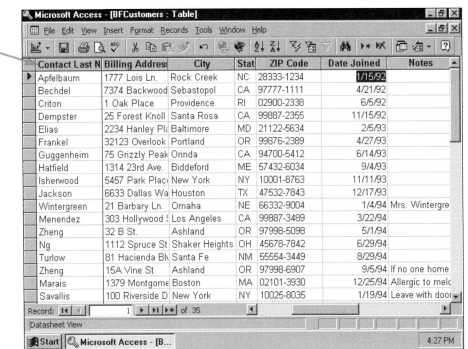

Frozen column stays on left

FIGURE 3-21

Freezing columns lets you lock fields on the screen

CANCELING CHANGES TO THE DATASHEET LAYOUT

Any changes you make to the datasheet layout can be saved or canceled. If you like, you can move columns back to where they were by using the techniques you just learned for moving columns. Alternatively, you can close the table without saving the changes to the datasheet layout.

At this point, you've finished experimenting with the datasheet layout.

HANDS ON

1. Close the BFCustomers table by clicking the Close button.

Access displays the dialog box shown in Figure 3-22, asking whether you want to save the changes you've made to the datasheet layout for the BFCustomers table.

FIGURE 3-22

Dialog box lets you save the changes to the Datasheet view

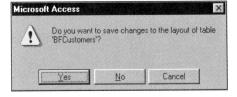

2. Click No to close the table without saving any of the changes to the datasheet layout.

Access returns you to the Be Fruitful Database window.

NOTE *Even if you don't save the datasheet layout, Access still saves any edits or additions to your data. Remember, these changes are saved automatically when you move to the next record.*

3. Close the **Be Fruitful** Database window.

4. Exit Access.

LESSON SUMMARY AND EXERCISES

After you complete this lesson, you should know how to do the following:

ADDING DATA TO A TABLE

- To add records to a table, open the table and type the data for each field. Press Tab to move to the next field.

RETRIEVING DATA FROM ANOTHER TABLE

- To copy records from one table into another, open the table containing the records you want to copy. Select the records and click the Copy toolbar button to place them into the Clipboard. Open the table you want to copy the records into and choose Paste Append.

COPYING TABLES FROM ANOTHER DATABASE

- To copy an entire table from another database, click the File menu, move to Get External Data, and then click Import. Locate the database that contains the table you want to copy and open it. Choose the table to be copied and click OK.

EDITING AND VIEWING RECORDS IN THE DATASHEET

- To move from record to record in the datasheet, click the navigation buttons at the bottom of the datasheet window.
- To Move from field to field, press Tab, Shift+Tab, End, Home, Ctrl+End, or Ctrl+Home.
- To change the contents of a field, press F2 and type your changes.
- To undo changes to a field, press Esc or click the Undo toolbar button.
- To undo changes to an entire record, press Esc twice or click the Undo toolbar button three times.
- To undo changes to the last record saved, click the Edit menu and choose Undo Saved Record.
- To remove a record from the table, select the row and click the Delete Record toolbar button.

SEARCHING FOR RECORDS BASED ON THEIR CONTENT

- To find a record that contains specific text, click the Find toolbar button and type text in the Find What box.
- To replace data in the table, click the Edit menu and choose Replace. Type appropriate text in the Find What and Replace With boxes.

CHANGING THE DATASHEET DISPLAY

- To change the width of a column, place the mouse pointer between the column selectors and drag left or right.
- To change the height of all the rows, place the mouse pointer between any two record selectors and drag up or down.
- To move a column in the datasheet, select the column and drag left or right to the new location.

■ To hide a column from view, select the column and click the Format menu and choose Hide Columns.

■ To freeze a column on the screen, select the column, click the Format menu, and choose Freeze Columns.

NEW TERMS TO REMEMBER

After you complete this lesson, you should know the meaning of the following terms:

Clipboard	ditto key	record selector
current record	freeze	reverse video
datasheet	import	select

MATCHING EXERCISE

Match each of the terms with the definitions on the right:

TERMS	DEFINITIONS
1. ditto key	**a.** Temporary storage area in your computer's memory
2. record selector	**b.** The command used to copy data from Clipboard into current table
3. frozen column	**c.** Column that has been removed from view on the datasheet
4. datasheet	**d.** Term describing current record—record that will be affected by any actions
5. focus	**e.** Repeats value from same field of previous record
6. Zoom window	**f.** Light text on dark background
7. reverse video	**g.** Column-and-row layout you can use to enter, edit, and view data
8. Paste Append	**h.** Column that has been locked into place so that it's always visible on screen
9. hidden column	**i.** Box on which you can click to select a record
10. Clipboard	**j.** Window that lets you view and edit field contents

COMPLETION EXERCISE

Fill in the missing word or phrase for each of the following:

1. To move to the previous field in the current record, press _____.

2. To move to the last record in a database, press the _____ key combination or click the _____ navigation button.

3. A(n) _____ in the record selector indicates a new, blank record into which you may type data.

4. After you have used the Copy command to save data in the Clipboard, you should use the _____ command to put the data into the table.

5. _____ means to copy data from another database or program into the current one.

6. To delete a record, select it and press the _____ key.

7. The _____ toolbar button lets you reverse your most recent changes.

8. The _____ command lets you substitute one set of characters for another throughout the table.

9. The _____ window makes the editing of large text or memo fields easier.

10. To change the width of a field, move the mouse pointer to the right of the _____ and drag left or right.

SHORT-ANSWER QUESTIONS

Write a brief answer to each of the following questions:

1. Describe the first step you would take to edit the current field without removing its original contents, assuming that the field is selected. After you had finished editing the field, what two steps would you need to take to move quickly to the first field of the first record in the table?

2. Describe how data is saved in Access. When might you use the Records, Save Record command?

3. Under what circumstances might you increase the height of rows in Datasheet view? When might you use the Zoom window instead?

4. What command do you use to reverse all changes you have made to the current record? What command would you use to reverse the changes to a record that has already been saved?

5. Briefly describe the advantages and disadvantages of using the Replace button rather than Replace All button in the Replace dialog box.

6. If you know that someone lives on Riverside Drive but don't know their street number, which option would you pick from the Match drop-down list box in the Find dialog box? (Hint: The available options are Any Part of Field, Match Whole Field, and Start of Field.)

7. How do you ensure that your changes to the datasheet layout will be retained?

8. Describe the steps you would take to copy records from a table called *Unpaid* to a table called *Payables*.

9. Describe the steps you would take to copy a table from a database called *Inventory* into a database called *Assets*.

10. Describe the difference between hidden and frozen columns.

APPLICATION PROJECTS

Perform the following actions to complete these projects:

1. Open the **Be Fruitful** database from the **Lessons** folder on your Student Data Disk. Use the Find feature to find all the records of customers who live in the state of New York in the BFCustomers table. Before you start your search, move to the last record in the database. Then, in the Find dialog box, choose the Up option in the Search box. Use the Find Next button to move to all the records that contain the state in question, noting the order in which Access tracks down the records.

2. Use the Hide feature to hide all columns in the BFCustomers table except for Contact Last Name, Contact First Name, Phone Number, and Notes. Then rearrange the columns so that Contact First Name is the left-most column. Widen the Notes column to display as much text as possible. Last, restore the Datasheet view window to its original state. (Hint: You could bring the hidden columns back into view, move the first name column back to its original position, and narrow the Notes column, but there's an easier way to do this all at once.) Close the **Be Fruitful** database.

3. Open the **Personal** database from the **Projects** folder on your Student Data Disk. Then open the To Dos table. Enter at least ten records in your To Dos table. Include any tasks which you should complete in the next few weeks and add one or two tasks that you have recently completed. Use priority values in which 1 means highest priority and 5 is the lowest priority. Add records to this table any time you have a new task to do. Do not remove records from the table when you have completed the task, instead, insert a check mark in the Task Complete field for that record. Print the data in your table by clicking the Print toolbar button and close the database. (Note: You must have completed Application Project 2 in Lesson 2 to do this project.)

4. Open the **Music** database from the **Projects** folder on your Student Data Disk. Then open the Recording Artists table.

Enter the following text in the Artist Name field:

Linda Ronstadt

Eric Clapton

New York Philharmonic

Raffi

Stan Getz

Julie Andrews

Boys II Men

Dean Martin

Seal

Add at least two additional artists of your choice. Print the data in the table by clicking the Print toolbar button. Close the table. (Note: You must have completed Application Project 3 in Lesson 2 to do this project.)

5. If it is not already open, open the **Music** database in the **Projects** folder on your Student Data Disk. Then open the Music Categories table.

Enter the following text in the Music Category field:

Jazz

Rap

Classical

Rock

Pop

Musical

Children's

Add any additional records for categories of your choice. Print the data in the table by clicking the Print toolbar button and then close the table. (Note: You must have completed Application Project 3 in Lesson 2 to do this project.)

6. If it is not already open, open the **Music** database in the **Projects** folder on your Student Data Disk. Then open the Recordings table.

Enter the following recording titles for each of the musical categories and artists you entered into the Music Categories and Recording Artist tables in Application Projects 4 and 5. Use the ID numbers from the Music Categories and Recording Artist tables to fill in the Music Category ID and Recording Artist ID fields.

Recording Title	Artist	Music Category	Recording Label	Year Released	Date Purchased	Price	Format
Blue Bayou	Ronstadt	Rock	Asylum	1977	6/12/81	$8.99	LP
When Will I Be Loved?	Ronstadt	Rock	Capitol	1975	3/28/76	6.75	LP
After Midnight	Clapton	Rock	Atco	1970	4/30/71	6.31	LP
I Can't Stand It	Clapton	Rock	RSO	1981	7/14/83	8.50	LP
Grieg: Piano Concerto	New York Philharmonic	Classical	RCA	1973	8/30/81	5.99	LP
Music for a Great City	New York Philharmonic	Classical	Columbia	1968	2/9/92	10.25	CD
Raffi on Broadway	Raffi	Children's	MCA	1993	12/4/95	9.99	Cassette
A Young Children's Concert with Raffi	Raffi	Children's	A&M	1984	11/21/92	8.42	Cassette
The Girl from Ipanema	Stan Getz	Jazz	Verve	1964	9/25/80	6.85	LP
Desafinado	Stan Getz	Jazz	Verve	1962	9/25/80	7.50	LP
My Fair Lady	Julie Andrews	Musical	Columbia	1978	10/3/95	12.71	CD
The Sound of Music	Julie Andrews	Musical	Columbia	1970	5/22/89	9.35	Cassette
II	Boyz II Men	Pop	Motown	1994	12/20/95	14.99	CD
Memories Are Made of This	Dean Martin	Pop	Capitol	1955	6/18/85	4.30	LP
I Will	Dean Martin	Pop	Reprise	1965	2/28/85	5.97	LP
Seal	Seal	Pop	Warner Bros.	1994	3/16/97	13.99	CD

Include data for at least one recording for each of the other artists that you added. Print the data in the table by clicking the Print toolbar button. Then close the Recordings table and the **Music** database. (Note: You must have completed Application Projects 4 and 5 in Lesson 3 to do this project.)

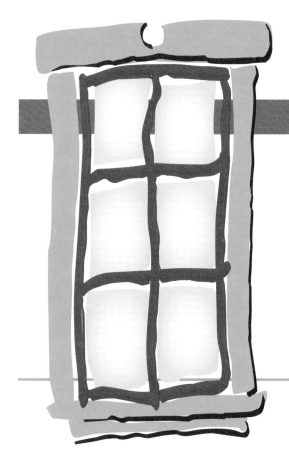

RETRIEVING THE DATA YOU NEED: SORTING AND SELECTING RECORDS

OBJECTIVES

After you complete this lesson, you will be able to do the following:

- *Use the Sort commands to sort your data in alphabetical, numerical, or chronological order.*

- *Use several types of filters to display specified records from a table.*

- *Devise criteria to select specified subsets of your data.*

- *Design basic queries that display and sort selected fields from a table.*

- *Use criteria in queries to select particular data from a table.*

- *Edit the data in a query's Recordset.*

- *Save your queries.*

- *Join tables so you can construct queries based on them.*

- *Create queries to sort and select the data from multiple tables.*

CONTENTS

Sorting and Selecting Data

Using the Sort Commands

Filtering Your Data

Designing Basic Queries

Querying Multiple Tables

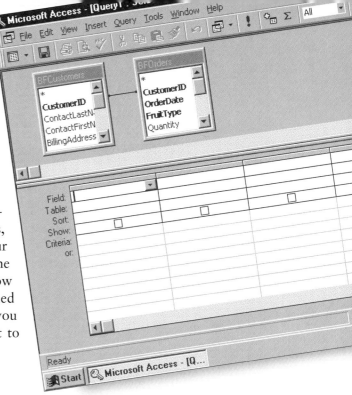

This lesson introduces the techniques you can use to sort your data into the desired order and to select just the records you need. You learn about everything from the Sort buttons, which enable you to sort your data with a single click of the mouse, to queries that allow you to devise very detailed instructions about what data you require and how you'd like it to be arranged.

SORTING AND SELECTING DATA

sort To rearrange records into alphabetical, numerical, or chronological order.

select To extract specified subsets of data based on criteria that you define. Alternatively, select can mean to choose an item to indicate to Access that you want to operate on that particular item.

filter A way of displaying your data to see only a selected portion of it.

In the previous lessons, you devoted a considerable amount of energy to setting up tables and gathering data into them. But no matter how well you've thought out your table structures, this raw data may not prove to be all that useful, especially as your database accumulates more and more information. In this lesson, you'll begin to learn how to make sense of your data. You'll discover several ways to **sort** your data—rearranging records into alphabetical, numerical, or chronological order. You'll also find out how to **select** the data you need—extracting specified groups of it based on factors that you define. You might want to see all customers who live in California, for example, or all orders placed after some designated date.

For both sorting and selecting data, Access is immeasurably more useful than even the most well-organized manual system. In a manual system, you can sort in only one way unless you create duplicate sets of data; for instance, you might arrange your records in alphabetical order by customer last name. In Access, by contrast, you can sort the same set of data in any number of ways—you could sort by last name, by data joined, and by ZIP Code, and could then consult the sorted data that best fits the task at hand. The same applies to extracting data: In a manual system, pulling out just the records you need can be a laborious task. In Access, with a little knowledge you can select the precise data you need and can also extract many different groups of the same data.

This lesson first describes the Sort commands, which enable you to sort the data in a single table. Next you'll learn how to create filters to both sort and select the data from a single table. A **filter** is pretty much what its name implies: a way to filter, or sift, your data so you can see only a selected portion of it. Last, you'll learn about queries: Remember, queries are a way of asking questions about your data. You can use queries to both sort and select data, and you'll learn as well how to build queries that ask questions of multiple tables.

USING THE SORT COMMANDS

Access automatically arranges the data in your tables according to the value in the primary key. In the BFCustomers table, for instance, the customers are arranged by customer ID, with customer 1 appearing before customer 2, and so on. Undoubtedly, however, at times you'll want to view your data in some other sequence—maybe in order by last name or by ZIP Code.

You can sort data on any field except for Memo, Hyperlink, and OLE Object fields. Access sorts Text fields into alphabetical order, considers lower- and uppercase letters to be the same, and lists digits before letters. An **ascending sort** arranges data from A to Z, and a **descending sort** arranges it from Z to A. Access sorts Number or Currency fields into numerical order— from lower to higher values in an ascending sort and from higher to lower values in a descending sort. Finally, Access sorts Date/Time fields into chronological order. An ascending sort places the earliest dates first, while a descending sort places the most recent dates first.

ascending sort A sort that arranges letters from A to Z, numbers from smallest to largest, and dates from earliest to most recent.

descending sort A sort that arranges letters from Z to A, numbers from largest to smallest, and dates from most recent to the earliest.

SORTING YOUR TABLE

Here you'll experiment with the Sort command to rearrange the records in the BFCustomers table in a variety of ways.

HANDS ON

1. Open the **Be Fruitful** database in the **Lessons** folder of your Student Data Disk.

2. Open the BFCustomers table.

You'll see the BFCustomers table in Datasheet view, as shown in Figure 4-1.

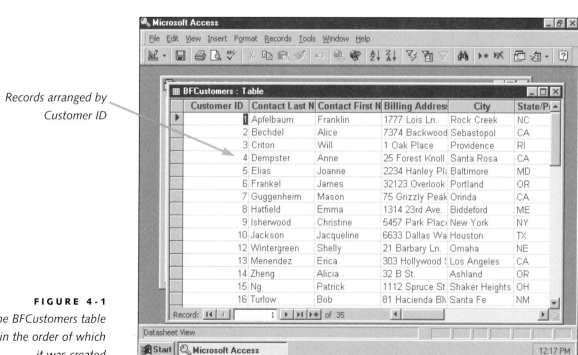

Records arranged by Customer ID

FIGURE 4-1

The BFCustomers table in the order of which it was created

3. Click the table's Maximize button.

4. Click anywhere within the Contact Last Name field.

5. Click the Sort Ascending toolbar button. Alternatively, you can click the Records menu, choose Sort, and then select Sort Ascending from the submenu.

Access rearranges the records in the table to display them in ascending order by last name, as shown in Figure 4-2. Notice, for instance, that the record for the customer named Alexander Everett is placed after the record for Joanne Elias.

Records sorted by last name

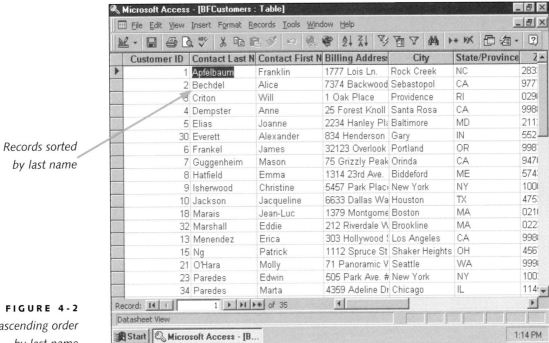

FIGURE 4-2
Records in ascending order by last name

N O T E   *The sort orders established by the Sort commands are not saved when you close the table, so you don't need to worry about rearranging your data and returning it to its original state.*

6. Scroll down through the records and notice that when there are duplicate last names, the first names are not in any kind of order.

7. Drag over the Contact Last Name and Contact First Name column selectors so that both fields are selected.

8. Click the Sort Ascending toolbar button.

Access sorts the records in order by last name, and, where there are duplicate last names, sorts the records in order by first name. The Smiths and the Zhengs are now in alphabetical order by first as well as last names. When you sort on more than one field, Access sorts first by the leftmost field, then by the field to its right, and so on.

9. Now click anywhere within the ZIP Code field and click the Sort Descending toolbar button.

As shown in Figure 4-3, Access rearranges the records in order by ZIP Code, with larger numbers first and smaller numbers last.

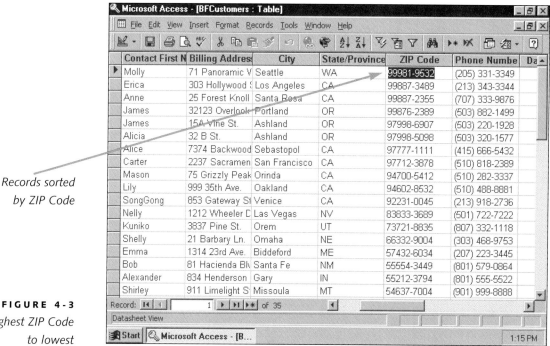

Records sorted by ZIP Code

FIGURE 4-3
Highest ZIP Code to lowest

10. Now click anywhere within the Date Joined field and click the Sort Descending toolbar button.

Access arranges the records in order by date joined. Notice that the most recent dates are displayed first. To see the earliest dates first, you would instead choose an ascending sort.

NOTE   *Access interprets the dates 1/1/30 through 12/31/99 as 1/1/1930 through 12/31/1999. The dates 1/1/00 through 12/31/29 are interpreted by Access as 1/1/2000 through 12/31/2029. To override these interpretations, you can enter dates with four-digit years such as 5/12/2032.*

11. Click anywhere in the Customer ID field and click the Sort Ascending toolbar button.

Access returns the records to their original sort order—in ascending order by the primary key field, Customer ID. You can also return a table to its original state just by closing the table, because the sort order established by a Sort command is not retained.

FILTERING YOUR DATA

If you want to sort all of the data in a single table, the Sort command works well. But if you want to do more—let's say you want to sort your records and view only those records for customers in California—a Sort command won't do the job. Instead, you could use a filter to sort your data into the desired order. Like the Sort commands, filters only work on the data in a single table; you usually use a filter to quickly and temporarily change the records you see.

There are four methods for creating a filter: Filter By Selection, Filter By Form, Filter For Input, and the Advanced Filter/Sort window. In the exercises that follow, you will see each method used.

USING THE FILTER BY SELECTION METHOD

The simplest way to choose the records you wish to view is to use the Filter By Selection option, which allows you to select specific data in a particular field. Access will display only those records that contain the same data in the specified field.

HANDS ON

1. Make sure your BFCustomers table is still open.

2. Double-click the first State/Province field that contains the state code for California—CA.

3. Click the Filter By Selection toolbar button.

Within a few moments only those records with the state code of CA are displayed, as in Figure 4-4.

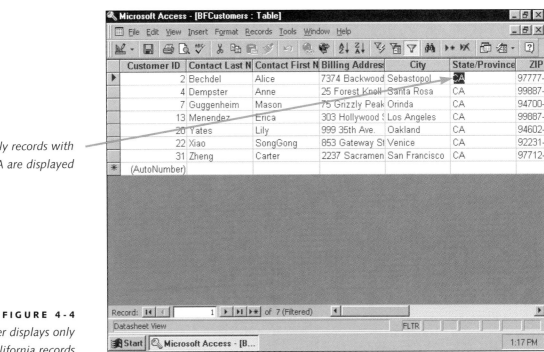

Only records with CA are displayed

FIGURE 4-4

Filter displays only California records

T I P   *If your first filter doesn't narrow the records enough, you can apply a new, different fil-*
ter to the filter results.

To display all the records on the datasheet, you must remove the filter.

4. Click the Remove Filter toolbar button.

All of the records now reappear on the datasheet.

The data you select does not have to be an entire field—you can select
only part of a field, and then Access will filter out any records not containing those characters in that field.

5. Select the last two digits of the date from any Date Joined field ending
in 92.

6. Click the Filter By Selection toolbar button.

Access displays only those records whose Date Joined field ends in 92,
as seen in Figure 4-5.

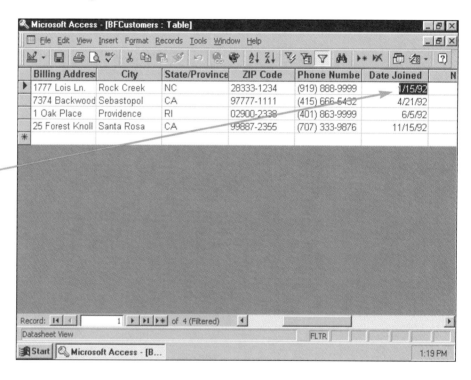

Only customers
who joined in
1992 are displayed

FIGURE 4-5

Filter shows customers
who joined in 1992

7. Click the Remove Filter toolbar button.

8. Select the telephone area code from record 26 (which is 901).

T I P   *Only select the digits 901; do not highlight the parentheses surrounding the area code.*

9. Pull down the Records menu and choose Filter. From the submenu
that appears, choose Filter By Selection.

Two records appear. The first record does have an area code of 901, but
the second record has an area code of 617. What happened?

As you may have noticed, the second record in the display has 901 as the last three digits of the phone number. When you use Filter By Selection, Access will show records that contain the selection *anywhere* in the field.

10. Click the Records menu and choose Remove Filter/Sort.

Filter By Selection is a convenient locating method—as long as you can select the exact data in a field you want to match. For more flexibility, you need to use another filtering method.

USING THE FILTER BY FORM METHOD

selection criteria Instructions that tell Access exactly which records you want to extract from the database.

The Filter By Form method lets you choose more than one selection criteria at once. **Selection criteria** are instructions that tell Access exactly which records to gather from the database. In the next exercise, you'll build some simple filters to get acquainted with the Filter By Form method.

NOTE *Even when a filter is in effect, you can work in the datasheet much as before: You can add and edit data; hide, move, and resize datasheet columns; and more.*

GETTING TO KNOW THE FILTER BY FORM WINDOW

This section illustrates how to set up a filter in the Filter By Form window.

HANDS ON

1. Make sure the BFCustomers table in the Be Fruitful database in your **Lessons** folder is still open.

2. Click the Filter By Form toolbar button.

You'll see the Filter By Form window, as shown in Figure 4-6.

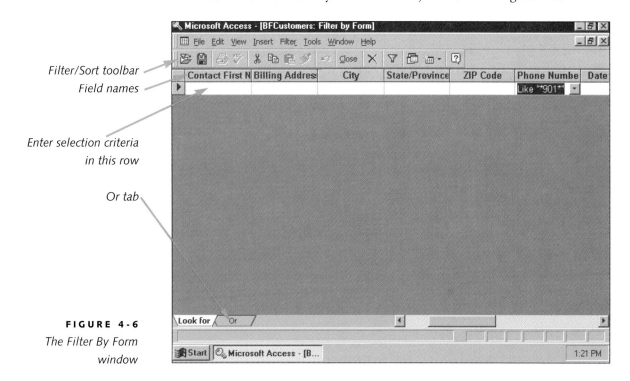

Filter/Sort toolbar

Field names

Enter selection criteria in this row

Or tab

FIGURE 4-6
The Filter By Form window

You may have noticed several changes to your screen: First, your menu bar now has a Filter option. Second, a new toolbar replaces the one that you have been working with; this new toolbar is called the Filter/Sort toolbar. Finally, the records do not appear in the Filter By Form window—only the field names remain in the top row, and beneath the field names is a row of blank text boxes. You will enter your selection criteria into these boxes.

N O T E *The characters **Like "*901*"** appear beneath the Phone Number field name. This entry is a holdover from the last Filter By Selection you performed in the previous exercise.*

N O T E *The Or tab at the bottom of the window allows you to select two or more values in a field.*

3. Press Delete to remove the previous selection criteria from the Phone Number field.

4. Click in the row beneath the Contact Last Name field.

A drop-down arrow appears in the box.

5. Click the drop-down arrow.

A list box appears that contains all the last names in the database, as shown in Figure 4-7. The Filter By Form method lets you see the selections in each of the fields, rather than having to search for them as you did in the Filter By Selection method.

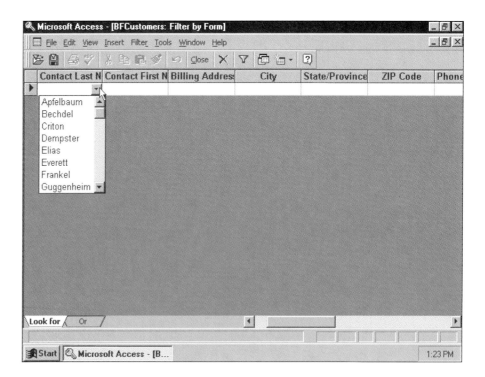

FIGURE 4-7
Drop-down list box shows field contents

6. Click in the row under the Contact First Name field.

7. Type **E**

The field fills with *Eddie*—the first name in the table that begins with the letter you typed. If you know what you are looking for, you can just type in the entry rather than using the drop-down arrow and searching through the list box.

8. Click the drop-down arrow in the Contact First Name field.

An alphabetical list of first names appears, beginning with *Eddie*. Even if you don't know the exact spelling of an entry, you can narrow your search by typing in the first few letters and selecting an entry from the list box.

9. Click the row beneath City, click the drop-down arrow that appears, and select the first city in the list, *Ames*.

 10. Click the Apply Filter button.

No records appear in the window. This means that no records were found that matched the selection criteria of Eddie as the first name in the city of Ames. You also may have noticed that your screen has reverted to the previous menu bar and toolbar.

11. Click the Records menu and select Filter. From the submenu, choose Filter by Form.

You're back to the Filter By Form window. This window only stays active until you apply the selection criteria you have entered.

SELECTING RECORDS IN FILTER BY FORM

In the next few steps, you will find some practical uses for the Filter By Form method.

 1. Click the Clear Grid toolbar button.

Your previous selection criteria disappear from the screen.

2. Click the row beneath the City field.

3. Click the drop-down arrow.

The list box contains all of the cities in the table.

4. Scroll down the list and select New York.

 5. Click the Apply Filter toolbar button.

You see all the records for the customers who live in the city of New York, as shown in Figure 4-8.

FILTERING FOR RECORDS THAT MEET ONE OF SEVERAL VALUES

You can also use the Filter By Form method to find any of several values in a field. In a selection criteria, the word *or* means that one or the other must be found. If you want to filter out all records except those containing the names Elias, Marshall, or Ng, you need to inform Access that one of three names should be displayed. You link these three names together using the Or tabs at the bottom of the Filter By Form window.

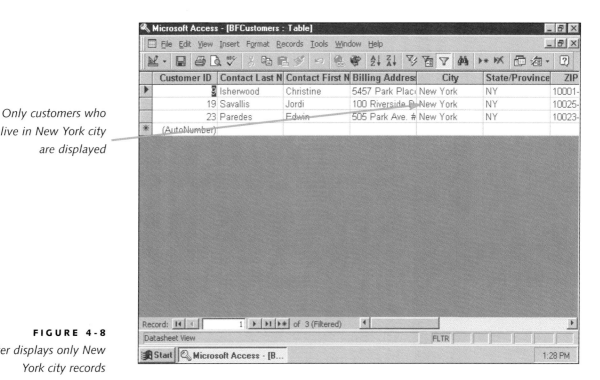

Only customers who live in New York city are displayed

FIGURE 4-8

Filter displays only New York city records

HANDS ON

1. Click the Filter By Form toolbar button.

2. Click the Clear Grid toolbar button.

3. Click the Contact Last Name field and select Elias from the drop-down list.

   At the bottom of your screen is the Look For tab. Beside it you should see an Or tab.

4. Click the Or tab.

   Your first selection criteria—Elias—disappears from view.

5. Click the drop-down arrow in the Contact Last Name field and select Marshall.

6. Click the *second* Or tab.

7. Click the drop-down arrow and select Ng.

   You have now informed Access that you want to see records with a last name of Elias *or* Marshall *or* Ng.

8. Click the Apply Filter toolbar button.

   Figure 4-9 shows that your screen contains three records—one for each of the last names specified in the selection criteria.

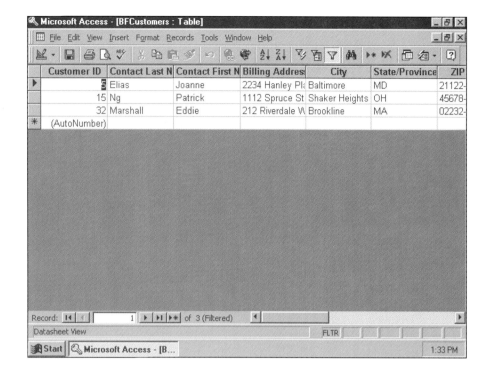

FIGURE 4-9

Filter showing records meeting any of three search criteria

FILTERING FOR RECORDS THAT MEET MULTIPLE CRITERIA

If, for example, you want to display all customers who live in Venice, California, you have to set up a filter based on two fields: The City field must be *Venice* and the State field must be *CA*. You could set up a selection criteria for a state code of CA but that would display records in any city in California. By entering values in both the City and State fields you link the two values in an *and* relationship. The *and* relationship means that both conditions must be met for a record to be displayed.

HANDS ON

1. Click the Filter By Form toolbar button and clear your selection criteria.

2. Click the box below City and select Venice from the drop-down list.

3. Click the box below State/Province and select CA from the drop-down list.

   Your selection criteria should look like that in Figure 4-10.

4. Click the Apply Filter button.

   You see only one record that meets both conditions.

5. Click the Remove Filter button.

   Your unfiltered table reappears.

OFFICE ASSISTANT   *You can also filter for records that do not contain a certain value. For help, ask the Office Assistant about the* **Filter Excluding Selection** *option.*

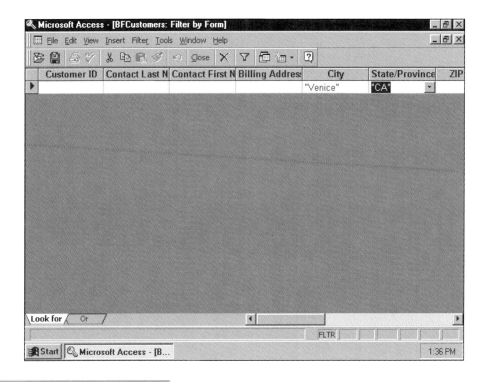

FIGURE 4-10

Multiple search criteria in the Filter By Form window

USING FILTER FOR INPUT

Using the Filter By Form method, you can specify criteria by selecting it from a list. Using the Filter For Input method, you can quickly access a shortcut menu and type the exact value or expression that you want to use as criteria.

Using the following steps, you'll create a filter by typing the exact criteria. You'll also learn how to use a wildcard character in a filter.

HANDS ON

1. Right-click anywhere in the Contact Last Name field.

A shortcut menu appears.

2. From the shortcut menu, click Filter For.

The insertion point jumps to the Filter For text box. You can use this box to specify filter criteria.

3. Type **Smith** and press Enter.

The records for all of the customers with the last name of Smith appear in the window.

4. Click the Remove Filter toolbar button.

Your unfiltered table reappears.

5. Right-click anywhere in the ZIP Code field.

6. Click Filter For from the shortcut menu and type **9***

The asterisk (*) is a **wildcard character** that finds any number of characters. Typing 9* will find all ZIP Codes that start with 9. You can also use wildcard characters to search for text strings.

7. Press Tab.

wildcard character A character used in searches and filters to find a variable string of characters. For instance, *we** would find all words that start with *we*, such as *weather*, *well*, and *weekday*.

The records for all of the customers with a ZIP Code beginning with 9 appear in the window. Notice that since you pressed Tab instead of Enter, the shortcut menu remains on the screen. You may press Tab when you want to create another filter, perform a sort, or perform another action on the same field.

8. Click Sort Descending on the shortcut menu.

The records are sorted in descending order by ZIP Code as shown in Figure 4-11.

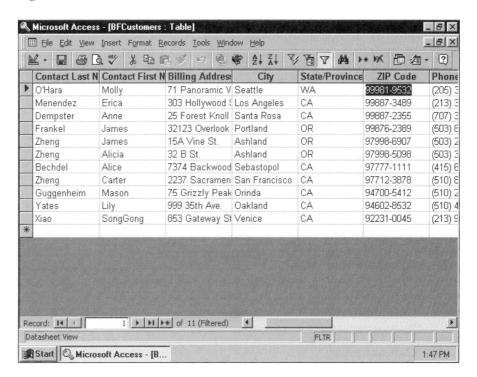

FIGURE 4-11

ZIP Codes beginning with 9 in descending order

9. Click the Remove Filter toolbar button.

Again, the unfiltered table appears.

OFFICE ASSISTANT

*Not sure which type of filter to use? Type **comparison of filtering methods** in the Office Assistant to view a table that summarizes the capabilities of each.*

USING ADVANCED FILTER/SORT

Using the Filter By Selection, Filter By Form, and Filter For Input methods, you have been able to display records using one or more criteria. You can also sort the data with these methods—but only after you apply the filter. For more complex filters, especially those where you want to sort multiple fields, an Advanced Filter/Sort works well. The Advanced Filter/Sort window allows you to choose criteria for one or more fields to filter as well as choose one or more sort arrangements—all in one window.

In this section, you'll learn how to perform an Advanced Filter/Sort. You'll also learn how to use an **expression** as criteria for a filter. An expression is a combination of field names, values, and comparison operators that

expression A combination of field names, values, and comparison operators that can be evaluated as criteria for most types of filters.

can be evaluated by Access. Expressions can be used as criteria not only in the Advanced Filter/Sort method but also in the Filter By Form and Filter For Input methods.

Expressions can be used as criteria in many instances. You may have a situation, for instance, in which you need to see records of customers who have joined the club after 1996. At other times, you might want to show records within a range of values—for example, you might want to find only those customers who joined between 1993 and 1995. In contrast, you might want to exclude particular records, such as when you want to display all records except those of customers in California.

comparison operator A symbol that is used to compare a value or text in the table to characters that you enter.

An essential part of most expressions is the **comparison operator**. A comparison operator is a symbol that is used to compare a value or text in the table to characters that you enter. Table 4-1 describes the common comparison operators used in Access.

TABLE 4-1: COMPARISON OPERATORS

OPERATOR	DESCRIPTION
=	Equal to
< >	Not equal to
>	Greater than
<	Less than
> =	Greater than or equal to
< =	Less than or equal to
Between...And	Between two specified values

SETTING UP AN ADVANCED FILTER/SORT

With the next few steps you will create a filter that uses comparison operators.

HANDS ON

1. Open the BFCustomers table, if necessary.

The unfiltered BFCustomers table should be on the screen.

2. Click the Records menu and choose Filter. Choose Advanced Filter/Sort from the submenu.

You will see the Advanced Filter/Sort window, as shown in Figure 4-12. The top portion of the window contains a **Field list** for BFCustomers. You will be able to select fields to include in the filter from the Field list. The bottom portion of the window shows the selection criteria from your previous filtering operation.

Field list A small window that lists all of the fields in a table or query. You can select fields to include in a filter or query from the Field list.

3. Click the Clear Grid toolbar button.

4. Scroll through the Field list at the top of the window until you see the DateJoined field.

5. Double-click DateJoined.

The DateJoined field name is listed in the first Field box in the bottom half of the window.

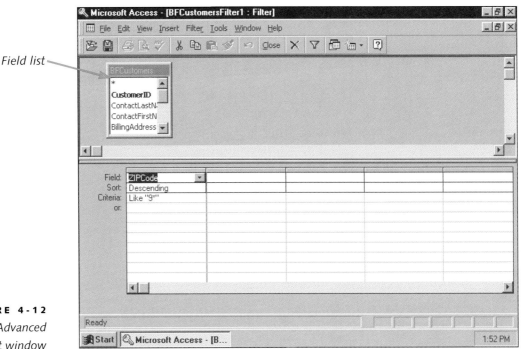

Field list

FIGURE 4-12
*The Advanced
Filter/Sort window*

T I P   *Access offers several ways to select fields from the Field list. You can double-click a field name in the Field list, drag a field from the Field list to the Field row, or use the drop-down arrow that appears when you click a box in the Field row.*

6. Click in the Sort box below the DateJoined entry.

7. Click the drop-down arrow in the Sort box.

You are given the options for sorting the records based on this field.

8. Click Descending.

This option will sort the records from the most recent to the oldest dates.

9. Click the Criteria field below the DateJoined field.

10. Type >=3/22/95

You are instructing Access to find all records for customers who joined on or after the date 3/22/95.

OFFICE ASSISTANT   *To create more complex expressions, Access provides a tool called the Expression Builder. Ask the Office Assistant for help with this feature.*

 11. Click the Apply Filter toolbar button.

12. Scroll to the right until you can see the Date Joined field. As you can see, Access has displayed the records shown in Figure 4-13, in descending order by the date joined.

13. Click the Records menu and choose Remove Filter/Sort. The table is displayed in its original form.

T I P   *To cancel both the filter and the sort, select Remove Filter/Sort from the Records menu. To keep the records sorted but remove the filter, use the Remove Filter toolbar button.*

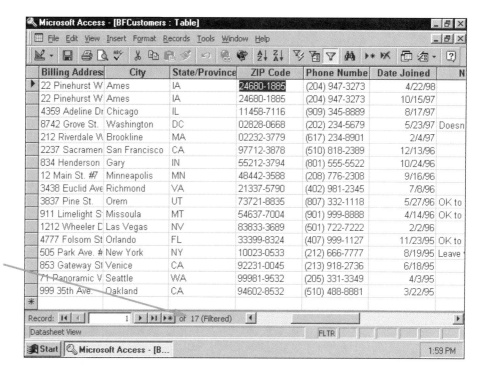

*17 records
meet the
criteria*

FIGURE 4-13
*Records filtered and sorted
by the Date Joined field*

FILTERING RECORDS WITHIN A RANGE

Sometimes you want to specify a range of values between beginning and ending values. In the following steps, you will display only those records whose ZIP Codes are between 50000 and 99999 and who have requested extra catalogs.

**HANDS
ON**

1. Click the Records menu and choose Filter, Advanced Filter/Sort.

The Advanced Filter/Sort window appears.

2. Click the Clear Grid toolbar button.

The bottom half of the screen is cleared of the previous search and sort criteria.

3. Drag the ContactLastName field from the Field list into the first Field box.

The mouse pointer turns into a small rectangle as you drag the field name into the grid.

4. Click in the Sort box beneath the ContactLastName field.

5. Click the drop-down arrow and choose Descending.

The display will be in reverse alphabetical order by the last name when you apply the filter. By leaving the Criteria box blank, you will not be excluding any of the last names from the filter.

6. Drag the ZIP Code field from the Field list to the second Field column.

7. Click in the Criteria box below the ZIPCode field.

8. Type **Between 50000 And 99999**

9. Click the top box in the third Field column.

10. Click the drop-down arrow and choose ExtraCatalogs from the list.

11. In the Criteria box for ExtraCatalogs, type **Yes**

Typing Yes in this Criteria box will display only those customers who have requested extra catalogs (indicated by a check mark in the ExtraCatalogs field check boxes).

The Advanced Filter/Sort window should look like the one in Figure 4-14.

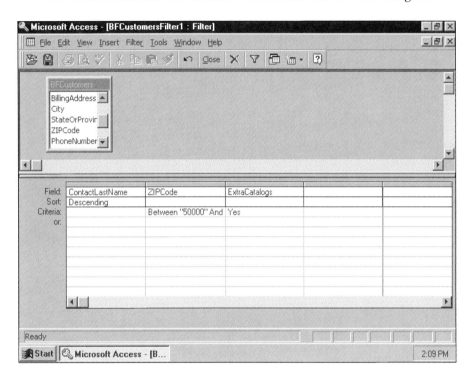

FIGURE 4-14
Advanced Filter/Sort window

 12. Click the Apply Filter toolbar button.

Access display 7 records, shown in reverse alphabetical order by last name. All of the records contain ZIP Codes between 50000 and 99999 and contain a check mark in the Extra Catalogs field.

13. Click the Close button to close the BFCustomers table.

14. When you are asked if you want to save changes to the design of your table, click No.

You are back to the Be Fruitful Database window.

DESIGNING BASIC QUERIES

Like filters, queries allow you to sort your data in a variety of ways and to extract the data you need by using all types of selection criteria. Queries, however, have several distinct advantages over filters: For one, queries permit you to select the fields that will be displayed. (Remember, filters let you select which fields to sort on but don't enable you to conceal fields.) In addition, you can use queries to perform calculations and to work with data from multiple tables. As you'll discover in the next few lessons, you can also use the results of queries in forms and reports. You can even save your queries so you can use them in the future—getting up-to-the-minute responses to questions about the data in your database.

Access allows you to create several different kinds of queries. This lesson concentrates on the most often used query type, **select queries.** Select queries can be used to sort, select, and view records from one or more tables. When you run a query, the result is called a Recordset. A **Recordset** is the portion of your data sorted and selected as spelled out in the query. This portion of data changes to reflect modifications to the data in your tables, so the data in the Recordset is always up-to-date. Recordsets are also dynamic in that you often can make changes to them and have those changes reflected in the underlying table(s).

select queries Queries that you can use to sort, select, and view records from one or more tables.

Recordset A subset of your data sorted and selected as specified by a query. Recordsets change to reflect modifications to the data in your tables, and you can often make changes to Recordsets that are reflected in the underlying table(s).

NOTE   *When you work with Recordsets, you can modify the datasheet much as you can when you work with a table. Among other things, you can move, freeze, and hide columns; change column widths and row heights; and add and edit data.*

OFFICE ASSISTANT   *Access provides several types of queries, including select queries, parameter queries, crosstab queries, action queries, and SQL queries. To learn about each type of query, ask the Office Assistant.*

SETTING UP A SIMPLE QUERY

You set up queries in the Query Design view window, which is very similar to the Advanced Filter/Sort window. It has an upper pane that includes lists of fields from one or more tables or queries on which the query will be based. Its lower pane consists of a grid—called the **query design grid**, which you use to make decisions about how to sort and select your data, and also about the fields to include in the Recordset.

query design grid The grid in the Query Design view window that you use to make decisions about how to sort and select your data and which fields to include in the Recordset.

Now you'll experiment with a variety of single-table queries to get used to working in the Query Design view.

HANDS ON

1. If it is not already open, open the **Be Fruitful** Database window.

2. Click the Queries tab.

   Access displays any queries in the Be Fruitful database; currently, none exist.

3. Click the New button.

   Access displays the New Query dialog box.

4. Make sure Design View is selected and click OK.

   Access displays the Show Table dialog box, which lists all tables in the open database, as shown in Figure 4-15. You choose tables and/or queries to base your new query on in this dialog box.

5. Double-click BFCustomers, or highlight its name and click the Add button.

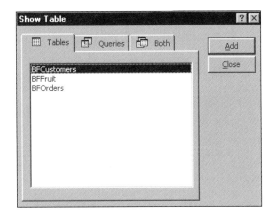

FIGURE 4-15

The Show Table dialog box

Access adds a Field list for BFCustomers to the Query Design view that you see in the background. You will be able to select fields to include in the query from the Field list.

6. Click the Close button in the Show Table dialog box.

Access removes the Show Table dialog box from view, leaving you in the Query Design view window, as shown in Figure 4-16. This window closely resembles the Advanced Filter/Sort window, with a Field list at the top and a grid at the bottom for entering field names, sorting instructions, and selection criteria.

Field list

Table where field is located

Sorting option

Click to display or hide field in results

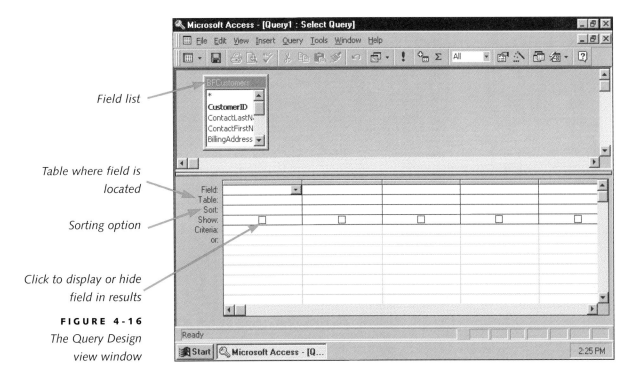

FIGURE 4-16

The Query Design view window

NOTE   *The Show Table dialog box doesn't close automatically, in case you want to include more tables in creating multi-table queries, as discussed later in this lesson.*

7. Double-click the ContactLastName field in the Field list.

Access adds the field name to the query design grid. Notice that the check box in the Show row is selected automatically indicating that Access will display the ContactLastName field in the Recordset.

8. Double-click the ContactFirstName field. It appears in the second box of the Field row in the query design grid.

9. Double-click the StateOrProvince field and then the PhoneNumber field to place them in the next boxes of the Field row in the query design grid.

10. Select Ascending order for the ContactLastName and ContactFirstName fields.

The query will display records alphabetically by the last name. If two or more records have the same last name, the records will be alphabetized by the first names.

11. Type **CA** in the Criteria row under the StateOrProvince field.

Only those records within California will be included in the query. Your Query Design view window looks like that in Figure 4-17.

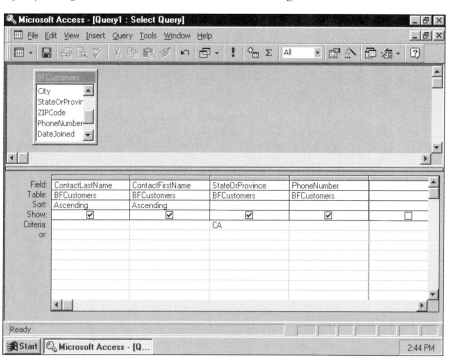

FIGURE 4-17

The Query Design view window with entries

12. Click the Run toolbar button.

Access displays the Recordset shown in Figure 4-18; notice that you see only the selected fields, rather than all of the fields in the table. Also note that the fields are displayed in the order in which you arranged them in the query design grid. On both of these counts, queries differ from filters.

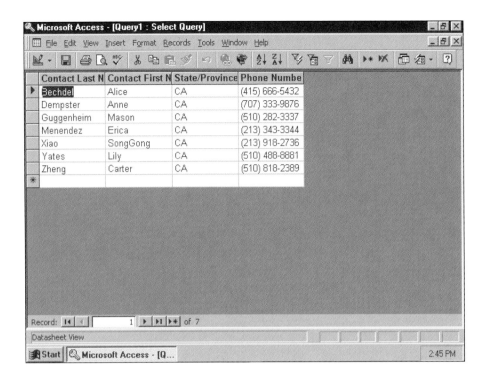

FIGURE 4-18

The Query Recordset display

MODIFYING AND SAVING A QUERY

The queries you create can be modified and saved. In the next few steps, you'll make a change to the query you just created. Then you'll save the query so you can view the Recordset at any time in the future.

1. Click the View toolbar button.

Clicking the View toolbar button switches to display Design view. Notice that after you click the button, the icon changes to indicate that clicking it again will switch back to Datasheet view. To check the available views, click the arrow next to the View button or click the View menu. Then make a choice from the available options.

Access returns you to Query Design view.

2. Click the Show check box under the StateOrProvince field.

Clicking this box deselects it. This lets you select records based on state without displaying the StateOrProvince field in the Recordset.

TIP *You can define sorting and selection instructions based on a field without displaying that field in the Recordset.*

3. Click the Run toolbar button.

Access displays the new Recordset shown in Figure 4-19; all customers in California are displayed as before, but this time the State Or Province field does not appear.

State/Province field not displayed

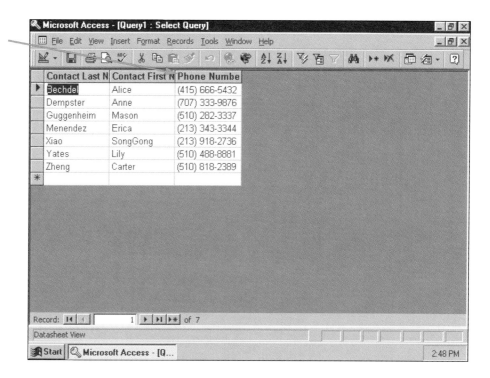

FIGURE 4-19
Modified Recordset does not show State/Province field

4. Click the File menu and then click Save As/Export.

TIP   *You can also use the Save toolbar button. When you click the Save toolbar button before giving the query a name, Access prompts you for a query name. Remember, saving a query doesn't save the data you currently see in the Recordset but instead saves a set of instructions for sorting and extracting a particular set of data.*

Access displays a Save As dialog box much like the one you saw when you saved your table structure. This time, however, Access requests a query name rather than a table name.

5. Make sure the Within the Current Database As option is selected; then type **California Phone Numbers** as the query name and click OK.

6. Click the View toolbar button to switch to Query Design view.

Access returns you to Query Design view and displays the new query name in the title bar. As when saving a table structure, you are prompted for a query name only when you save for the first time.

ADDING AND DELETING FIELDS FROM QUERY DESIGN VIEW

You can easily add new fields to Query Design view and remove them as well.

HANDS ON

1. In the query design grid, drag across the column selectors for the PhoneNumber and StateOrProvince fields and press Delete.

NOTE   *In the query design grid, the column selectors are the small, blank, gray boxes above the names of the fields.*

Access deletes the PhoneNumber and StateOrProvince fields from the query design grid.

2. Click the DateJoined field in the Field list to select it, drag it down so that it's directly over the ContactLastName field, and then release the mouse button.

Access adds the DateJoined field to the query design grid, placing it in the ContactLastName field's former position and pushing all other fields to the right.

3. In the Sort row of the DateJoined column, choose an Ascending sort.

4. In the Criteria row of the DateJoined column, enter **>12/31/95**

5. Click the View toolbar button.

Access runs the query, displaying the names for customers who joined after 12/31/95, as shown in Figure 4-20.

Dates after 1995

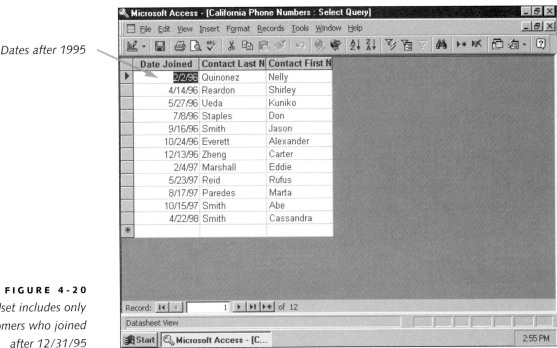

FIGURE 4-20

Recordset includes only customers who joined after 12/31/95

6. Click the View toolbar button to switch to Design view.

7. Click the column selector for the DateJoined field to select the field.

8. With the mouse pointer still over the column selector, drag to the right until the heavy vertical line is just to the right of the ContactFirstName field, and then release the mouse button.

Access moves the DateJoined field to the right end of the query design grid. Remember, this will change the arrangement of data in the Recordset as well as affecting the sort order.

9. Click the Run toolbar button.

Access displays the revised Recordset shown in Figure 4-21. The same records are included, but now last names are displayed first and the records are first sorted by last name.

Field moved to right

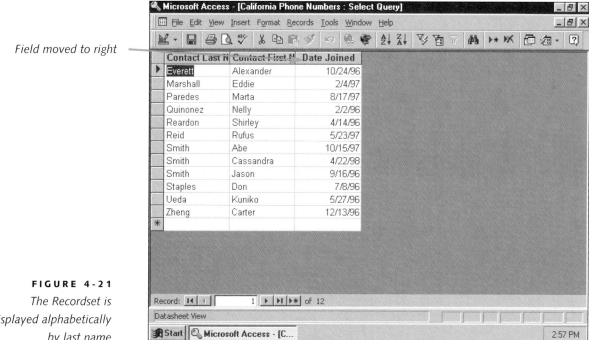

FIGURE 4-21

The Recordset is displayed alphabetically by last name

10. Click the file menu and choose Save As/Export.

You see the Save As dialog box. This dialog box lets you save your queries in the database under a new name. You want to save this query without overwriting the California Phone Numbers query on which it is based.

11. Type **Joined After 1995,** and click OK.

Access returns you to Datasheet view and displays the new query name in the title bar.

12. Click the Close button.

Access returns you to the Be Fruitful Database window, which now includes the two queries California Phone Numbers and Joined After 1995.

OPENING A SAVED QUERY

As mentioned, one of the great benefits of a query is that you can save it to view the Recordset at a later date. In the next few steps, you will open one of your saved queries and make changes to the data inside it.

HANDS ON

1. Double-click California Phone Numbers from the Queries tab.

When viewing your queries in the Database window, you can run them either by double-clicking the name or by selecting the query name and clicking the Open button. Now you'll try changing data in the Recordset, noting that your changes are reflected in the underlying table.

Access displays the California Phone Numbers query in Datasheet view.

2. Change the phone number for Alice Bechdel to **(415) 777-6543**

3. Close the datasheet by clicking on the Close button to the right of the menu bar.

4. In the Be Fruitful Database window, click the Tables object tab.

5. Double-click the BFCustomer tables to open it.

6. Scroll to the right until you can see the phone number for Alice Bechdel.

As you can see, the new number that you just entered through the Recordset is reflected in the table.

7. Close the table by clicking its Close button.

QUERYING MULTIPLE TABLES

You've just spent a fair amount of time building queries based on a single table. With just a little more effort you can create queries that display data from more than one table. Essentially, you add the Field lists for the desired tables to the top of the Query Design window and then choose fields and specify the sort and selection instructions as you do for a single-table query. However, it's critical that you also **join** the tables—that is, you must tell Access how to match up records from one table with the appropriate records from any other tables. Otherwise, Access wouldn't have a clue which orders corresponded with which customers, for example.

> **join** A method of notifying Access how to match up records from one table with the appropriate records from any other tables.

You can join tables by means of their common fields. In some cases, Access joins the tables for you automatically. This happens if one table has a field of the same name and the same data type as the primary key in the other or if you've already defined a formal relationship between the tables. (You'll learn about defining relationships between tables in Lesson 7.)

BUILDING A MULTI-TABLE QUERY

Now you'll build a query that draws data from both the BFCustomers and BFOrders tables. Before you can enter your selection criteria, you need to display Field lists from both tables and join the tables. Then you can select the fields and values upon which to extract and/or sort your data.

DISPLAYING FIELD LISTS FROM TWO TABLES

During this exercise, you'll tell Access to display Field lists from both tables and to join them based on a common field.

1. Make sure that the BFCustomers table is selected in the Be Fruitful Database window.

2. Click the drop-down arrow beside the New Object toolbar button on the far right side of the toolbar.

3. Select Query from the drop-down list.

Access displays the New Query dialog box, which you saw earlier.

4. Select the Design View option and click OK.

Access opens the Query Design window. The BFCustomers Field list is already displayed; you must add the second Field list.

OFFICE ASSISTANT

You can also create queries using a Query Wizard. For information on the Query Wizards available in Access, ask the Office Assistant.

5. Click the Show Table toolbar button to display the Show Table dialog box.

6. Double-click the BFOrders table and then click the Close button on the Show Table dialog box.

Access closes the Show Table dialog box. You can see that the Field list for the BFOrders table has been added to the Query Design view window, as shown in Figure 4-22.

Join line

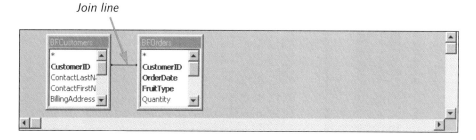

FIGURE 4-22
The Query Design view window with Field lists from two tables

Notice the line connecting the two tables; this line indicates that the tables are joined. Access guessed that you wanted them joined because they both have a field with the same name and data type.

7. Click the line between the CustomerID fields in BFCustomers and BFOrders and press Delete .

Access removes the join line.

If Access can't guess where to place the join and you want to establish one, you can drag to introduce a join line like the one you just saw.

8. Click the CustomerID field in the BFCustomers Field list.

9. Drag from the field over to the CustomerID field in the BFOrders table.

As you drag, the mouse pointer takes on the shape of a small rectangle. When you release the mouse button, Access reestablishes the link between the two tables, drawing a join line between the two CustomerID fields.

CREATING SELECTION CRITERIA FROM TWO TABLES

Now that you have Field lists from both tables in the window and have joined them together, you are ready to set up your selection criteria.

HANDS ON

1. In the BFCustomers Field list, double-click the ContactLastName field and then double-click the ContactFirstName field.

Access adds both of these field names to the query design grid.

2. Choose a sort order of Ascending for the ContactLastName field and also for the ContactFirstName field.

3. Double-click the FruitType field in the BFOrders Field list to add that field to the query design grid.

4. In the Criteria row for the FruitType field, enter **Apples**

N O T E   *You can expand the selection criteria by joining two or more criteria with the word "And." For instance, if you wanted to list all of the records except those ordering peaches and strawberries, you could type < > Peaches And < > Strawberries.*

5. Click the Run toolbar button.

Access displays the Recordset shown in Figure 4-23, which lists records for customers who have ordered apples. Notice that customers who ordered apples more than once are listed more than once.

Fields from BFCustomers table   Field from BFOrders table

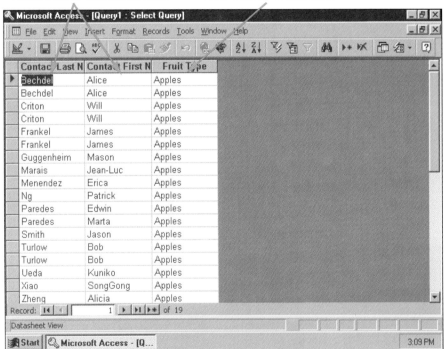

FIGURE 4-23
Recordset that includes data from more than one table

6. Click the File menu and choose Save As/Export.

7. Type **Apple Orders** as the query name and click OK.

8. Click the Close button to close the datasheet.

You are back to your Be Fruitful Database window. Even though you created the new query from the Tables tab, you do not see the new query in the tab. It's there, however, under the Queries tab.

QUERYING FOR BLANK DATA

Sometimes you need to set your selection criteria for data that is missing rather than comparing to data that has been entered. For example, in your BFOrders table, a field contains the date the order was paid. In the next steps, you will create a query that uses data from two tables, and lists records that do not have a date entered in the payment date field.

HANDS ON

1. Click the drop-down arrow on the New Object toolbar button in the Be Fruitful Database window.

2. Select the Query option.

TIP *If the Query icon is displayed on the New Object toolbar button, you can click the button itself rather than its drop-down arrow. The appearance of this button changes depending on the last new object type created.*

3. With Design View selected in the New Query dialog box, click OK.

4. Click the Show Table toolbar button.

Access displays the Show Table dialog box with the Query Design view window in the background.

5. Double-click the BFOrders table to display its Field list.

6. Click the Close button in the Show Table dialog box.

The BFOrders and BFCustomers Field lists should both appear in the Query Design view window. As before, Access introduces a join line between the two CustomerID fields.

7. Add the ContactLastName, ContactFirstName, and PaymentDate fields to the query design grid, in that order.

NOTE *The ContactLastName and ContactFirstName fields are in the BFCustomers table, while the PaymentDate field is in the BFOrders table.*

8. Choose an Ascending sort for both the ContactLastName and ContactFirstName fields.

9. Deselect the Show check box for the PaymentDate field.

10. In the Criteria row for the PaymentDate field, type **Is Null**

You're going to display all customers who have unpaid orders. *Is Null* is the expression to use to display records where the specified field is empty.

11. Click the Run toolbar button.

Access displays the Recordset shown in Figure 4-24. This is a list of all customers who have ordered fruit but have not yet paid for it. Note that you can make a selection based on the PaymentDate field without including it in the Recordset.

12. Click File, click Save As/Export, type the query name **Unpaid Orders**, and click OK to save the query.

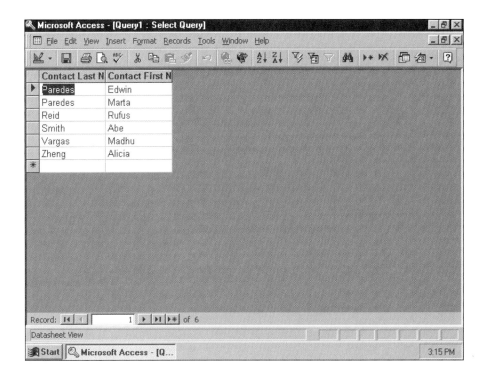

FIGURE 4-24

Recordset of unpaid orders

13. Click the Close button.

You are back to the Database window. Your queries are saved in the Queries tab and you can view them at any time.

14. Close the **Be Fruitful** Database window and exit Access.

LESSON SUMMARY AND EXERCISES

After you complete this lesson, you should know how to do the following:

SORTING AND SELECTING DATA

■ To display all records in a particular sequence, use the Sort command.

■ To display specific records from tables, use the Filter or Query command.

USING THE SORT COMMANDS

■ To sort your records, click anywhere in the field you want to sort on in Datasheet view and click the Sort Ascending or Sort Descending toolbar button.

FILTERING YOUR DATA

■ To filter a table based on data in one of the fields, select the data in the field and click the Filter By Selection toolbar button.

■ To redisplay all the records in the table, click the Remove Filter toolbar button.

■ To filter a table using multiple criteria, click the Filter By Form toolbar button. Enter the selection criteria for the field or fields upon which you want to filter the data. To base a filter on more than one value in a field, click the Or tab and enter the additional value. Click the Apply Filter toolbar button.

■ To type exact criteria to use as a filter, right-click within a field, choose Filter For from the shortcut menu, type the criteria, and press Enter.

■ To set up a filter and sort or use more complex selection criteria, click the Records menu, choose Filter, and then select Advanced Filter/Sort.

DESIGNING BASIC QUERIES

■ To create a new query, select the Queries tab in the Database window and click the New button.

■ To select the tables to be used in the query, double-click them in the Show Table dialog box.

■ To choose the fields to sort, select, or display data in the query, double-click each field in the Field lists at the top of the Query Design view window.

■ To sort a query based on a particular field or fields, select Ascending or Descending under each field in the query design grid.

■ To hide a field from the Recordset, deselect the Show box under the field in the query design grid.

■ To save a query, click the File menu and choose Save As/Export. Enter the name for the query.

■ To open a query, double-click its name in the Queries tab in the Database window.

QUERYING MULTIPLE TABLES

■ To base a query on more than one table, click the Show Table toolbar button and add each additional table's Field list to the Query Design view window.

■ To join tables, click the common field in the first table and drag to the common field in the second table.

NEW TERMS TO REMEMBER

After you complete this lesson, you should know the meaning of the following terms:

ascending sort	query design grid
comparison operator	Recordset
descending sort	select
expression	select queries
Field list	selection criteria
filter	sort
join	wildcard character

MATCHING EXERCISE

Match the terms with the definitions on the right:

TERMS	DEFINITIONS
1. sort	a. Order in which characters are shown from A to Z
2. filter	
3. selection criteria	b. Way to link tables in a query so that Access knows how to match up corresponding records
4. Recordset	
5. join	c. Expression used in selection criteria to query a table for empty fields
6. ascending sort	
7. query design grid	d. To rearrange records into alphabetical, numerical, or chronological order
8. descending sort	e. Area of Query Design view window in which you enter sorting and selection criteria
9. Is Null	
10. show	f. Subset of your data that is the result of a query
	g. Area of the query design grid that enables you to choose whether fields are displayed in the Recordset
	h. To extract a selected subset of your data
	i. Instructions used to determine records to be filtered or queried
	j. Order in which dates would be listed from most recent to oldest

COMPLETION EXERCISE

Fill in the missing word or phrase for each of the following:

1. When you want to extract records and sort them into some order that you can use again in the future, you should use a(n) _____.

2. To remove criteria from the last sort, click the _____ toolbar button.

3. To type specific filter criteria, right-click within a field and select _____ from the shortcut menu.

4. Filtering a table based on data you have highlighted in the table is called a Filter By _____.

5. In order to use a query at a future date, you must _____ it.

6. To extract and sort records all at once with a filter, you must use the _____ option from the Records menu.

7. To select Field lists for tables in Query Design view, click the _____ toolbar button.

8. The symbol used in selection criteria that means greater than or equal to is _____.

9. To filter for records that meet one of several values, use the _____ tab at the bottom of the Filter By Form window.

10. To return the display to the original order and contents after creating a filter, choose _____ from the Records menu.

SHORT-ANSWER QUESTIONS

Write a brief answer to each of the following questions:

1. Name at least two reasons for using a query rather than a filter to sort and/or select data.

2. Describe the purpose of the Show row in the query design grid.

3. List the differences between Filter By Selection, Filter By Form, Filter For Input, and the Advanced Filter/Sort options.

4. Provide the selection criteria you would use to find all customers who joined the club before (but not on) 2/2/92.

5. Describe how you would change the order in which fields are displayed in the datasheet when you work with a filter. (Think about whether this can be accomplished.) Then describe how you would change the order of fields with a query. (For extra credit, describe two ways of doing this.)

6. Describe how you would create an Advanced Filter/Sort in the BFCustomers table that shows all customers living in Massachusetts. Then describe how you would change the filter to show all customers not living in Massachusetts.

7. Describe how you would create a filter using the Filter By Form method to show all customers who joined on 5/18/93 from New York state.

8. Describe how you would modify the filter to show all customers who joined on 5/18/93 and lived in either New York or Illinois.

9. Describe how you would create a query to display the last and first names of customers who have a ZIP Code of less than 45000.

10. Describe how you would create and save a query using both the BFCustomers and BFOrders tables to show all customers who did *not* order Apples, Grapefruit, or Pears. The query should show the first and last names, in that order.

APPLICATION PROJECTS

Perform the following actions to complete these projects:

1. Open the **Be Fruitful** database in the **Lessons** folder of your Student Data Disk. Devise a filter that extracts records with an order date after 6/15/95. Create the filter so that it sorts the orders in the BFOrders table by quantity (in descending order) and then by order date (in ascending order). Print the resulting records. Revise the filter so that orders for oranges are excluded. Do not save changes to the table design.

2. Devise a query that displays customers in the BFCustomers table in descending order by the DateJoined field. Include the dates joined, last names, first names, and phone numbers in the Recordset. Save the query, naming it **Join Date**. Print the results of the query. Then revise the query so that it displays records for only those customers who joined before 1994 and print again. There's no need to save the revised query.

3. Devise a multi-table query that lists all customers who have placed orders after 1997. Sort these customers in ascending order first by last name and then by first name. Display the last names, first names, and order dates in the Recordset. Save the query as **Post 1997 Orders**. Print the Recordset. For extra credit, rearrange the fields in the Recordset so that order dates are displayed first; then resave the query.

4. Open the **Personal** database in the **Projects** folder on your Student Data Disk. Create a filter that displays data from the To Dos table. (You can only do this project if you have completed the Application Projects in Lessons 2 and 3 that created this table.) In the filter, show only those records that have a priority of 1. Then modify the filter to show records with a priority of less than 3 in ascending order by ending date. Print the results of the filter.

5. Open the **Music** database in the **Projects** folder on your Student Data Disk. Build a query that displays selected categories from the Music Categories, Recordings, and Recording Artists tables. (You can only do this project if you have completed the Application Projects in Lessons 2 and 3 that created these tables.) Join the Recording Artists table to the Recordings table based on the RecordingArtistID. Join the Music Categories table to the Recordings table using the MusicCategoryID. Display the artist name and recording title for all records in the Rock category. Save your query as **Rock Albums** and print the results of the query.

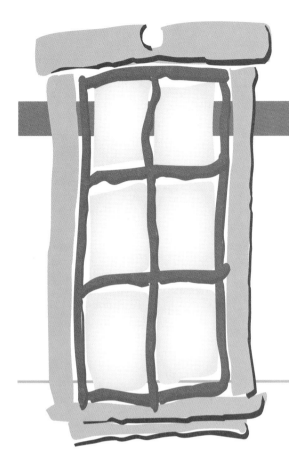

VIEWING, ENTERING, AND EDITING DATA WITH FORMS

OBJECTIVES

After you complete this lesson, you will be able to do the following:

- *Create an AutoForm.*
- *Use a Form Wizard to create a columnar form.*
- *Use a Form Wizard to create a tabular form.*
- *Add and edit data with forms.*
- *Sort and view subsets of your data with a form.*
- *Preview and print forms.*

CONTENTS

When and Why to Use Forms

Creating an AutoForm

Using the Form Wizard

Adding and Editing Data by Use of Forms

Sorting and Selecting Data with Forms

Previewing and Printing Forms

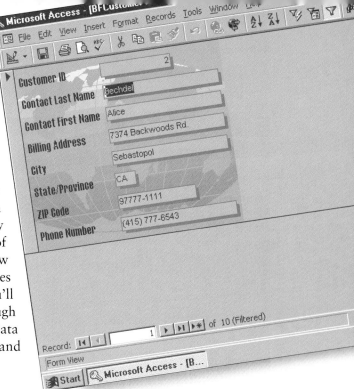

This chapter provides a thorough introduction to Access's form-making capabilities. You'll take advantage of the Access Form Wizard—a quick and easy way to produce a wide variety of form layouts. You'll learn how to build several different types of forms. In addition, you'll learn how to edit data through forms, view groups of your data with forms, and preview and print forms.

WHEN AND WHY TO USE FORMS

As you probably remember from Lesson 1, Access forms are display versions of paper forms. You can use forms to view, edit, and enter data into your tables. So far, you've only used the datasheet to work with your data. Although this setting provides a fine overview, generally it doesn't permit you to see all fields at once—making assessing or editing your data awkward. To create a more comfortable working environment, you can make a custom form and determine how it will present the data from a table or query. Among other things, you can build forms that display a single record at a time as well as forms that reveal only selected fields from the chosen table or query. Forms are particularly helpful when you want to simplify data entry or when you need to control which data is displayed.

Access makes creating basic forms easy. You can produce one with the click of a button. In addition, Access supplies a number of Form Wizards for creating various types of forms. Like the Table Wizard you used in Lesson 2, the Form Wizards enable you to build several standard forms with minimal effort.

Although you're just now learning about forms, you will find that many of the mouse actions and keystrokes are similar to those you already know. In forms, you move through fields and records much as you do in Datasheet view. In fact, you can switch any time to the form's Datasheet view to see multiple records at once. (This view is identical to the Datasheet view of the table but displays only the information that you would see in the form.) And, since you already know how to add, edit, delete, sort, and select data in the datasheet, you should have no trouble learning how to do these things with forms—the procedures are much the same.

CREATING AN AUTOFORM

AutoForm A form that Access builds for you automatically; the AutoForm gathers the information it needs by examining the selected table or query.

To create AutoForms, Access simply requires you to choose the table or query on which you want to base the form and then click a single button. An **AutoForm** is actually a specialized type of Form Wizard that doesn't request any special choices on your part but instead gathers the information it needs by examining the selected table or query. The Wizard builds a very basic— but perfectly good—form that includes every field from the table or query arranged in columns. The field names (or captions) appear on the left side of the form to identify the fields, and the name of the table or query appears at the top as a heading. Most fields are displayed as text boxes; Memo fields are displayed as slightly larger text boxes, and Yes/No fields show up as check boxes that you can click to either select or deselect.

EXPLORING AN AUTOFORM

Now you'll explore an AutoForm based on the BFCustomers table, and you'll learn to view and move through your data using the form.

TIP   *If your Student Data Disk is almost full, copy your* **Be Fruitful** *database file to a blank, formatted disk before proceeding with the following Hands-On activity.*

HANDS ON

1. Open the **Be Fruitful** database in your Lessons folder on the Student Data Disk. Access displays the Be Fruitful Database window.

2. If the BFCustomers table is not already selected, make sure the Tables tab is selected and click once on the BFCustomers table.

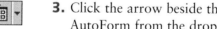

3. Click the arrow beside the New Object toolbar button and select AutoForm from the drop-down list, as seen in Figure 5-1.

TIP   *If the AutoForm icon appears on the New Object toolbar button, you can click the button rather than its drop-down arrow.*

After a while, Access displays a form like the one shown in Figure 5-2. Notice that it displays the data for the first record in the BFCustomers table. The form will include all of the fields for a single record.

TIP   *You can just as easily create AutoForms from within Datasheet view.*

4. Click the Maximize button on the right side of the form's title bar if your form is not already maximized.

TIP   *If most, but not all, fields show up in your form, you may be able to bring them all into view by maximizing the form window.*

5. Click the Last Record navigation button.

Access displays the information for the last record in the table. All the navigation buttons at the bottom of the form work as they do in the datasheet.

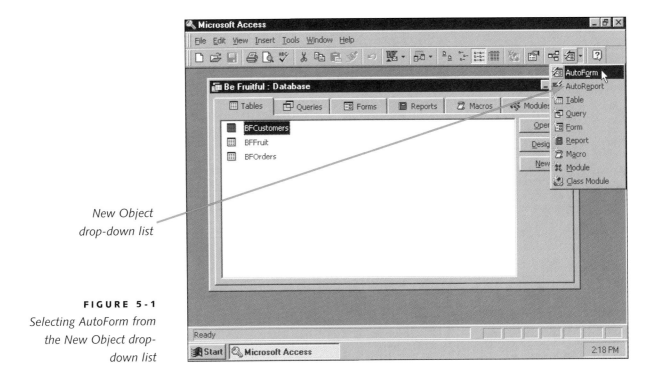

FIGURE 5-1

Selecting AutoForm from the New Object drop-down list

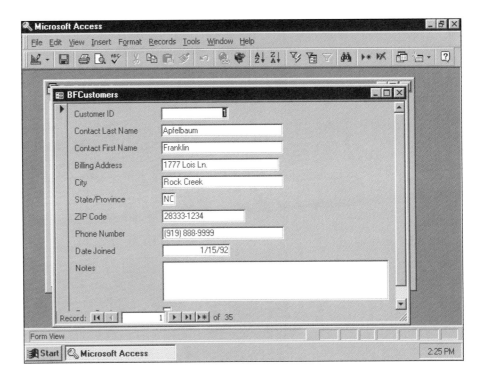

FIGURE 5-2

AutoForm created this form to display each record

6. Click twice on the Previous Record button.

Access moves up two records in the table.

The Notes field has a larger text box because it's a Memo field, and the Extra Catalogs field is displayed as a check box because it's a Yes/No field. You can click this check box to turn it on (a ✔ appears) or turn it off (the ✔ disappears).

7. Click the arrow next to the View toolbar button and select Datasheet View, or click the View menu and choose Datasheet View.

Access displays the form in Datasheet view, as shown in Figure 5-3. You'll see the portion of the data that you were viewing in Form view. In the Datasheet view, the data appears in columns and rows.

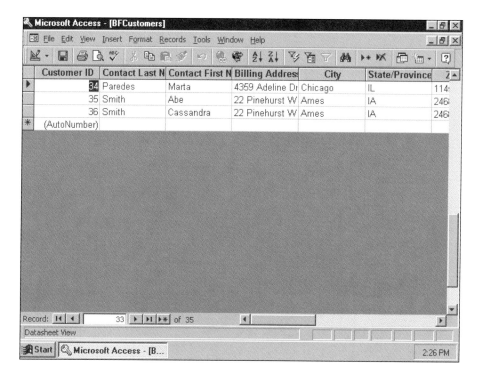

FIGURE 5-3

Datasheet view shows more than one record at a time

If you like, you can also scroll up and down (and left and right) through your data, as you can when working on a table in Datasheet view.

8. Click the arrow next to the View toolbar button and select Form View.

Access returns you to Form view. In the Form view, the data appears like a paper form.

9. Click the Form view window's Close button.

Because you haven't saved the form, Access displays a warning box. You can select Yes to save the form, No to close the form without saving it, or Cancel to back out of the operation and return to the form.

10. Click Yes.

Access displays a Save As dialog box prompting you for a form name.

T I P   *You can also choose Save As/Export from the File menu to save an AutoForm.*

11. Type **BFCustomer AutoForm** as the form name and click OK.

Access saves and then closes the form, returning you to the Be Fruitful Database window. The form you just created becomes one of the objects under the Forms tab.

USING THE FORM WIZARD

If you have uncomplicated needs and simple tables, AutoForms might do the job. Often, however, you'll want more control over your forms—you might want to choose their layout, decide the fields to include, and more. If so, you can take advantage of the Form Wizard built into Access.

Using the Form Wizard is much like using the Table Wizard; the Form Wizard prompts you for information, and Access builds a form based on your responses. The Form Wizard does much of the work for you; at the same time, it gives you some say in the final results.

When using a Wizard, keep in mind that you can click the Back button any time you want to move back one step.

With the following steps, you'll create a simple single-column form. A little later, you'll experiment with some other types of forms that Access supplies.

CREATING A COLUMNAR FORM WITH THE FORM WIZARD

columnar form A form that displays each field on a separate line with field labels or captions to their left as identifiers.

Now you will create a single-column form using the Form Wizard. A **columnar form** is one that displays each field on a separate line with the label or caption to the left of the field.

HANDS ON

1. Choose the Forms object tab in the Be Fruitful Database window and click the New button.

Access displays the New Form dialog box.

2. Click Form Wizard in the list box.

3. Click the drop-down arrow beside the text, "Choose the Table or Query Where the Object's Data Comes From."

Access displays an alphabetical list of the available tables and queries, as shown in Figure 5-4. This list includes the queries you created in the previous lesson, as well as the tables you created earlier.

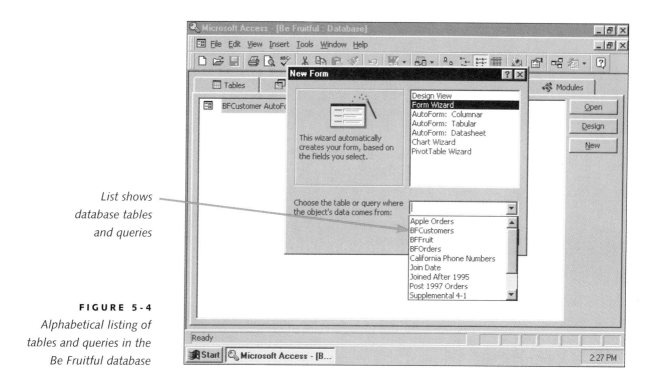

*List shows
database tables
and queries*

FIGURE 5-4
*Alphabetical listing of
tables and queries in the
Be Fruitful database*

4. Click the BFCustomers table and then click OK.

After a moment, Access displays the Form Wizard dialog box shown in Figure 5-5.

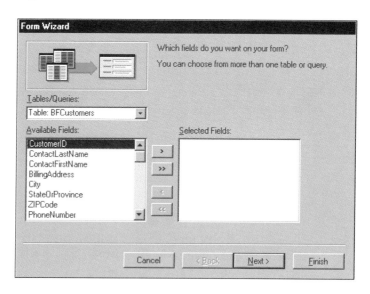

FIGURE 5-5
*The first Form Wizard
dialog box*

You can choose the fields to include in the form, as well as the order in which to display them. This dialog box works much like the first Table Wizard dialog box, although in this case, you can only choose fields from the selected table or query.

5. Click the >> button.

Access moves all of the field names over to the Selected Fields list box. If you want to include all or most fields in the form, this button quickly adds them all at once, and then you can remove a few with the < button.

TIP *The order of fields in the Selected Field list box determines their order in the form itself. If you want to change the existing order of fields, you must use the > button to add them one by one in the desired order.*

6. Click the DateJoined field and click the < button.

Access removes the DateJoined field from the list of fields to be included in the form and returns it to the Available Fields list box. Notice that the Notes field is selected.

7. Click the < button to remove the Notes and then remove the ExtraCatalogs fields.

Access removes the Notes and ExtraCatalogs fields from the list of fields to be included in the form.

OFFICE ASSISTANT *You can organize your forms so that they contain two or more tabs or pages of information. You can also create a form within a form (called a subform). Ask the Office Assistant for help.*

8. Click the Next button to move to the next Form Wizard dialog box.

You see the next Form Wizard dialog box, as shown in Figure 5-6.

Type of layout

Preview of
selected layout

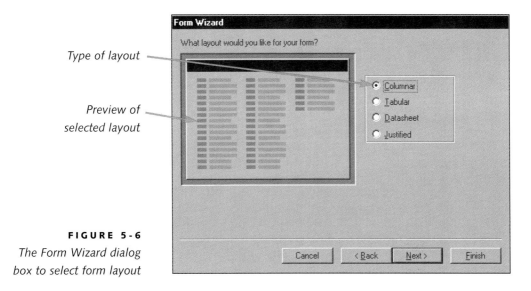

FIGURE 5-6
The Form Wizard dialog box to select form layout

This dialog box allows you to choose the type of form you want to create. When you click a layout option button, Access gives you a preview of how the layout will look.

9. Make sure the Columnar layout button is selected and click Next.

You see the next Form Wizard dialog box.

This dialog box lets you choose a style for your form. Styles include pictures, shading, and colors to give a special "look" to the form. When you select an option button, a preview of the style appears in the dialog box.

10. Click International and click Next.

Access displays the final Form Wizard dialog box shown in Figure 5-7.

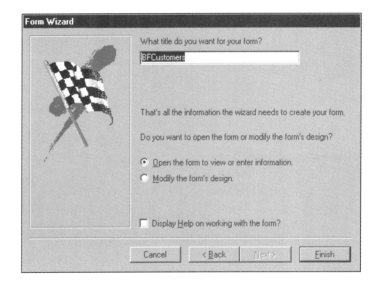

FIGURE 5-7

Thr final Form Wizard dialog box

In this dialog box you supply a title for your form and decide whether to open the form with data or edit the form's design. In either case, you can choose to view helpful information while you work with the form.

11. Type **BFCustomer Names and Addresses** as the title for the form.

The title you type replaces the one that Access chose. Access uses the name of the table as a suggestion for the form title.

12. Make sure you select the option button "Open the Form to View or Enter Information," and click the Finish button.

In a moment, Access displays the form you just created, as shown in Figure 5-8. The form contains data from the BFCustomers table that you selected via the Form Wizard. Also, note that the form displays only the designated fields.

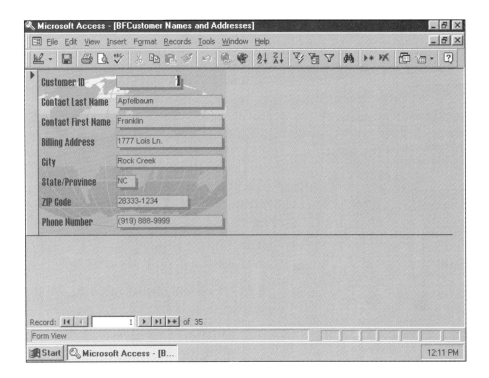

FIGURE 5-8

Columnar form created with the Form Wizard

SWITCHING FROM FORM TO DATASHEET VIEW

Once you have created a form, you can still use the Datasheet view, as with the AutoForm you created earlier in this lesson.

HANDS ON

1. Click the arrow next to the View toolbar button and select Datasheet View.

You switch to the form's Datasheet view.

2. Scroll to the right through your data.

You will notice that Access only displays the fields included in the form.

3. Click the arrow next to the View toolbar button and select Form View.

You return to Form view.

OFFICE ASSISTANT   *You can also use the View toolbar button to switch to Design view. For information on modifications you can make to a form's layout in Design view, ask the Office Assistant.*

4. Click the form's Close button.

You return to the Be Fruitful Database window.

NOTE   *Even though only some of the table's data is displayed in this form, all of it is still there in the underlying table. Always remember that a form just displays your data; it doesn't contain it. You might want to think of a form as a window to your data.*

BUILDING A TABULAR FORM WITH THE FORM WIZARD

tabular form A form that displays all of the fields for a single record in one row, field names or captions as column headings, and data in the table or query as a tabular arrangement of rows and columns.

The two forms you've created so far display the fields in columns and show only one record at a time. On some occasions, however, you might want to see multiple records at once but not in Datasheet view. If so, you might want to use a tabular form. A **tabular form** displays all of the fields for a single record in one row and displays multiple records at once. You see field names or captions displayed as column headings—much as they are in Datasheet view. These forms work particularly well for tables or queries that don't include many fields.

Follow these steps to create a tabular form based on the Joined After 1995 query using the Form Wizard.

HANDS ON

1. Make sure you're still in the Be Fruitful Database window and click the Queries object tab.

You'll see a list of queries in the Be Fruitful database. You should see all of the queries that you created in Lesson 4.

2. Click the Joined After 1995 query to select it.

Remember, this query sorts customers in ascending order by last name and displays only records whose Date Joined field is greater than 1995.

3. Click the arrow next to the New Object toolbar button and select Form.

Access displays the New Form dialog box you saw earlier. This time, however, the Joined After 1995 query is already selected in the "Choose the Table or Query" drop-down box.

4. Select Form Wizard in the list box and click OK.

Access brings up the initial Form Wizard dialog box, as shown in Figure 5-9, where you can choose the fields to include in the form.

5. Click the ContactFirstName field to select it and then click > to move it to the Selected Fields list box.

6. In the same manner, select the ContactLastName and DateJoined fields, in that order, and use the > button to move them to the Selected Fields list box.

WARNING *In this instance, you can't just use the >> button to select all these fields because you need to change the order in which they appear.*

7. Click the Next button.

Now you will see the Form Wizard dialog box you use to choose your layout.

8. Click Tabular and then click Next.

Access displays the Form Wizard dialog box for selecting a style.

9. Click the Clouds option and then click Next.

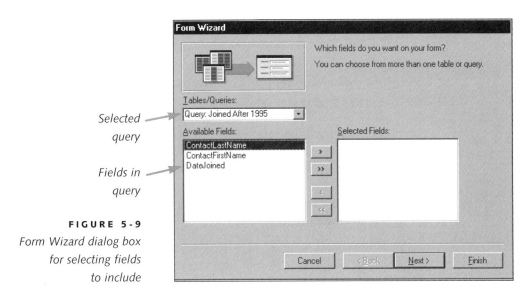

Selected
query

Fields in
query

FIGURE 5-9
Form Wizard dialog box
for selecting fields
to include

Access displays the final Form Wizard dialog box. As when you created a columnar form, you now can enter a title for the form, and you can choose to view data with the form or to view the form's design.

10. Type **Joined After 1995 Tabular Form** as the form's title; make sure the "Open the Form to View or Enter Information" option button is selected, and click the Finish button.

You see the tabular form, as shown in Figure 5-10, which displays the data from your Joined After 1995 query in a tabular layout.

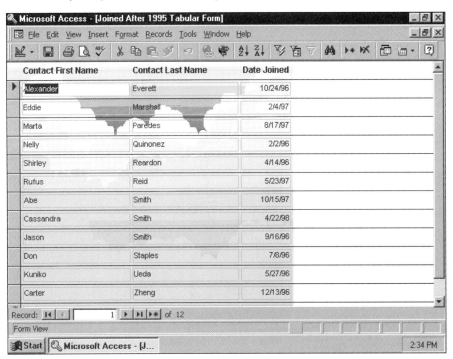

FIGURE 5-10
Tabular form created
from a query

11. Scroll through the data to view the available records.

12. Click the form's Close button.

Access returns you to the Be Fruitful Database window.

ADDING AND EDITING DATA BY USE OF FORMS

Sometimes you may want to use forms to browse through your data. The real purpose of forms, however, is to facilitate the entering and editing of data.

In forms, as in the datasheet, you need to know how to find the records that you want to edit. Once you're there, you need to know a few editing strategies. Fortunately, the techniques for navigating in forms are basically the same as those for moving around in the datasheet. Refer to Lesson 3 if you need a refresher course on how to navigate or how to edit data.

ADDING DATA USING A FORM

In this exercise, you'll use the BFCustomer AutoForm you created earlier to add some new customers to the BFCustomers table.

HANDS ON

1. Click the Forms object tab in the Be Fruitful Database window to select it and then double-click BFCustomer AutoForm.

Access displays the selected form and shows the first record for the underlying table, as you see in Figure 5-11.

T I P   *If you want to see more fields at once, you can either resize or maximize the form window.*

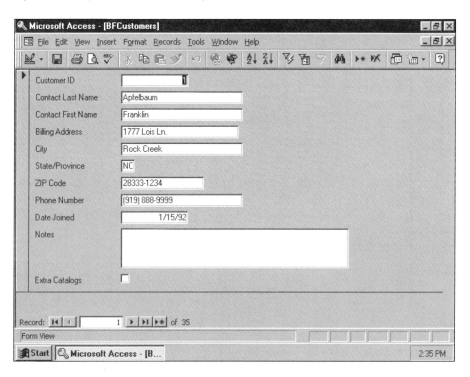

FIGURE 5-11
The BFCustomer AutoForm displaying the first record

2. Press Ctrl+End.

Access moves you to the last field of the last record.

3. Press Tab or click the New Record toolbar button.

Access presents you with a new, blank record. As in Datasheet view, Access also saves any changes to the record you were working on when you move to another record.

4. Press [Tab] to move to the Contact Last Name field and type
Myrianthopoulos

Notice that Access automatically enters the next record number in the Customer ID field. (If you're confused about why there are more customer IDs than customers, don't forget that you deleted a record in Lesson 3. Also, if you completed Supplemental Activity 4-1, you added and deleted records.)

5. Press [Tab] to move to the Contact First Name field, and type **Zoe**

6. Pressing [Tab] to move from field to field, type the address **1357 Birch St. #7**, the city **Woodstock**, the state **NY**, the ZIP Code **11223-4432**, and the phone number **(917) 333-1234**

7. Finally, enter the date **4/19/98** in the Date Joined field, leave the Notes field blank for now, and leave the Extra Catalogs field deselected (the default).

You now have a new record in the table. (Make sure you enter the record by moving to another record.)

OFFICE ASSISTANT   *Once you add all the necessary records to your database, you may want to lock the form so that other users can view your data but can't change it. To get instructions on this process, ask the Office Assistant about* **read-only forms***.*

EDITING RECORDS USING A FORM

You can also make changes to data already in the table with use of a form. Once the record you want to edit is displayed, you can change it with the same basic steps you completed in Lesson 3.

HANDS ON

1. Press [F5].

Access highlights the current record indicator in the lower-left corner of the screen.

2. Type 7 and press [Enter].

Access moves you to the seventh record in the table—the record for Mason Guggenheim.

3. Click the label for the Notes field.

Access selects this field. Although there's no text (if there were, it would become selected), Access places the insertion point within the field and adds a vertical scroll bar.

4. Type the following text:

11/4/96: Mr. Guggenheim reported not receiving his order of pears, although the fruit was delivered to his front door. Perhaps this is a question of a hungry neighbor or passerby. Please send him a replacement box, rush delivery, and include a half dozen extra pears. Leave all packages at the back door in the future.

5. Click the Last Record navigation button.

Access displays the record you just added for Zoe Myrianthopoulos.

6. Click the record selector—the long vertical bar on the left side of the window.

The record selector should turn a darker shade of gray, which indicates that this entire record is selected. You can see this effect in Figure 5-12.

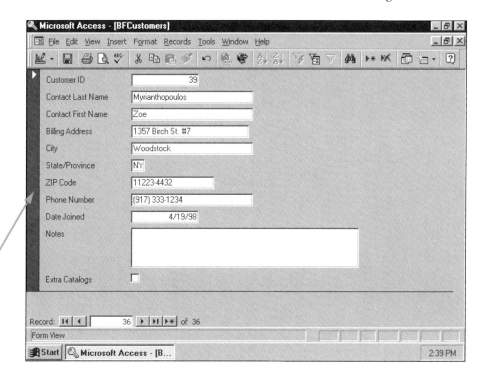

Record selector

FIGURE 5-12

The left side of the screen shows the record is selected

7. Press [Delete] to remove the new record.

It turns out that Zoe had requested a catalog but hadn't actually placed an order.

Access displays the dialog box shown in Figure 5-13; you see the identical dialog box when you delete records in Datasheet view.

FIGURE 5-13

Dialog box asks if you want to delete the selected record(s)

8. Click Yes.

The record is deleted from the table. A blank form appears.

9. Click File and choose Close.

The BFCustomer AutoForm is closed and you return to the Database window.

SORTING AND SELECTING DATA WITH FORMS

You've just learned how to use forms to show selected fields from an underlying table or query. You may have noticed that the forms include data from all of the records and that the records are sorted by the primary key. At times, you'll want to view selected groups of data from the form sorted in some other order. To accomplish this, you can use the Sort commands and filters that you learned about in Lesson 4. As you experiment with these commands, keep in mind that you're changing which records are displayed and the order that they're displayed in, but you are not changing which fields are displayed or the order that the fields are displayed in. In other words, you're not modifying the form itself.

SORTING RECORDS THROUGH A FORM

Here you will learn to sort the data being viewed through a form. Most of the techniques used here should seem similar to the sorting exercises in Lesson 4.

HANDS ON

1. Make sure that you're in the Be Fruitful Database window; click the Forms object tab if it's not already selected, and double-click BFCustomer Names and Addresses to open this form.

Access displays the first record in BFCustomers, as shown in Figure 5-14.

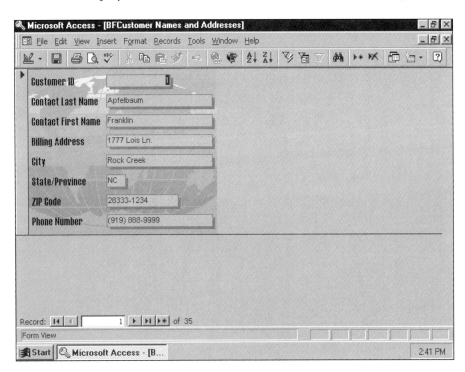

FIGURE 5-14

The first table record appears first in the form

Suppose you want to view the records in order by last name instead of Customer ID.

2. Press ⌊Tab⌋ to move to the Contact Last Name field.

3. Click the Sort Ascending toolbar button.

If you want to sort on more than a single field, you can switch to Datasheet view and select the desired fields using the techniques you learned in Lesson 4.

4. Click the Last Record button.

Access moves you to the last record; note that it's now the record for Carter Zheng, even though he's not the last customer listed when the records are arranged by customer ID number.

5. Click the Previous Record button repeatedly.

You see that Access has rearranged the records in ascending alphabetical order by last name (although not by first name).

SELECTING RECORDS THROUGH A FORM

The steps you will use to set up a filter for your form are very similar to those you used to create the filter while in Datasheet view.

HANDS ON

1. Click the Records menu, choose Filter, and then select Advanced Filter/Sort.

Access displays the Filter Design window, as shown in Figure 5-15. This is the exact same filter window you worked with in Lesson 4. Note that the ContactLastName field already appears in the grid—as a result of the Sort command of a moment ago.

Fields from table, not just from form

From previous sort

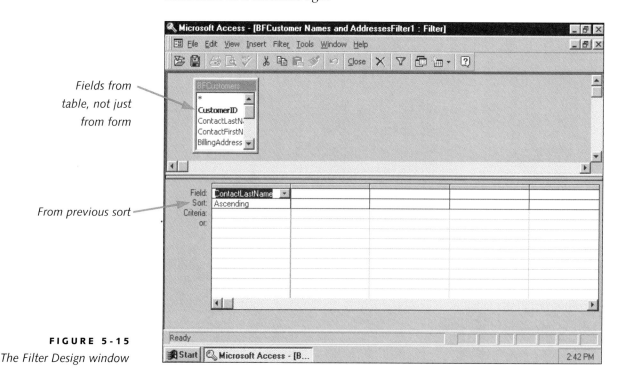

FIGURE 5-15

The Filter Design window

2. Scroll through the list of fields in the Field list at the top of the Filter Design window.

All of the fields in the underlying table are included here, not only those displayed in the form.

TIP *If you select a field that does not appear in the form, Access will sort or select based on that field but will not display it.*

3. Double-click the ContactFirstName and StateOrProvince fields—in that order—to add them to the grid at the bottom of the Filter Design window.

4. Choose Ascending order for the ContactFirstName field.

5. Type CA in the Criteria row for StateOrProvince.

6. Type NY in the Or row of the StateOrProvince field.

 7. Click the Apply Filter toolbar button.

Access returns you to the form, as shown in Figure 5-16. This time, however, only 10 records can be viewed. You can see the number of viewable records by looking to the right of the navigation buttons.

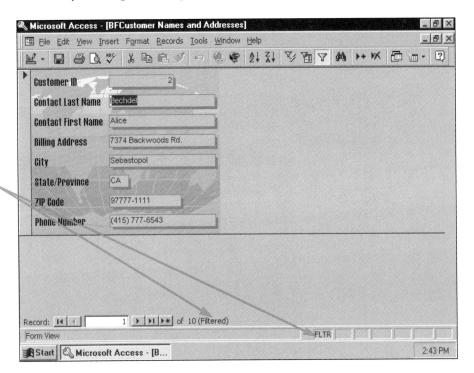

Shows filter is in effect

FIGURE 5-16
This form sorts and filters records in the table

 8. Scan through the records by clicking the Next Record button repeatedly.

Notice that the records are in order by last name, not customer ID, and that only records for customers from either New York or California are displayed.

9. Click the form's Close button.

Access closes the form and returns you to the Database window.

PREVIEWING AND PRINTING FORMS

Usually, when you want printed output, you create a report; you'll learn how to do this in Lesson 6. Sometimes, though, you may want to print some of the forms you've created. Also, often you might want to see an on-screen preview of the form before you print—to get a sense of what it will look like when printed. Previewing a form before printing can help you save time and paper. While previewing, you may notice errors that can be fixed before printing. You'll learn how to both preview and print a form in the next exercise.

GENERATING A PRINTOUT OF A FORM

Now you will learn how to preview and then print one of the forms that you created earlier in this lesson.

HANDS ON

1. If it's not already selected, click the Forms object tab in the Be Fruitful Database window.

Access displays all the forms in the Be Fruitful database.

2. If it is not already selected, click BFCustomer Names and Addresses to select it.

TIP *If you click the name of an object that is already selected, a blinking cursor appears and Access thinks that you want to edit the name. Press* Esc *to remove the cursor.*

3. Click the Print Preview toolbar button.

You should see a preview of your form, much like the one pictured in Figure 5-17.

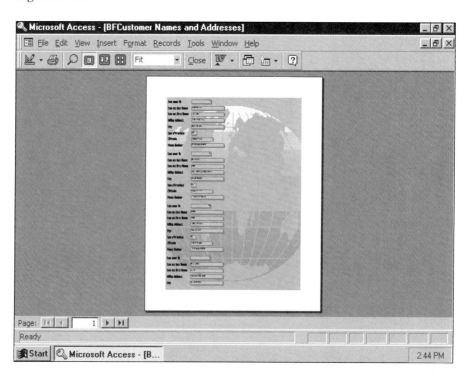

FIGURE 5-17

Preview of the printed form

TIP *You can also issue the Print Preview command from Form view to see a preview of the printed form.*

4. To view part of the form closely, move the cursor over any portion of the form so that its shape changes to that of a magnifying glass and click once.

5. To return to the full-page view, click anywhere in the form again.

6. To view two pages at once, click the Two Pages toolbar button.

7. To view even more pages at once, click the Multiple Pages toolbar button and drag to select the number of pages that you want to view.

8. Make sure that your printer is turned on and click the Print toolbar button.

   You'll see a message box, indicating that your data is being printed.

   Eventually, your printer will generate a hard copy of the form, complete with all records in the underlying table or query.

TIP *You can also choose Print from the File menu in order to see the Print dialog box. This dialog box allows you to specify the number of copies to print, which pages to print, and more.*

OFFICE ASSISTANT *You can print just one or a few records at a time by first selecting them. For more help, start the Office Assistant and type* **print a form***.*

9. Choose Close to close the Print Preview window and return to the Database window.

10. Close the Database window and exit Access.

LESSON SUMMARY AND EXERCISES

After you complete this lesson, you should know how to do the following:

WHEN AND WHY TO USE FORMS

- You should use a form to display one record at a time, to reveal only selected fields, or to simplify data entry and editing.

CREATING AN AUTOFORM

- To create an AutoForm, select the table or query on which you want to base the form, click the arrow next to the New Object toolbar button, and choose AutoForm.

USING THE FORM WIZARD

- To create a columnar form, select the Form tab in the Database window and choose New. Click Form Wizard, add the fields you want to include, and select the Columnar option button in the Form Wizard dialog box.

- To create a tabular form, select the Form tab in the Database window and choose New. Click Form Wizard, add the fields you want to include, and select the Tabular option button in the Form Wizard dialog box.

ADDING AND EDITING DATA BY USE OF FORMS

- To open a form, click the Forms object tab in the Database window. Double-click the form you want to open.

- To add a record to a table by use of a form, click the New Record toolbar button or press [Tab] when in the last field of the last record in the table.

- To delete a record from a table by use of a form, click the record selector, press [Delete], and click Yes in the dialog box that appears.

- To edit data in a table by use of a form, use [F5] to go to the record to be edited, [Tab] to or click the field you want to edit, and make your modifications.

SORTING AND SELECTING DATA WITH FORMS

- To sort the table by use of a form, open the form, click in the field you want to sort, and click the Sort Ascending or Sort Descending toolbar button.

- To filter records by use of a form, click on the Records menu, choose Filter, and select Advanced Filter/Sort. In the Filter Design window, complete the grid and click the Apply Filter toolbar button.

PREVIEWING AND PRINTING FORMS

- To preview a printed form, click the Print Preview toolbar button.

- To quit the preview, click the Close toolbar button.

- To print a hard copy of the form, click the Print toolbar button.

NEW TERMS TO REMEMBER

After you complete this lesson, you should know the meaning of the following terms:

AutoForm

columnar form

tabular form

MATCHING EXERCISE

Match the terms with the definitions on the right:

TERMS	DEFINITIONS
1. tabular form	**a.** A form that Access creates automatically based on the fields in the selected table or query
2. Form view	
3. Design view	**b.** An Access tool that creates a form based on your responses to a series of questions
4. style	
5. columnar form	**c.** Form in which each record is displayed on a single row
6. Print Preview	
7. Form Wizard	**d.** View in which you can modify a form's layout
8. Datasheet view	
9. AutoForm	**e.** Vertical bar at left side of a form that you can use to activate designated record
10. record selector	
	f. View in which your form looks much like a paper form
	g. View in which data in any type of form is laid out in series of columns and rows
	h. Form in which each field is on a separate line
	i. View in which your form looks much as it will look when printed
	j. Pictures, shading, and colors that give a form a special "look"

COMPLETION EXERCISE

Fill in the missing word or phrase for each of the following:

1. _____ fields are automatically displayed as check boxes in forms.

2. _____ forms display all fields in a single row.

3. When you click on the AutoForm button, Access generates a simple _____ form.

4. To show only selected records in a form, you can set up a _____.

5. Click the _____ before you press ⌈Delete⌉ to remove a record from the table using a form.

6. In the final Form Wizard dialog box, Access displays the _____ name as the suggested name for the form.

7. The _____ determines the background and colors of a form.

8. Before you print a hard copy of a form, you should display it on the screen using the _____ toolbar button.

9. To add a new record to a form, click the New Record toolbar button or press _____ in the last field of the last record.

10. The _____ automates the process of creating a tabular or columnar form while letting you choose the fields to include.

SHORT-ANSWER QUESTIONS

Write a brief answer to each of the following questions:

1. Describe briefly what Access does for you when you click the AutoForm button. What type of form does it create? What fields are included? What's used as the form title?

2. If the screen doesn't show all of the fields in a form at once, how can you fix the form? Name one possible solution.

3. How do you create a new, blank record in which to enter data when you are working in Form view? Mention both a mouse and a keyboard technique.

4. What type of form do you use to display multiple records at once? Does this type of form work well for tables or queries that contain many fields? Explain your answer.

5. Describe the exact steps involved in first previewing and then printing a form.

6. Why should you preview forms before printing them?

7. If you want to use a form to view only the records for those customers who had joined after 12/31/96, would you make this request to Access

while using the Form Wizard or with a filter? Which criteria would you use?

8. Explain how you'd use a Sort command to sort the records in the BFCustomers AutoForm into ascending order first by last name and then by first name. (Hint: Think about whether you can do this in Form view.)

9. Describe the differences between using AutoForms and Form Wizards.

10. Describe the benefits of creating a form for data entry. What are the advantages over working on the table in the Datasheet view?

APPLICATION PROJECTS

Perform the following actions to complete these projects:

1. Open the **Be Fruitful** database in the **Lessons** folder on your Student Data Disk. Create a columnar form based on the BFOrders table, and include only the CustomerID, OrderDate, FruitType, and Quantity fields. Give the new form a style of your choice, and save it as **Order Type and Quantity**. Sort the orders into ascending order by fruit type.

2. Create a tabular form based on the Joined After 1995 query. Include the ContactLastName, ContactFirstName, and DateJoined fields; choose any style; and save it as **Customers Joined After 1995**. With the form still open, create a new record and enter the last name **Wildershaw**, the first name **Oscar**, and the date joined **12/31/95**. Now close the form and then open it again. Can you find the record you just added? Now open the BFCustomers table and see if you can find the "missing" record. Can you explain why it shows up in the table but not in the form? Also, what happened to those fields from the table that weren't included in the form? When you're finished, delete the record.

3. Sort the records in BFCustomer AutoForm into descending order by DateJoined, and display only those records for customers in California, Oregon, or New York state. Print the form.

4. Open the **Personal** database in the **x** folder on your Student Data Disk. Create an AutoForm for the To Dos table. Save the form as **To Do List** and then print the form. (To complete this project you must have completed the Application Projects in Lessons 2 and 3 that created this table.)

5. Open the **Music** database in the **Projects** folder on your Student Data Disk. Create tabular forms for the Recordings, Recording Artists, and Music Categories tables. In the forms for the Music Categories and Recording Artists tables, include all fields available. In the form for the Recordings table, include the RecordingArtistID, MusicCategoryID, and RecordingTitle fields, in that order. Use the table names as the names of the forms. Choose a common style for the forms. Print the forms. (To complete this project you must have completed the Application Projects in Lessons 2 and 3 that created these tables.)

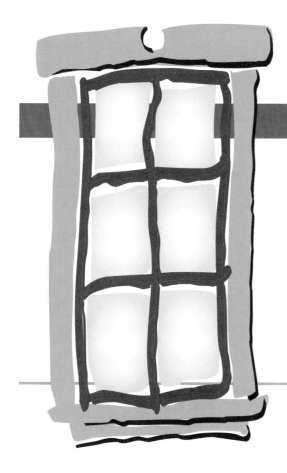

GENERATING REPORTS AND MAILING LABELS

OBJECTIVES

After you complete this lesson, you will be able to do the following:

- *Create an AutoReport.*
- *Use the Report Wizard to create a columnar report.*
- *Use the Report Wizard to create a tabular report.*
- *Use the Report Wizard to create a report with totals.*
- *Use the Label Wizard to generate mailing labels.*
- *Preview and print reports and mailing labels.*

CONTENTS

When and Why to Use Reports

Creating an AutoReport

Using the Report Wizard

Creating Totals in Reports

Generating Mailing Labels

Printing Reports and Mailing Labels

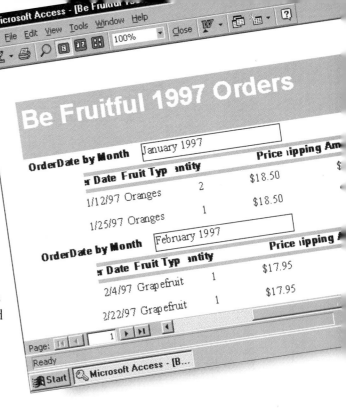

n this chapter, you will produce many types of printed output. You'll discover how to generate AutoReports with the click of a mouse button. You'll also use the Report Wizard to create columnar reports, tabular reports, and reports that have totals. Finally, you'll learn how to produce mailing labels, as well as how to print reports and mailing labels.

WHEN AND WHY TO USE REPORTS

As mentioned in Lesson 1, you generally use reports when you need professional-looking printed output. You might have to provide handouts for a presentation. Or, perhaps you need to share information with someone who isn't familiar with Access, doesn't have access to a computer, or simply prefers to spread pages out on a desk rather than view them on a computer screen. Although you can print datasheets and forms, reports look more polished and give you much more control over how your data is presented. In addition, you can take advantage of reports that automatically generate summary data such as totals and grand totals.

When you create reports, as with forms, you will be able to do much of what you need by using a Wizard—the Report Wizard. The reports that you create with the Report Wizard may require a certain amount of fine-tuning, however. The next lesson explains how to modify existing reports in Design view.

CREATING AN AUTOREPORT

AutoReport A report that Access builds for you automatically, based on the selected table or query.

AutoReports are basic reports generated automatically by Access. To create an AutoReport, you choose the table or query on which to base your report and then you click a single button. Like the AutoForm, the AutoReport tracks down the information it needs by examining the selected table or query—without asking you for any input. Access then builds a basic report that includes every field from the table or query arranged in columns. The field names (or captions) show up on the left, to identify the fields. You can also create a second type of AutoReport that contains a header and a footer. In this type of report, the name of the table or query appears at the top, as a report header. A **header** is text information that is printed at the top of every page of the report; a report header appears at the top of the first page only. On the bottom of the report is the date of the day the report is printed, the page number, and the number of pages in the entire report as a footer. A **footer** is text information that is printed at the bottom of every page of the report.

header Text information that is repeated at the top of every page in a report.

footer Text that appears at the bottom of every printed page in a report.

EXPLORING AN AUTOREPORT

In this exercise, you'll create an AutoReport based on the BFCustomers table.

HANDS ON

1. Open the **Be Fruitful** database in the **Lessons** folder of your Student Data Disk.

   You'll see the Be Fruitful Database window.

2. Click the Tables object tab, and make sure the BFCustomers table is selected.

3. Click the New Object toolbar button's drop-down arrow.

   You see a list of new objects from which to choose.

4. Click AutoReport.

   Access generates a report that contains all fields of all records. The toolbar at the top of the screen has changed to indicate that you are in Print Preview view.

OFFICE ASSISTANT   *You can also view a report in Layout Preview and Design views. To find out more about working in various views, ask the Office Assistant.*

5. Click the Maximize button to enlarge the Report view window.

6. Click the Zoom toolbar button so that you can see the entire page at once, as shown in Figure 6-1.

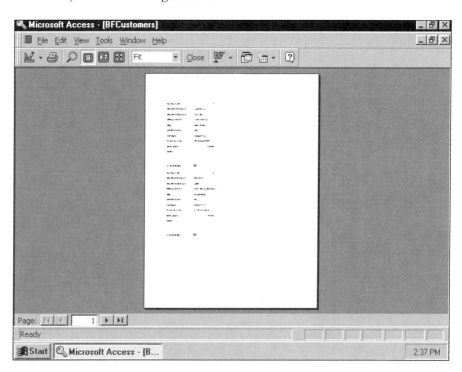

FIGURE 6-1
Report in Print Preview view

This display gives you a much better sense of the page layout, even though you can't really read what is on the page. However, you can see that two records fit on this first page of the report. Also, notice that no header or footer appears when you use this method to create a report.

7. Click Close on the toolbar to exit Print Preview view.

The Design view window of the report appears.

8. Click the report's Close button to close the report.

Since you haven't yet saved your report, a warning box appears asking if you want to save the design of the report.

9. Click No.

Access returns you to the Be Fruitful Database window.

You can also create an AutoReport that contains a header and a footer.

10. With the BFCustomers table still selected, click the arrow next to the New Object toolbar button and choose Report.

You will see the New Report dialog box.

11. Double-click the AutoReport: Columnar option in the list box.

After a while, Access displays a print preview of the report similar to the one shown in Figure 6-2. All fields in the table are laid out in a single column. The field names or captions are to the left of the field contents. The table name is the report header.

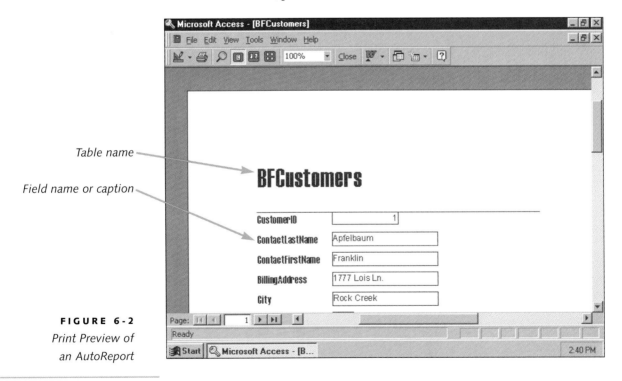

Table name

Field name or caption

FIGURE 6-2
Print Preview of an AutoReport

NOTE *Depending on the actions taken by others who have used Access before you, the style of your text in your AutoReports may be different than the style of the text in the illustrations shown in this book. However, the actual text (the labels, record data, and headings) should read the same.*

Notice that you're looking at the data for the first record in the BFCustomers table. In an AutoReport, records always occur in the same order as in the underlying table or query.

TIP   *You can also create AutoReports from within Datasheet view.*

12. Scroll down using the down arrow on the vertical scroll bar.

You'll see the second record in the table. Access fits as many records as possible (in this case, two) on a single page.

13. Scroll down to the end of the page.

You will see the footer created for the report. You may need to scroll to the right to see the entire footer.

VIEWING PAGES IN THE REPORT

At the bottom of this Print Preview window are navigation buttons. These navigation buttons allow you to move from page to page in the report, rather than from record to record (as they did in Form view).

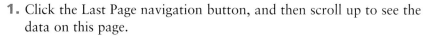

1. Click the Last Page navigation button, and then scroll up to see the data on this page.

Access displays the last page of the report, and you can verify that the records are in the same order here as in the underlying table.

2. Click twice on the Previous Page button.

Access moves up two pages in the report.

3. Press F5 or double-click the Current Page indicator.

4. Type **6** and press Enter.

Access moves you to the sixth page of the report.

5. Scroll down until you see the Notes field for Shelly Wintergreen.

The Notes text is wrapped so that it appears in several rows.

6. Place the mouse pointer over the report (so that the pointer takes on the shape of a magnifying glass).

7. Click anywhere in the report.

Access shrinks the report so that you can see an entire page on the screen at once, as shown in Figure 6-3. Notice that you can see that this report contains a footer. No header appears on this page.

8. Click the First Page navigation button.

Both the header and footer appear on the first page. Remember, a report header appears only on page 1 of a report.

9. Click the Zoom toolbar button or click the report again.

Access returns the report to its original magnification. The portion of the page that you see enlarged depends on where you click.

10. Click the report's Close button to close the report.

Because you haven't saved the report, Access displays a warning box asking whether you want to save the new report.

11. Click Yes to save the report.

Access displays a Save As dialog box that prompts you for a report name.

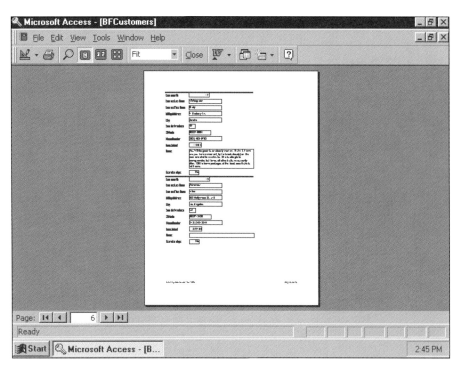

FIGURE 6-3

*Zooming displays an entire
page on the screen*

12. Enter **BFCustomers AutoReport** as the report name and click OK to
save the report.

Access saves and then closes the report, returning you to the Be Fruitful
Database window.

13. Click the Reports object tab.

Access displays any reports associated with the Be Fruitful database. As
you can see in Figure 6-4, the BFCustomers AutoReport that you just created
and saved is displayed here.

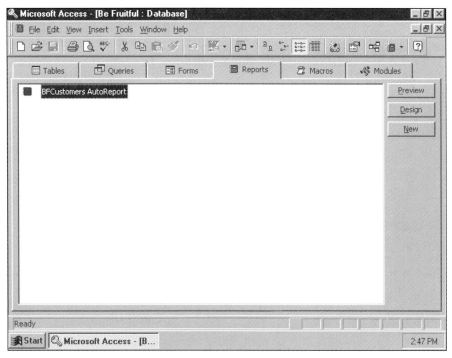

FIGURE 6-4

*AutoReport name
in Database window*

USING THE REPORT WIZARD

If you need a basic report, an AutoReport might do the job. Often, however, you'll want to have more control over your reports—to choose their layout, decide the fields to include and their order, determine the text layout on the page, and more. If so, you can use the Report Wizard. Using the Report Wizard is very similar to using the Form Wizard: Access prompts you for information and then constructs a report based on your replies.

As in any other Wizard, you can click the Back button any time you want to move back one step.

CONSTRUCTING A COLUMNAR REPORT WITH THE REPORT WIZARD

Next you will create a columnar report with the Report Wizard. In a **columnar report**—as in a columnar form—all of the fields for a record are displayed as you look down the page. Actually, the AutoReport you created earlier is a simple columnar report.

columnar report A report that displays all fields in a single column with field labels or captions to their left as identifiers.

STARTING THE REPORT WIZARD

To use the Report Wizard, you must first tell Access the tables, queries, and fields to use in the report.

HANDS ON

1. Click the Tables tab in the Be Fruitful Database window and select BFCustomers.

2. Click the New Object button's drop-down arrow.

3. Select Report.

TIP   Remember, if the Report icon appears on the New Object toolbar button, you can click the button rather than its drop-down arrow.

4. Double-click Report Wizard.

Access displays the first Report Wizard dialog box, as shown in Figure 6-5.

Choose table or query on which to base report

List of fields in selected table or query

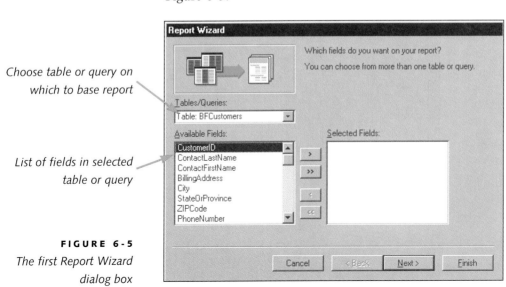

FIGURE 6-5
The first Report Wizard dialog box

5. Since you selected the BFCustomers table before issuing the command to create a new report, its name should appear in the Tables/Queries text box. If not, click the drop-down arrow and select it from the list box.

6. Click the >> button.

Access moves all of the field names to the Selected Fields list box. If you want to include all or most fields in the report, the quickest way is to add them all and then remove a few.

TIP *To change the existing order of fields, you can't use the >> button. You must instead use the > button to add the fields one by one in the desired order.*

7. Click the CustomerID field in the Selected Fields list to select it and click the < button.

Access removes the CustomerID field from the list of fields to include in the report.

8. Select the DateJoined field and click the < button.

Access removes the DateJoined field from the list of fields to include in the report.

9. Click the < button two more times.

Access removes the Notes and ExtraCatalogs fields from the list of fields for the report.

10. Click the Next button to move to the next Report Wizard dialog box.

After a moment, Access displays the Report Wizard dialog box shown in Figure 6-6.

Add selected field to grouping list

Choose field on which to group

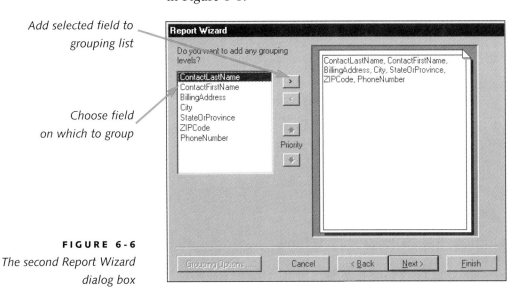

FIGURE 6-6
The second Report Wizard dialog box

In this dialog box, you tell Access how to group the records. You will learn more about grouping for reports later in this lesson.

11. Click Next.

You see the next Report Wizard dialog box.

This dialog box allows you to sort records by up to four fields. You will learn more about sorting for reports later in this lesson.

12. Click Next.

COMPLETING THE REPORT WIZARD

Now that you have told Access the data you want to include in the report, you are ready to choose the overall layout for it.

In this Report Wizard dialog box you must choose either a columnar, tabular, or justified layout. The columnar layout displays the records one after another, as in the AutoReport you created earlier in this lesson. The tabular layout shows the fields of each record in rows, as in the Datasheet view. The justified layout displays each record in its own small box. This dialog box also has options to print either in portrait or landscape orientation. In **portrait orientation**, pages print like the pages in this tutorial. In **landscape orientation**, pages print across the wide side of the paper, as if you held this tutorial sideways.

portrait orientation A method of printing a report across the width of the page or vertically.

landscape orientation A method of printing a report across the length of the page or horizontally.

HANDS ON

1. Select the Columnar and Portrait option buttons.

2. Click Next.

The next Report Wizard dialog box appears, as shown in Figure 6-7.

Selected style

Preview of selected report style

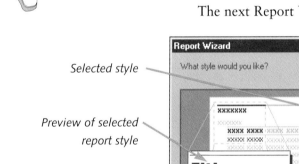

FIGURE 6-7
Report Wizard dialog box for choosing a style

As in the Form Wizard, you can choose a style for your report.

3. Click the Corporate style and click Next.

The final Report Wizard dialog box appears.

Here, you enter the title of the report and tell Access what you want to do next.

4. Type **Customer Names and Addresses** in the Title text box.

5. Make sure the Preview the Report option is selected and click the Finish button.

In a moment, Access displays the first page of the report you just created, as shown in Figure 6-8. The report contains data from the selected BFCustomers table. Unlike the AutoReport you just created, this report displays only designated fields from the underlying table.

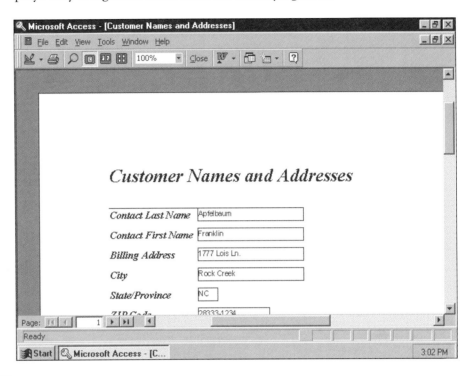

FIGURE 6-8
First page of the report

N O T E   *You can rename your report later by selecting it in the Database window and then clicking its name again so that an insertion point appears. Once you see the insertion point, use* Backspace *on* Delete *to delete the existing name and type a new one. If you want to create a copy of the same report using a different name, open the report, choose Save As from the File menu, and type a name for the new copy of the report.*

OFFICE ASSISTANT   *To add some pizazz to your report, add a background picture or color. For instructions, ask the Office Assistant.*

6. Click the Last Page button.

Access shows the last page in the report. Note that you see the report title on the first page only.

7. Scroll to the bottom of the page.

The date and page number appear as a footer in the report.

8. Click the report's Close button to close the report.

Access closes the report and returns you to the Be Fruitful Database window.

CREATING TABULAR REPORTS

tabular report A report that displays the fields for a single record in one row, field names or captions as column headings, and all data in the table or query as a tabular arrangement of rows and columns.

The two reports you've created so far display the fields in a single column. While this layout is pretty easy to read, it doesn't use space all that economically. To view more records at once, consider using a tabular report. Like a tabular form, a **tabular report** displays the fields for a single record in one row and presents multiple records at once. Field names or captions appear near the top of the report as column headings. Tabular reports don't tend to work well with a lot of long Text or Memo fields nor with too many fields to fit on a single page. At the same time, tabular reports can be an excellent means of presenting a large amount of data in a relatively small amount of space.

CREATING A QUERY FOR A REPORT

You will use the Report Wizard to create a tabular report based on a portion of Be Fruitful's orders data. Before you can create the table, you need to create a query to select the portion of the data that you want the report to print.

HANDS ON

1. Make sure you're still in the Be Fruitful Database window, and click the Tables object tab.

2. Click the BFOrders table.

3. Select Query from the New Object drop-down list.

   Access displays the New Query dialog box.

4. Click Design View and click OK.

   Access displays the Query Design view window, which you learned about in Lesson 4.

5. Double-click the BFOrders Field list title bar at the top of the Query Design view window.

   Access selects all of the fields in the Field list.

6. Drag the selected list of fields to the first column in the query design grid.

   Access inserts all fields into the query design grid.

7. In the Sort row of the OrderDate column, choose Ascending.

8. In the Criteria row of the OrderDate column, type **>12/31/96 and <= 12/31/97**

   You're selecting all orders after 12/31/96 and on or before 12/31/97—that is, all orders in 1997.

9. Click the Run toolbar button.

   Access displays a Recordset that includes only the orders from 1997.

10. Click File and choose Save As/Export.

11. Type **1997 Orders** as the query name and click OK.

12. Click the query's Close button.

CREATING A TABULAR REPORT BASED ON A QUERY

Now that you have created a query to control which records to print, you can create a report for that query.

1. Click the Queries object tab in the Database window.

2. Click the 1997 Orders query you just created.

3. Click the arrow next to the New Object button in the toolbar.

4. Click Report from the New Object drop-down list.

You'll see the New Report dialog box that you saw earlier; but this time, the 1997 Orders query is already selected as the one containing the data on which to base the report.

5. Click Report Wizard and click OK.

Access displays the initial Report Wizard dialog box, where you can choose the fields to include in the report.

6. Add the OrderDate, FruitType, Quantity, Price, ShippingAmount, and PaymentAmount fields to the Selected Fields list.

Remember, the sequence in which the fields are placed in the Selected Fields list box determines the order in which they'll print on your report.

7. Click the Next button.

In the following dialog boxes, you will determine how the records are grouped and sorted.

GROUPING RECORDS IN A TABULAR REPORT

Your 1997 Orders query contains records with orders for all months within the year. Because the query has sorted the records by order date, your report will appear in that sequence. However, you can group or sort the records into a different order if you wish. **Groups**, as the name implies, are collections of records with like information. Examples of groups include records with a city field of Philadelphia or records with the same order date. As you continue working in this exercise, you will create a report that groups the orders by the month.

groups Categories of information from the table or query that you can use to arrange records and show subtotals in a report.

1. Click OrderDate and click >.

The top of the screen now reads *OrderDate by Month*, as you can see in Figure 6-9.

You may also have noticed that the Grouping Options button in the lower-left corner of the dialog box is no longer grayed. You'll use this button later in this lesson.

2. Click the Next button.

In this dialog box, you can control the order in which records appear within each group. In this case, you want the records to be in chronological order within each month.

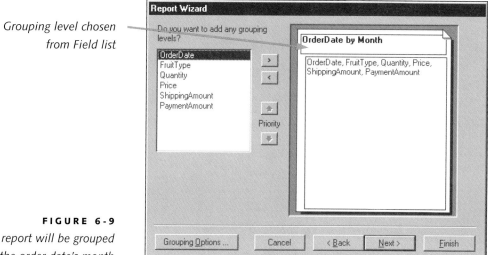

Grouping level chosen from Field list

FIGURE 6-9

The report will be grouped by the order date's month

3. Click the drop-down arrow beside the number 1 field.

A Field list appears.

4. Click the OrderDate field.

The OrderDate field will determine the sequence of the records within each group. Notice the button beside each field lets you sort in ascending or descending order. Ascending order is the default.

5. Click Next.

The next Report Wizard dialog box appears, as shown in Figure 6-10.

Choose layout   *Choose orientation*

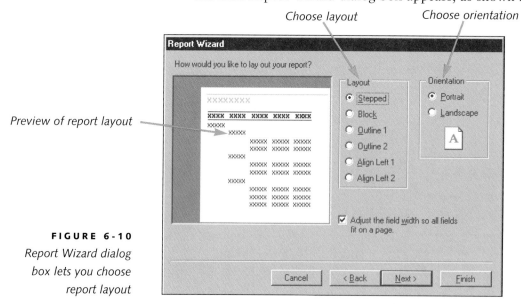

Preview of report layout

FIGURE 6-10

Report Wizard dialog box lets you choose report layout

In this dialog box you choose the layout for the tabular report. As you can see, when you create a report that groups and sorts the records, a tabular report is selected automatically. The preview box inside the dialog box illustrates what the Stepped layout looks like.

6. Click the Align Left 1 option button.

The layout of the Align Left 1 tabular report is shown in the preview box.

7. Leave the Orientation set at Portrait.

8. Click Next.

The next dialog box appears, asking you to choose a style.

9. Click Soft Gray, and then click the Next button.

The final Report Wizard dialog box appears.

10. Type **Be Fruitful 1997 Orders** as the title.

11. Click the Finish button.

In a moment, Access displays the tabular report that you can see in Figure 6-11; it shows the data from your 1997 Orders query in a tabular layout.

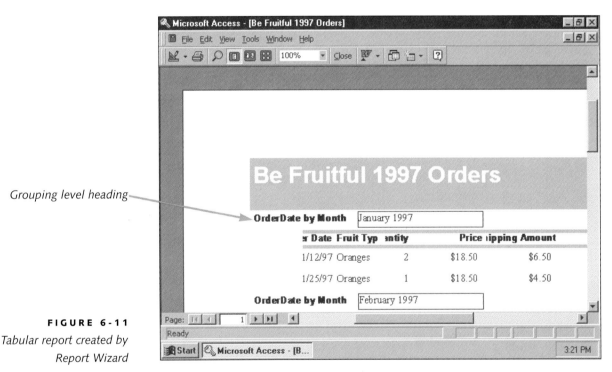

Grouping level heading

FIGURE 6-11
Tabular report created by Report Wizard

PREVIEWING A TABULAR REPORT

With the next few steps you will see some of the features that the Report Wizard has added to your tabular report.

HANDS ON

1. Scroll through the report.

Access has grouped the records by month and sorted each month's records by order date, as shown in Figure 6-12.

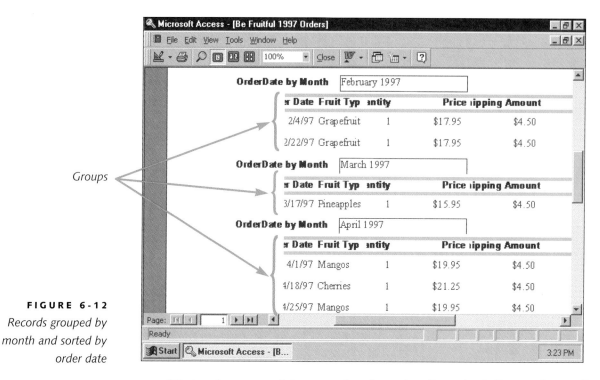

FIGURE 6-12
Records grouped by month and sorted by order date

Notice that some of the report's column headings don't line up that well with the data and some letters are missing from them. This problem is easy enough to fix in Design view, as you'll learn in the next lesson. Although you'll frequently want to revise tabular reports in Design view, using the Report Wizard is still the quickest way to put together the basic report.

OFFICE ASSISTANT   *Access allows you to control the page breaks in a report. The Office Assistant can give you guidance on inserting page breaks.*

2. Click anywhere on the page to zoom out. Although much of the text is not readable, you can use this view to preview the layout of an entire page.

3. Click Close to close the report and return to the Be Fruitful Database window.

CREATING TOTALS IN REPORTS

As you just saw, Access can easily group records in tabular reports. Sometimes, however, you may want to include totals of the numeric fields in the report as well. In the report you just created, you might want subtotals for each month's orders and a grand total for all of the records in the query or table. As another example, you might like to see the total sales per year rather than only the entire sales over the life of the company. In such cases, you can simply add totals to a report.

BUILDING A REPORT WITH TOTALS

Next you will use the Report Wizard to put together a report that sorts and totals orders by year.

HANDS ON

1. Select the BFOrders table in the Tables object tab of the Be Fruitful Database window.

2. Click the Insert menu and choose Report.

Access displays the New Report dialog box, this time with the BFOrders table selected in the drop-down list box.

3. Double-click the Report Wizard option.

You should see the first Report Wizard dialog box, asking you to choose the fields you want to include in the report.

4. Use the > button to include the OrderDate, FruitType, Quantity, Price, ShippingAmount, and PaymentAmount fields, in that order.

Access places all of the selected fields in the Selected Fields list box.

5. Click Next.

In the dialog box that appears you choose the field or fields to use as the basis for grouping data in your report. You can pick anywhere from zero to four fields. Access sorts on the first designated field first and then on each designated field in the order you choose them.

6. Select OrderDate and click the > button.

7. Select FruitType and again click >.

Both fields are added to the list box on the right. What you have told Access is that you want the records in the table grouped by OrderDate. Within each group, you want the orders grouped by FruitType.

TIP   *Access provides a wide variety of ways to group the data in the* **group by** *fields: for example, you can group by the first letter (or first several letters) of a Text field; you can group Date/Time fields by year, quarter, month, and more; and you can group Number fields by ranges (by tens, fifties, hundreds, and so on).*

8. Click the Grouping Options button.

You see the Grouping Intervals screen, as shown in Figure 6-13.

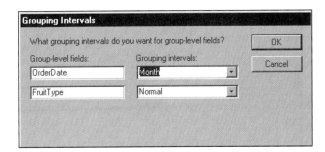

FIGURE 6-13
Grouping Intervals dialog box

9. Choose Year from the drop-down list box to the right of the OrderDate field.

10. Click OK.

The records will be grouped by the year in which the orders were placed.

11. Click the Next button.

You'll see the Report Wizard dialog box that lets you choose the fields to sort by.

12. Select the Quantity field.

The Quantity field will be used to sort records that have the same order year and type of fruit.

ADDING TOTALS AND SUBTOTALS TO THE REPORT

In the Report Wizard sorting dialog box there is a button called *Summary Options*. By clicking this button you can choose to have totals and subtotals displayed for any of the numeric fields in your report. Because you have created a group within a group, Access will display totals for each year's order and totals for each type of fruit ordered within each year. You will get grand totals at the end of the report as well.

HANDS ON

1. Click the Summary Options button.

You will see the Summary Options dialog box, as shown in Figure 6-14.

Click check boxes to choose summary values for each numeric field

Number fields in report

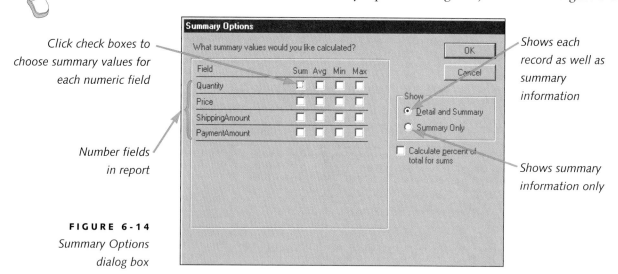

Shows each record as well as summary information

Shows summary information only

FIGURE 6-14
Summary Options dialog box

Check boxes in this dialog box let you select from four different types of summary information: totals (Sum), average (Avg), minimum value (Min), and maximum value (Max) for each numeric field. The option buttons on the right allow you to choose between Detail And Summary or Summary Only. If you choose Detail And Summary, you will see the data for each record as well as summary information for each group, subgroup, and final totals. If you choose Summary Only, you will see the summary information for each group, subgroup, and final totals, but you will not see the data for individual records.

OFFICE ASSISTANT   *If you're not sure how some of the functions such as Avg, Min, and Max work, ask the Office Assistant to describe them.*

2. Click the Sum check boxes for Quantity, ShippingAmount, and PaymentAmount.

3. Click OK; then click Next.

In the next Report Wizard dialog box, you set the layout and orientation for the report.

4. Click Stepped layout and Landscape orientation. Then click Next.

You see the dialog box that allows you to choose a style.

5. Click Compact style and click Next.

You are now at the final Report Wizard dialog box.

6. Type **Orders by Year and Fruit Type** as the title of the report.

7. Click Finish.

After a few moments, the Report Wizard displays a preview of your report on the screen.

8. Scroll through the report.

Note the totals and subtotals as you move through the pages of the report, which you see a portion of in Figure 6-15.

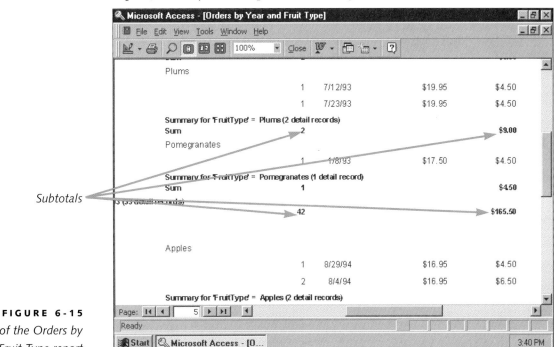

FIGURE 6-15

Portion of the Orders by Year and Fruit Type report

NOTE   *As in the tabular report, the columns aren't aligned very well in this report. This problem is not hard to fix, as you'll learn in the next lesson.*

9. Click File and then choose Close.

You return to the Database window.

OFFICE ASSISTANT   *Another efficient way to illustrate summaries and details is to create subreports. For more information on these reports within reports, ask the Office Assistant.*

GENERATING MAILING LABELS

In the course of your work, you may need to mail anything from brochures to invoices to invitations. Fortunately, Access provides a Wizard, the Label Wizard, that makes it extremely easy to generate mailing labels from any name and address information—of customers, employees, business associates, or friends—that you have stored in a table or query. You can even use the Label Wizard to create other labels, such as file folder labels and name tags. The steps you use with the Label Wizard are much like those you used with the Report Wizard in this lesson. You'll soon find out, however, that the Label Wizard gives you more freedom to determine not only the contents but also the appearance of your mailing labels.

In the next three exercises, you will create mailing labels for the customers in Be Fruitful's database. First, you must choose the table or query that contains the data you wish to use for the labels. You must tell the Label Wizard the kind of labels you have and the lettering style you want to use. In the second set of steps, you will choose the fields to include and their arrangement on each label. Finally, you will choose an order in which to sort the labels and you'll preview them on the screen.

SELECTING MAILING LABEL FORMS AND APPEARANCE

During the next few steps you will set up the general characteristics of your labels—you'll choose the table that contains the data, the type of label paper, and the font to use in printing the labels.

HANDS ON

1. Select the BFCustomers table from the Be Fruitful database in your **Lessons** folder.

2. Click the Insert menu and choose Report.

Access displays the New Report dialog box, with the BFCustomers table already selected.

3. Double-click Label Wizard.

You see the first Label Wizard dialog box, as shown in Figure 6-16.

Label paper number

Manual paper feed

Automatic paper feed

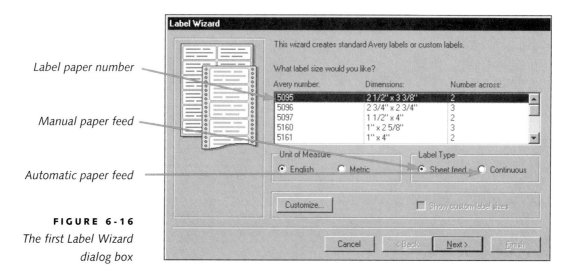

FIGURE 6-16
The first Label Wizard dialog box

sheet feed The process that feeds paper into a printer one sheet at a time, such as with inkjet and laser printers.

In this dialog box you choose the size of the mailing labels you will use and the way the mailing label paper will be fed into the printer. **Sheet feed** means the paper is taken into the printer one sheet at a time, as in an inkjet or laser printer. **Continuous** label paper has pages of paper attached to each other, as in the paper used by most dot-matrix printers.

W A R N I N G

The choices you should make here depend upon the kind of printer you have. You will be able to create and display mailing labels from this exercise but you may need to modify the instructions in order to print the labels on your printer.

continuous The process that feeds into a printer pages of paper attached to each other, as in the paper used by most dot-matrix printers.

4. In the top portion of the dialog box, scroll down and select the option for Avery Number 5198.

As shown in the Dimensions and Number Across columns, these labels are 1⅔ inches by 3½ inches each and print two-across on the page.

N O T E

Avery is the name of a company that produces many sizes of printer labels. If your labels are manufactured by a company other than Avery, you can use the descriptions in the Dimensions and Number Across columns to select the label size.

5. Make sure that Sheet Feed is selected and click Next.

N O T E

If you are using a different Label type and/or a dot matrix printer, your instructor may give you other settings to use.

The next Label Wizard dialog box appears, as shown in Figure 6-17.

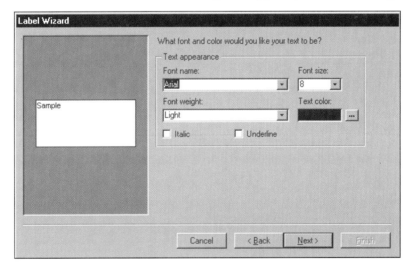

FIGURE 6-17
Label Wizard dialog box for setting the appearance of characters

6. Select the font Times New Roman from the Font Name drop-down list box.

7. Select 12 from the Font Size drop-down list box.

8. Select Bold from the Font Weight drop-down list box.

Notice that the preview box on the left side of the dialog box changes to reflect your new selections. This feature is especially handy if you're not sure what a particular font looks like.

9. Click Next.

The next dialog box appears.

ARRANGING FIELDS ON THE LABELS

Now you must decide which fields to include on each label and how the fields should be placed on each line of the label.

HANDS ON

1. Click the ContactFirstName field and click >.

The field is placed on the upper-left corner of the Prototype Label box. The Prototype Label box shows you where your fields will be printed on the label. When you preview the label, you will see the contents of each record instead of the field names.

2. Press `Spacebar`.

3. Click the ContactLastName field and click >.

Access adds the last name field to the Prototype Label box, on the same line as the ContactFirstName field. Pressing `Spacebar` makes sure that the first and last names on the labels are separated by a space.

4. Press `Enter`.

Your insertion point moves to the next line in the Prototype Label box.

5. Double-click the BillingAddress field and press `Enter`.

The address appears on its own line.

6. Double-click the City field.

7. Type , (a comma character) and press `Spacebar`.

8. Double-click the StateOrProvince field.

9. Press `Spacebar` twice.

10. Double-click the ZIPCode field.

At this point, the Prototype Label box should resemble the one shown in Figure 6-18.

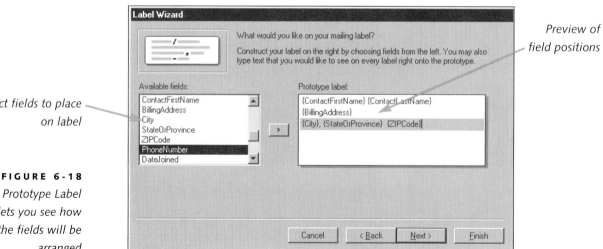

Select fields to place on label

Preview of field positions

FIGURE 6-18
The Prototype Label box lets you see how the fields will be arranged

SORTING MAILING LABELS

The post office gives a discount for mass mailings that have been pre-sorted by ZIP Code. The Label Wizard makes it easy to take advantage of this discount with the next dialog box.

1. Click Next.

You see the Label Wizard dialog box that allows you to sort your labels by one or more fields.

2. Double-click the ZIPCode field.

3. Click Next.

Access displays the final Label Wizard dialog box, as shown in Figure 6-19. From here, you can give the labels report a name. You can also choose to view how the mailing labels should look when printed or you can select to change their design.

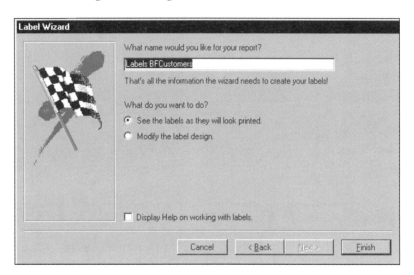

FIGURE 6-19
*Final Label Wizard
dialog box*

4. Type **Two Across Customer Labels** as the labels report name and make sure the SeeThe Labels As They Will Look Printed option is selected.

5. Click the Finish button.

Access will name your labels report with the name you have specified and display the labels on the screen.

6. Click the Maximize button for the label window.

A portion of the label preview appears in Figure 6-20.

7. Click the Zoom toolbar button.

This display clearly shows that the labels will print two labels across by six labels down the page.

8. Click between the top two labels.

9. Click File and choose Close.

You return to the Database window. Your label report appears in the Reports tab.

Labels printed two across each page

Jean-Luc Marais
1379 Montgomery Ave. #3
Boston, MA 021013930

Eddie Marshall
212 Riverdale Way
Brookline, MA 022323779

Rufus Reid
8742 Grove St.
Washington, DC 028280668

Will Criton
1 Oak Place
Providence, RI 029002338

FIGURE 6-20
Preview of mailing labels

WARNING   *If you use too large a font size some lines won't be placed. If this happens, omit some of the data from the label, reduce the font size, or both, and then try again.*

PRINTING REPORTS AND MAILING LABELS

Although you can print forms and even datasheets, you'll usually use reports when you want to present professional-looking printed output. When you printed forms in Lesson 5, you first previewed them to get a sense of how they would look when printed. When you work with reports, though, they are displayed in Print Preview mode by default. As you learned, you can use the Zoom feature for either an overview or a close-up view of the report before you decide to go ahead and print.

Now you'll print the Be Fruitful 1997 Orders report that you created earlier in this lesson.

HANDS ON

1. Click the Reports object tab in the Be Fruitful Database window.

Access displays all of the reports in the Be Fruitful database.

2. Double-click the Be Fruitful 1997 Orders report.

You should see your report in Print Preview view.

3. Click the Zoom toolbar button.

Access displays a reduced view of the report, so you can see what an entire page looks like.

T I P *If you want to see more of the report at once without zooming, you can resize or maximize the report window. You can also click the arrow next to the zoom box on the toolbar and select a percentage to zoom to.*

4. Click the Two Pages toolbar button.

You can see both pages of the report.

5. Make sure the printer is turned on and online.

When the printer is online it is ready to accept output from the computer. The printer is online when its Online or Ready button is lit.

6. Click the File menu and choose Print.

You'll see a Print dialog box like the one shown in Figure 6-21. Note that you can print while viewing the report in Print Preview mode, and you can also simply select the report in the Database window and print from there.

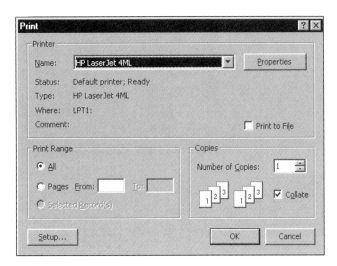

FIGURE 6-21
The Print dialog box

In the Print dialog box you can choose to print only selected pages of the report; you also can choose to print multiple copies of the pages or full report.

7. Leave all the default settings selected and click the OK button.

Access will display a message to tell you that it is printing your report, and eventually your printer will generate a hard copy of the report.

T I P *If you don't plan to change the default settings in the Print dialog box, you can simply click the Print button on the toolbar.*

8. Click the Close button.

You are back at the Database window.

9. Close the **Be Fruitful** database and exit Access.

LESSON SUMMARY AND EXERCISES

After you complete this lesson, you should know how to do the following:

WHEN AND WHY TO USE REPORTS

■ You should create a report when you need professional-looking output or want to share data with someone who is not using a computer.

CREATING AN AUTOREPORT

■ To create an AutoReport without a header and footer, select the table or query that contains the data you need to print, click the arrow next to the New Object toolbar button, and choose AutoReport.

■ To create an AutoReport that contains a header and a footer, select the table or query that contains the data you need to print, click the arrow next to the New Object toolbar button, and select Report. When the New Report dialog box appears, select either AutoReport: Columnar or AutoReport: Tabular.

■ To move among the pages of the report, use the navigation tools at the bottom of the preview window.

■ To see more of the preview on screen, click the Maximize button, click the Zoom button, or click anywhere in the report.

USING THE REPORT WIZARD

■ To make a columnar report, select the table or query that contains the data you want to print; choose Report from the New Object drop-down list; then double-click Report Wizard. Answer the Report Wizard dialog boxes to select the fields, style, and title of the report. Do not choose to group the report.

■ To make a tabular report, select the table or query that contains the data you want to print; choose Report from the New Object drop-down list; then double-click Report Wizard. Answer the Report Wizard dialog boxes to select the fields, style, and title of the report. If desired, choose the field to group the report on and choose the field you want to use to sort the records within each group.

CREATING TOTALS IN REPORTS

■ To add totals to a report, create a tabular report. Click the Summary Options button and choose the fields you want totaled.

GENERATING MAILING LABELS

■ To create mailing labels, select the table or query that contains the data you want to print; click the Insert menu; click Report; then double-click Label Wizard. Answer the Label Wizard dialog boxes to select the fields, style, sorting options, and title of the labels.

PRINTING REPORTS AND MAILING LABELS

- ■ To preview your report or mailing labels, double-click the report name to open it. The report is automatically displayed in Print Preview view.

- ■ To print your report or mailing labels, double-click the report name to open it. Choose Print from the File menu and select the appropriate options in the Print dialog box or click the Print toolbar button.

NEW TERMS TO REMEMBER

After you complete this lesson, you should know the meaning of the following terms:

AutoReport

columnar report

continuous

footer

groups

header

landscape orientation

portrait orientation

sheet feed

tabular report

MATCHING EXERCISE

Match the terms on the left with the definitions on the right:

TERMS	DEFINITIONS
1. tabular report	**a.** Text that is printed at the bottom of each page in a report
2. zoom	
3. landscape orientation	**b.** Single-column report that Access generates for you
4. groups	**c.** Printing setup in which report text is printed vertically across a page
5. columnar report	
6. Print Preview	**d.** Access feature that can aid you in sending mass mailings
7. portrait orientation	**e.** Report in which all information for a single record is laid out in one row
8. footer	
9. AutoReport	**f.** Collections of data with similar information
10. Label Wizard	**g.** To enlarge or decrease the size of a report so you can see less of it in more detail or more of it in less detail
	h. Printing setup in which report text is printed horizontally across a page
	i. Report Wizard type in which one record is printed after another with the data in a single column
	j. View in which you see a report much as it will look when printed

COMPLETION EXERCISE

Fill in the missing word or phrase for each of the following:

1. The AutoReport option from the New Object drop-down list automatically creates a(n) _____ report.

2. The _____ Wizard lets you set the font name, the font size, and the font weight used in your report.

3. Reports can use data from tables or _____.

4. Most laser printers use the _____ process; that is, paper is fed into the printer one sheet at a time.

5. You can calculate totals and averages for fields that contain _____.

6. Click the _____ Options button in the Report Wizard dialog box to change the way records are collected.

7. Click the _____ Options button in the Report Wizard dialog box to display totals and subtotals.

8. A(n) _____ displays text information at the top of each page in the report.

9. Clicking the _____ buttons will move you from page to page in a report.

10. The _____ toolbar button increases or decreases the amount of the report that you can preview in one screen.

SHORT-ANSWER QUESTIONS

Write a brief answer to each of the following questions:

1. List at least two limitations of an AutoReport.

2. Describe the differences between a tabular and a columnar report.

3. What must you do to group records in a report? On what kind of report can you do this?

4. What must you do to display totals in a report? What option would you choose if you want individual records displayed as well?

5. What name will the Report Wizard suggest for a new report? After the report is created, how can you rename the report?

6. If you created a report with the following fields and records, would you likely want to group any of the records? If so, which field(s) would you choose to group? Explain your answer.

First Name	Last Name	Address	City	State
Mary	Martin	11890 Oakwood Drive	Cincinnati	OH
Charles	Parker	909 State Street	Cleveland	OH
Suzanne	Casper	34 Greens Farm Lane	Columbus	OH
Mia	Sanchez	899 Merwin Drive	Cincinnati	OH
Gunnar	Hopkins	2028 Kitchen Place	Columbus	OH
Grace	Jaehnen	7889 Reinders Street	Youngstown	OH
Clark	Martin	11890 Oakwood Drive	Cincinnati	OH
Penny	Mitchel	77 First Street	Cleveland	OH

7. What unique Wizard dialog boxes do you see when you use the Label Wizard?

8. List at least two different ways to access the New Report dialog box.

9. What two ways can you increase the amount of the report you see in Print Preview?

10. Describe the difference between landscape and portrait orientations.

APPLICATION PROJECTS

Perform the following actions to complete these projects:

1. Open the **Be Fruitful** database in the **Lessons** folder on your Student Data Disk. Use AutoReport to create a report based on the BFFruit table. The report should not contain a header or a footer. Save the report with the name **BFFruit Report**. Print the report.

2. Create a report based on the BFOrders table. Include the FruitType, Quantity, Price, ShippingAmount, and PaymentAmount fields in the report. Group the orders by the FruitType field, and tell Access to calculate the total of the Quantity field. Choose a style and choose Portrait orientation for the report. Name the report **Fruit Summary**. Print the report.

3. Create a query that includes customers in the BFCustomers table that joined in either 1995 or 1996. Name the query **Customers Joined in 1995 and 1996**. Then create mailing labels based on this query, sorting the labels by ZIP Code. Assume that the labels you are using are 1" x 2⅝" each and are laid out three across a page. Choose any font characteristics you wish and save the label report as **1995 to 1996 Customer Labels**. Print the report.

4. Open the **Personal** database in the **Projects** folder on your Student Data Disk. Create a tabular report based on the To Dos table including all of its fields except TaskID. Sort the records in descending order by EndDate within Priority. (Hint: Priority field should be selected *before* the EndDate field in the sorting dialog box.) Save the report as **To Do List**. Print the report. (Note: To complete this project, you must have created the database and table in the Application Projects in Lessons 2 and 3.)

5. Open the **Music** database in the **Projects** folder on your Student Data Disk. Create a columnar report for the Recordings table including all of the fields in the report. Sort by RecordingArtistID in ascending order and use the Casual style. Select Landscape orientation. Save the report as **Album Collection**. Print the report. (Note: To complete this project, you must have created the database and table in the Application Projects in Lessons 2 and 3.)

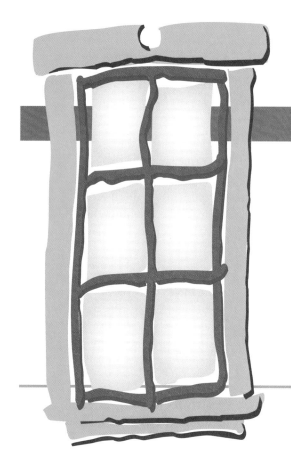

LESSON 7

ADVANCED

TOPICS

CONTENTS

Modifying Forms in Design View

Modifying Reports in Design View

Working with Multiple Tables

Creating Main Forms and Subforms

OBJECTIVES

After you complete this lesson, you will be able to do the following:

- *Modify forms in Design view.*

- *Modify reports in Design view.*

- *Identify the different types of relationships between tables.*

- *Understand the concept of referential integrity.*

- *Establish formal relationships between tables.*

- *Create main forms and subforms.*

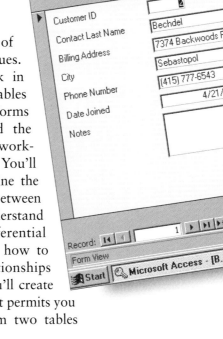

his chapter introduces a variety of more advanced techniques. First you learn to work in Design view, which enables you to modify existing forms and reports. You spend the remainder of the chapter working with multiple tables: You'll find out how to determine the types of relationships between tables; you'll learn to understand the concept of referential integrity; and you'll see how to establish formal relationships between tables. Last, you'll create a special type of form that permits you to display the data from two tables at once.

MODIFYING FORMS IN DESIGN VIEW

In Lesson 5, you spent a considerable amount of time creating forms with the help of the Access Form Wizard—a tool that makes it remarkably easy to construct quite polished forms. Most often, however, the results could use some fine-tuning—columns might not line up just right, text-box sizes may need adjusting, and fonts and font sizes may leave room for improvement. This lesson teaches you how to do these things.

To modify forms, you need to work in Design view for forms, which is similar to Design views that you've already used for tables and queries. Design view is where you see and modify the appearance of the object in question, rather than viewing or editing your actual data. You can move and change the size of objects such as text boxes and column headings; change the wording of labels; alter text attributes such as fonts, font sizes, and text alignment; and alter the colors of text, borders, and backgrounds. These simple skills help you put the finishing touches on your forms.

NOTE   *You can also create forms from scratch in Design view. For the most part, however, it's easier to create a basic design with the Form Wizard and then make necessary changes in Design view.*

SECTIONS IN DESIGN VIEW

You can view your forms by selecting the form in the Forms tab of the Database window and clicking the Design button. If the form is already open, you can click the View button to switch to Design view. Figure 7-1 shows BFCustomer AutoForm in Design view. (In the figure, the Form Design view window has been maximized.)

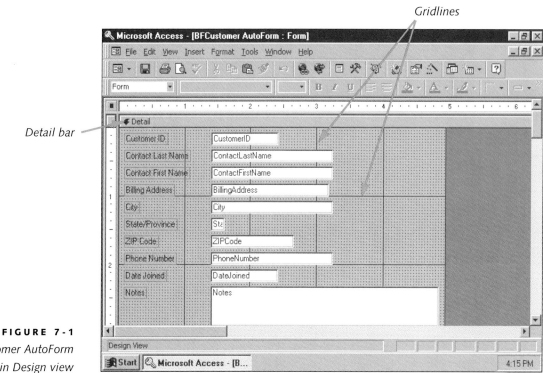

Gridlines

Detail bar

FIGURE 7-1
*BFCustomer AutoForm
in Design view*

sections Areas of a report or form. Can be a Report or Form Header, Report or Form Footer, Page Header, Page Footer, Group Header, Group Footer, or Detail section.

A bar called the Detail bar appears near the top of the Design view window. This bar identifies one of several separate areas of the form. Forms generally are divided into several **sections**, and you need a basic knowledge of what these sections are in order to modify the elements that they contain. Because reports, too, can be modified in Design view, Table 7-1 lists and describes each of these sections for both forms and reports.

TABLE 7-1: SECTIONS OF DESIGN VIEW

Report and Form Headers	Information that appears just once at the beginning of the report or form. In the figure, the Form Header is blank.
Report and Form Footers	Information that appears just once at the end of the report or form. The Report or Form Footer may contain information such as grand totals.
Page Headers	Information that appears at the top of each printed page, such as column headings in a tabular report.
Page Footers	Information that appears at the bottom of each printed page. A typical Page Footer would contain the date and page number.
Group Headers and Footers	Information that is to appear at the beginning or end of each group, respectively.
Detail section	The section of the report or form that displays the records.

OFFICE ASSISTANT

To see examples of various sections in Design view, Form view, and a printed form, start the Office Assistant and type **sections of a form***.*

grid lines A set of lines in Design view that lets you precisely align the data in your form or report.

Snap to Grid An option in Design view that limits the freedom of dragging to predefined intervals.

On the left and top of the Design view window, you see rulers. These rulers let you move and position items precisely within the form. By default, the rulers show inches. Inside the form you also can see **grid lines**. The grid lines are drawn every one inch horizontally and vertically. Dashes between the inch marks on the rulers allow you to measure in eighths of an inch. Dots within the grid lines allow you to measure even more precisely. By default, Access displays 24 dots per inch (vertically and horizontally). A feature called **Snap to Grid** will allow you to move or create items so that they align on these dots.

TIP   *If you have a steady hand and feel restricted by this limitation, you can turn off Snap to Grid from the Format menu.*

OFFICE ASSISTANT   *You can change the number of dots per inch within the grid to more precisely align items. For instructions on changing the number of dots, ask the Office Assistant.*

WORKING IN DESIGN VIEW

You can add labels, such as Form Headers or Page Headers, to any form in Design view—even if you created the form with AutoForm or Form Wizard. You simply use the Design view tools in the correct section.

To change items already in the form, you need to select the item before you make the change. In the exercises that follow, you will modify an AutoForm by adding a Form Header and then change the appearance of the label you add.

ADDING A FORM HEADER TO AN AUTOREPORT

In the next few steps, you'll open a form in Design view and you'll add a form header. You may remember how easy it was to create a form using AutoForm. Improving on the form's appearance, however, must be done in Design view.

HANDS ON

1. Open the **Be Fruitful** Database window and click the Forms tab.

2. Double-click **BFCustomer AutoForm** to open the form.

   Sort the BFCustomer AutoForm in ascending order by Customer ID, so that it looks like the one in Figure 7-2.

3. Click the arrow next to the View toolbar button and choose Design View.

TIP   *When the choices appear under the View toolbar button, notice the icon that appears next to Design View. When this icon appears on the toolbar button (without clicking the arrow), you can click directly on the button to switch to Design view.*

You see the Design view of the form.

4. Click the form's Maximize button, unless your form is already maximized.

   You must place the header you want to add in the Form Header section. As of now, that section is not displayed on the screen.

5. Click the View menu and choose Form Header/Footer.

6. Click the Form Header bar that appears directly below the horizontal ruler.

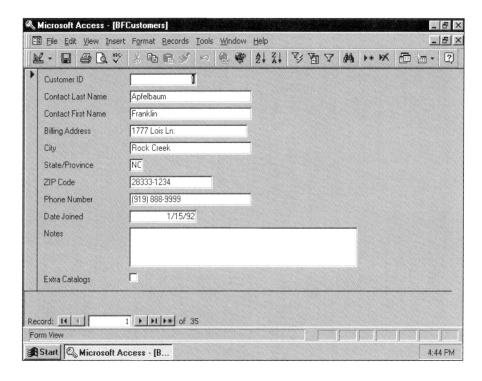

FIGURE 7-2
BFCustomer AutoForm

The bar becomes dark gray.

7. Move the mouse pointer over the last row of dots under the Form Header bar (just above the Detail bar) so that the arrow cursor is replaced by a set of crossed lines with a double-headed vertical arrow.

8. Hold down the left mouse button and drag the line down so that it lines up in the middle of the CustomerID field as shown in Figure 7-3; then release the button.

Cursor takes new shape

Line indicates new size of Form Header section

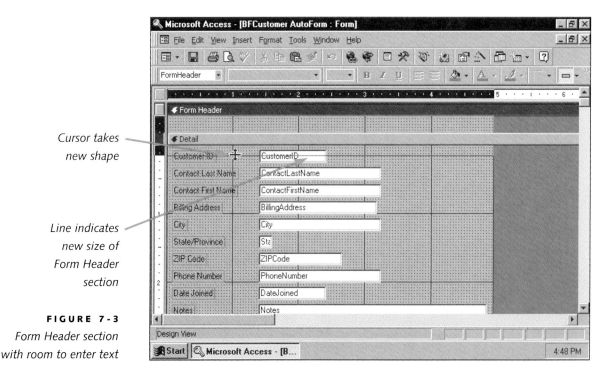

FIGURE 7-3
Form Header section with room to enter text

Now you have lengthened the Form Header section as shown in Figure 7-4.

To add the text in the Form Header, you'll need to use the toolbox—a special toolbar used to create and modify objects in Design view.

9. If the toolbox is not displayed on screen, click the Toolbox toolbar button.

The toolbox shows up on the screen.

T I P   *You can also right-click the toolbar and select the toolbox from there.*

10. If the toolbox covers part of the Design view window, click its title bar and drag it to the right side of the window, as shown in Figure 7-4.

Drag toolbox to move it

Increased size of Form Header

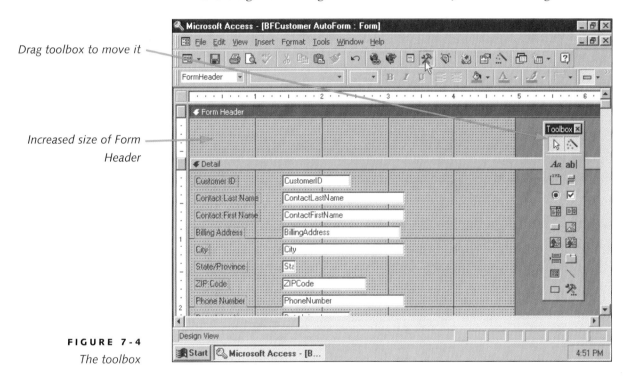

FIGURE 7-4
The toolbox

11. Click the Label button in the toolbox.

As you move your mouse pointer, it becomes a capital *A* with crossed lines next to it. The crossed lines indicate that you can click and drag to create a box. Once the box is in place, the *A* means you can type a label into the box.

12. Click and hold down the mouse button near the upper-left corner of the Form Header section. Drag down and to the right to form a box approximately 2" wide by ⅜" long.

Use the horizontal and vertical rulers to judge the size of the box; when the darkened bar that shows the cursor's position reaches the 2" mark on the horizontal ruler and the third dash in the vertical ruler (as shown in Figure 7-5), release the mouse button.

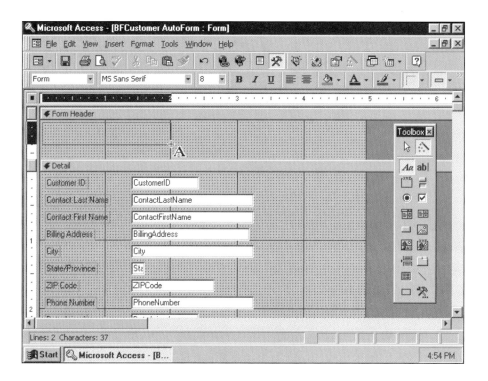

F I G U R E   7 - 5
Creating a label box

When you release the mouse button, a box appears in the Form Header section.

13. Type **BF Customers**

The text appears within the box you created, as shown in Figure 7-6. Now this text will appear as a title at the top of the form when you view, edit, or enter data into it.

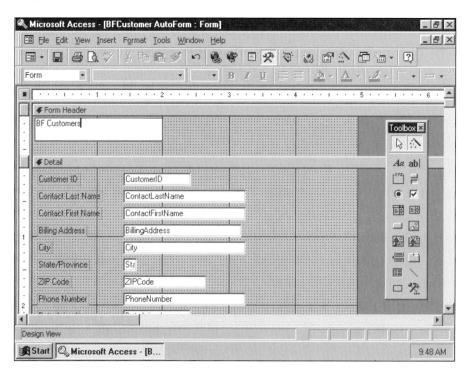

F I G U R E   7 - 6
*Title added to Form
Header*

14. Click the View toolbar button. Since the Form View icon was displayed in the View button, Access switches to Form view.

Notice that the text you typed in the Form Header box appears at the top of the form.

15. Click the View toolbar button again.

Access switches back to Design view.

SELECTING FORM CONTROLS

controls Form or report elements that display data, perform actions, or decorate the form or report. You can manipulate controls in Design view.

Within each section, the parts of the form or report—such as labels, text boxes for displaying data, and form or report titles—are represented as objects that are also known as **controls**. Controls are simply the different form elements that you can manipulate individually. As you'll soon find out, most often you will first select one or more controls in order to modify a form. Then you'll use the mouse, a menu command(s), or a toolbar button(s) to manipulate the selected controls.

Selecting controls is simple. Table 7-2 shows some of the basic keystrokes and mouse actions for selecting controls.

TABLE 7-2: SELECTING CONTROLS

Select a single control	Click it. This deselects any other selected controls.
Select additional controls	Hold down Shift while clicking them.
Select all controls	Click the Edit menu and choose Select All or press Ctrl+A.
Deselect all selected controls	Click away from any objects.
Deselect a single control	Hold down Shift while clicking it.

handles A set of boxes that encloses a control in a form or report when you're in Design view to indicate that the control is selected. These handles enable you to change the control's size and location.

sizing handles Handles that are used to enlarge or reduce the size of a control in Design view.

move handles Handles that are used to drag a control to another location in Design view.

When you select a control, it is surrounded by a set of **handles**—square boxes that indicate the control is selected and enable you to change its size and location. The smaller handles that completely surround a control are called the **sizing handles**. As the name implies, you can use these handles to increase or decrease the size of a control. The larger handles that appear at the top of the control are called **move handles**. Move handles are used to drag a control to another location. Figure 7-7 shows a selected text box control.

CHANGING THE APPEARANCE OF A LABEL

The label you added to the Form Header is quite small and plain. You can enlarge the label and make it more interesting by formatting the label, as you will do in the next few steps.

Move handles

Drag this handle
to change the height

Drag this handle
to change the width

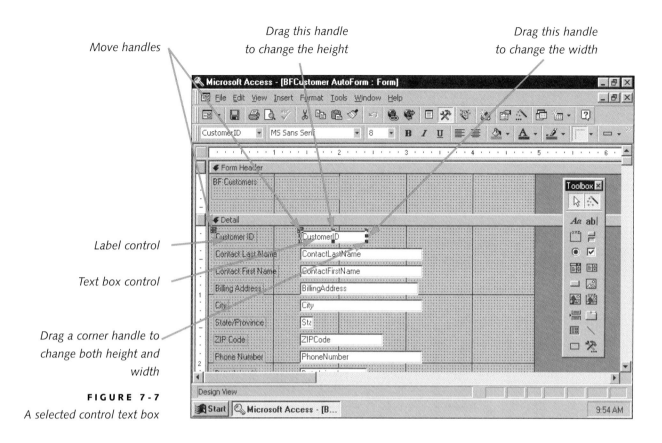

Label control

Text box control

Drag a corner handle to
change both height and
width

FIGURE 7-7
A selected control text box

**HANDS
ON**

1. Right-click the toolbox.

A shortcut menu appears.

2. If Formatting (Form/Report) does not have a check mark next to it,
click it.

The Formatting toolbar appears just above the horizontal ruler.

3. If it is not already selected, click the BF Customers label in the Form
Header.

As you can see by the handles that surround it, the label is selected.

MS Sans Serif ▾

4. Click the Font drop-down arrow on the Formatting toolbar; then click
Arial.

The text inside the label box changes font.

8 ▾

5. Click the Font Size drop-down arrow and choose 18.

The label changes to a larger size.

B

6. Click the Bold button.

A ▾

7. Click the Font/Fore Color drop-down arrow and click a bright blue
shade.

Your label now looks like that in Figure 7-8.

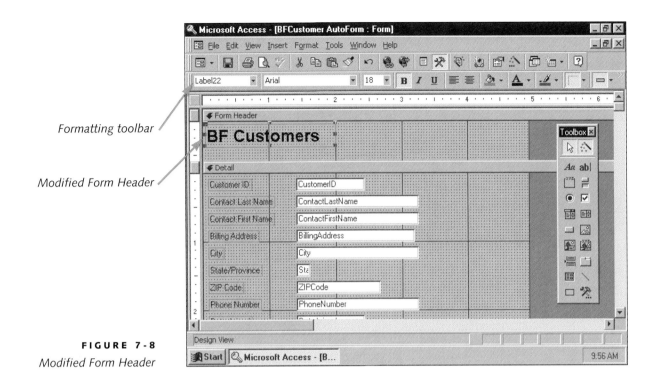

Formatting toolbar

Modified Form Header

FIGURE 7-8
Modified Form Header

CHANGING DETAIL CONTROLS IN DESIGN VIEW

When you create forms with the Form Wizard, you have a decent amount of control over the contents of the form but are limited to a few very specific layouts. Most often, your forms will feature all fields lined up in a single column or fields laid out in a series of rows and columns. The best thing about Design view is that it permits you to create alternatives to these standard layouts. You can move fields around at will and arrange them in ways that use space more economically and please the eye.

Changing the arrangement of fields is just one possibility. You also can increase or decrease the size of text boxes so that they suit their data.

In the next few exercises, you'll reposition, resize, and change the way your form works.

RESIZING CONTROLS IN DESIGN VIEW

You can move and resize selected controls by dragging on the appropriate handle. When you drag any side handle, the control's height or width changes. Dragging the corner handles changes the height and width at the same time.

TIP *You can also select multiple controls and then move or resize them simultaneously by dragging the handles of just one of them.*

HANDS ON

1. Make sure your BFCustomer AutoForm is displayed in Design view.

2. Close the toolbox by clicking its Close button.

T I P *If you make a change that you decide to reverse, you can choose Undo from the Edit menu. If you've made a number of changes that you decide to discard, click the Close button and respond with No when asked if you want to save your changes.*

3. Click the CustomerID text box to the right of the Customer ID label.

   Access displays handles around the text box.

4. Place the mouse pointer over the handle on the right edge of the control—the middle handle, not one of the corner handles.

   The mouse pointer changes to a double-headed arrow with arrows pointing to the right and the left.

5. Press and hold down the mouse button, drag to the left until the text box is about half of its original size, and then release the mouse button.

6. Click the City text box, and using the same technique, reduce its size by about a third.

7. Reduce the ZIPCode text box by about a third.

8. Click the ContactLastName text box to select it.

9. Hold down Shift and click the ContactFirstName text box. Then release Shift.

   Both text boxes remain selected.

10. Drag to reduce the size of either of the selected fields by about a third.

    Access resizes both of the selected fields.

11. Click outside of the controls to deselect all of the text boxes.

    The boxes are now narrow enough that more than one box can fit across the screen.

MOVING CONTROLS IN DESIGN VIEW

To move an individual control, you can drag on the move handle—the somewhat larger handle in the upper-left corner. However, when two controls are linked (such as the label and text-box pairs in Figure 7-7) you probably want to move them together. Notice that the selected CustomerID text box in the figure has an associated label, which also has a move handle when you select the text box. When you drag the move handle for a control, you move only that control. The other control in the pair remains in its original location. If you instead want to move the controls together, place the mouse pointer over the border of the selected control (the one with a full set of handles), and when the pointer looks like an open hand, drag both controls to the desired spot.

In the next series of steps, you will rearrange the controls on the form. If you have trouble lining up the controls, check the alignment of the fields in Figure 7-9.

HANDS ON

1. Select the ContactFirstName text box.

2. Place the mouse pointer over the border of the text box, avoiding the selection handles.

   The mouse pointer should take on the shape of an open hand.

3. Click and drag the ContactFirstName text box up and to the right, noting that the Contact First Name label is moving with it.

4. Release the button when the controls are to the right of and on the same line as the Contact Last Name controls. Don't worry if the text box seems to hang off the grid. The grid will automatically resize itself.

NOTE   *When you want to move two associated controls, you can select and drag either one of them using this method. If you use the control's border rather than the move handle, both controls move together.*

5. Drag the Billing Address controls (both the label and text box) up underneath the Contact Last Name controls; keep the BillingAddress and ContactLastName text boxes lined up on the left side.

6. Click outside of the controls to deselect all of them.

7. Hold down (Shift), position the mouse pointer in the middle of the City text box, and press and hold down the mouse button.

8. Drag the City controls up, so that they are placed directly below the Billing Address controls.

Holding (Shift) allows you to move controls in one direction only. If you were to continue holding down (Shift) and tried to move the controls to the left or right, they would not move. This method comes in handy when you want to move controls without changing their alignment.

9. Next, drag the State/Province controls up and to the right, and place them just to the right of the City controls.

10. Then, move the ZIPCode controls up and to the right, placing them directly to the right of the State/Province field.

11. Move the PhoneNumber controls up underneath the City field.

12. Drag the DateJoined controls so that they're directly underneath the Phone Number field.

13. Finally, drag the Notes controls, placing them immediately underneath the DateJoined field.

You can also move one control at a time rather than a pair.

14. Click the State text box to select it.

15. Place the mouse pointer over the move handle of the State text box (the large handle at the top-left corner of the text box) so that the pointer changes to the shape of a closed hand with one pointing finger.

16. Drag the text box to the left so that it is positioned close to its label.

17. Use the same method to drag the ZIPCode text box close to its label.

TIP   *Remember, you can use (Shift) to keep the controls bottom aligned.*

18. Scroll to the top of the Design view.

Your form should now look similar to that in Figure 7-9.

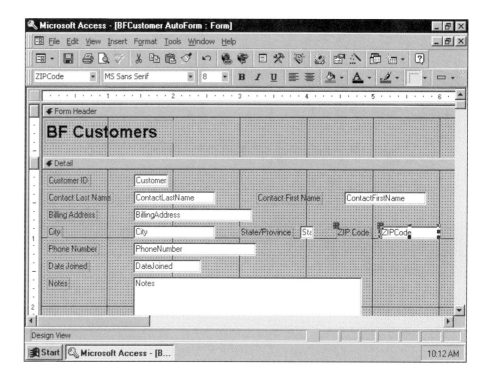

FIGURE 7-9

Fields repositioned on the form

CHANGING THE TAB ORDER

tab order The order in which Access moves from field to field when you press [Tab].

The **tab order** is the order in which Access moves from field to field when you press [Tab]. Unless you modify the tab order, Access moves from field to field in the order that the fields appear in the underlying table, instead of the order they appear in the revised form.

In the next exercise, you will move the Extra Catalogs field so it appears to the right of the Date Joined field. If you do not change the tab order, [Tab] will cause the insertion point to move from the Date Joined field to the Notes field, the next field in the underlying table.

HANDS ON

1. Drag the Extra Catalogs controls to the right of the DateJoined text box.

2. Click the View toolbar button to switch to Form view.

You now see your form as it has been changed.

3. Press [Tab] repeatedly to move through all of the fields in the form.

You will see that the Extra Catalogs field is selected after the Notes field—not after the Date Joined field that it is next to.

4. Click the View toolbar button to return to Design view.

5. Click the View menu and choose Tab Order.

The Tab Order dialog box appears, as shown in Figure 7-10. Note that the Detail option button is selected because you are working in the Detail section of Design view.

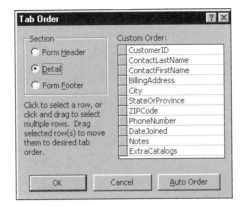

FIGURE 7-10

The Tab Order dialog box

Notice too that the Notes field is listed before the Extra Catalogs field in the Custom Order list, even though the Notes field now falls after the Extra Catalogs field on the form.

6. Click the selector to the left of the Extra Catalogs field in the Custom Order list.

7. Drag this field up to the position currently occupied by the Notes field, and then release the mouse button.

Access switches the positions of the Notes and Extra Catalogs fields in the Custom Order list.

NOTE *If you click the Auto Order button in the Tab Order dialog box, Access will change the tab order to move from left to right and top to bottom through the fields on the form.*

8. Click OK.

The change takes effect and the Tab Order dialog box closes.

9. Click the View toolbar button to switch to Form view.

10. Press Tab repeatedly to move through all the fields in the form.

You will see that the Extra Catalogs field is now selected after the Date Joined field—not after the Notes field as it was previously. This new order will be easier to use when entering data for new records.

11. Click the View toolbar button to switch back to Design view.

OFFICE ASSISTANT *When you press Tab after the last field in a record, the cursor moves to the first field in the next record. However, you can change the tab behavior so that it stays in the current record or page. Ask the Office Assistant for help on changing this default setting.*

MODIFYING THE APPEARANCE OF THE DETAIL SECTION

You can make many other changes to the appearance of your form. Previously, you added and modified the Form Header. In Design view, you can choose a style for the form—much as you did using the Wizards. You already learned how to change the color, size, and font of a control; you can also change border thickness and the color surrounding a control, as well as the background color of the section.

CHANGING BORDERS AND BACKGROUND

To finish the modifications to the form, you'll make changes to the border and background with the following steps.

HANDS ON

1. If it is not already selected, click the Extra Catalogs label control.

2. Click the Line/Border Width drop-down arrow on the Formatting toolbar.

Several boxes of border width choices appear.

3. Click border width 1.

Border width 1 is a thin line that will surround the control.

4. Click the Line/Border Color drop-down arrow on the Formatting toolbar.

A number of small color boxes appear.

5. Click the red box.

A thin red line surrounds the Extra Catalogs label.

6. Click the Special Effect drop-down arrow on the Formatting toolbar.

Several boxes appear showing the available special effects. Among other choices, you can have a sunken or raised look for your control.

7. Click the Shadowed box.

8. Click outside of any controls to deselect the Extra Catalogs label control.

The Extra Catalogs label is now surrounded by a shadowed, red border, as in Figure 7-11.

Shadowed, red border

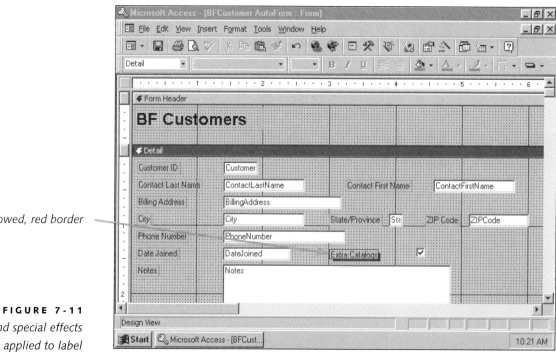

FIGURE 7-11
Border and special effects applied to label

9. If the Detail bar is not selected (dark gray), click it.

10. Click the Fill/Back Color drop-down arrow on the Formatting toolbar.

You see boxes that show the available colors.

11. Click the pale yellow box.

12. Click the View toolbar button to see your finished form in Form view.

At this point, your form will look something like the one shown in Figure 7-12.

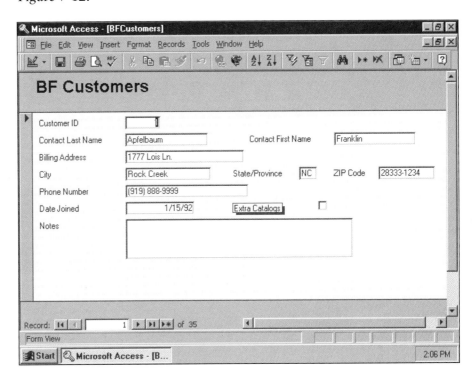

FIGURE 7-12
Color changes in Form view

SAVING AND PRINTING DESIGN CHANGES

Changes made in Design view must be saved in order for the modifications to be stored. During the next few steps you will save your changes and print the finished form.

HANDS ON

1. Click the Save toolbar button.

Access saves the design changes you have made to the form.

2. Click the Print Preview toolbar button.

You see a preview of your form on the screen.

NOTE   *If a dialog box appears warning that the section width is greater than the page width, return to Design view by clicking the View toolbar button and modify your form. You may need to move some of the controls closer together and then adjust the section width. To adjust the section width, drag the right border of the page (in Design view) to the left.*

3. Zoom in, if necessary, to view your form at 100%. Check all of the labels and text boxes to make sure no letters are cut off.

4. If necessary, return to Design view by clicking the View toolbar button and enlarge any labels or text boxes that appeared too small. Then return to Print Preview view.

5. If you are satisfied with the appearance of your form, click the Print toolbar button. Otherwise, close the Print Preview screen, make any necessary changes, and then print the form.

A hard copy of the modified report is printed.

6. Click the form's Close button. If you are asked whether you want to save the changes you made, click Yes.

Access returns you to the Database window.

MODIFYING REPORTS IN DESIGN VIEW

Modifying reports is pretty similar to modifying forms. You work with controls—either dragging them to move or resize them or selecting them and then choosing toolbar buttons or menu options to modify them. There are a few differences, however. For one, you're less likely to modify the colors in reports, unless you have a printer that can print more than one color. In addition, tabular reports with totals or summaries have group headers which are labeled with the name of the *Group By* field. Otherwise, you should feel pretty much at home changing a report in Design view.

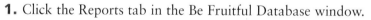

VIEWING A REPORT IN DESIGN VIEW

Here you will take a look at the Be Fruitful 1997 Orders report you created using the Report Wizard. This tabular report needs some minor adjustment to fix the alignment and width of the column headings.

HANDS ON

1. Click the Reports tab in the Be Fruitful Database window.

2. Select the Be Fruitful 1997 Orders report and click the Preview button.

3. Maximize the window and then use the Zoom box on the toolbar to view the report at 75%.

Notice that many of the column headings don't line up well with the data below and some of the text is cut off.

4. Click the Close toolbar button.

Access returns you to the Database window.

5. With the Be Fruitful 1997 Orders report still selected, click the Design button in the Database window.

Access displays the report in Design view. As you'd expect, the report design is divided into several different sections, most of which contain a number of different controls.

CHANGING THE REPORT HEADER AND PAGE FOOTER

You can change the size and font of a report title in much the same way you changed the form header earlier in this lesson.

HANDS ON

1. Click the text in the Report Header *Be Fruitful 1997 Orders.*

The Report Header is selected as you can see by the handles that surround it.

Arial

2. Choose Times New Roman from the Font drop-down list box.

Access changes the font used for the Report Header.

24

3. Choose 16 from the Font Size drop-down list box.

Access changes the size of the font used for the Report Header.

4. Scroll down until you can see the entire Page Footer section.

=Now() is a code that stands for today's date. The code at the right of the footer is set to make the footer read *Page 1 of 6* at the bottom of the first page of a six-page report.

5. Click the text =Now().

I

6. Click the Italic toolbar button.

The date is both bold and italic. (It was bold to begin with.)

N O T E *Both the Bold and Italic buttons now look as though they have been pressed in. When it doesn't look pressed in, you can click the Italic button to italicize the selected text. Both of these buttons are toggles: You can click them once to turn them on and again to turn them off.*

7. Click the View toolbar button to switch to Print Preview view.

8. Scroll down to view the Page Footer, which now appears in bold, italicized text.

CHANGING MARGINS FOR A REPORT

One way to improve the appearance of a report with several fields that don't fit neatly on a page is to decrease the size of the page margins. In the following steps, you'll decrease the right and left margins by ¼" each.

HANDS ON

1. While in Print Preview view, click the File menu and choose Page Setup.

The Page Setup dialog box appears.

2. Make sure the Margins tab is selected.

The Page Setup dialog box allows you to change options such as margins, page orientation, and row spacing in the report.

3. Double-click the Left text box, and then type .75 (Don't forget the decimal point.)

4. Double-click the Right text box and type **.75** (Don't forget the decimal point.)

5. Click **OK**.

The left and right margins decrease from 1 inch to ¾ of an inch (.75 inch).

ADJUSTING HEADER WIDTHS AND DETAIL CONTROLS

Now that you have increased the amount of space that you have to work with by decreasing the margins, you can fix the column widths and alignment of data. In the next few steps, you'll correct these problems.

HANDS ON

Text15

1. Click the View toolbar button to see the Be Fruitful 1997 Orders report in Design view.

2. Click the drop-down arrow next to the Select Object box on the toolbar.

The Select Object box is the first box on the Formatting toolbar; it provides an easy way to select any section or control on a report.

3. Scroll down and choose Order Date by Month Label from the list.

Access selects the label. Of course, you could have selected it yourself by clicking on it, but the Select Object button allows you to find the label easily.

4. Drag the middle-right sizing handle to widen the label by ⅛". Use the ⅛-inch marks on the horizontal ruler to determine the correct size.

You can now see the entire label in the box.

5. Scroll to the right and click the Payment Amount label in the OrderDate Header section.

Selection handles appear around the label.

6. Hold down (Shift) and click the Payment Amount control in the Detail section.

Handles remain around the Payment Amount label in the OrderDate Header section and new handles appear around the Payment Amount control in the Detail section.

7. Drag the middle-right handle of either of the selected items to the 7-inch mark on the horizontal ruler.

NOTE *Since you decreased each margin by ¼ of an inch, you now have a total of ½ of an inch of extra space in which you can place labels and controls. For that reason, you can drag items up to the 7-inch mark on the ruler. (They previously extended to the 6½-inch mark.)*

8. Drag the middle-left handle of either of the selected items to the 5⅝-inch mark on the ruler.

Both of the selected items are narrowed in size. Any action that you take in Design view affects all of the labels or controls that are selected.

9. Click the Shipping Amount label in the OrderDate Header section.

10. Hold down (Shift) and click the ShippingAmount control in the Detail section.

You should see handles around both of the Shipping Amount items.

11. Drag the middle-right handle of either of the selected items to the $5^{1}/_{2}$-inch mark on the ruler.

12. Drag the middle-left handle of either of the selected items to the $4^{1}/_{8}$-inch mark on the ruler.

T I P *Working from right to left when changing control and label widths may help you to avoid overlapping fields.*

13. Select both the Price label in the OrderDate Header and the Price control in the Detail section.

14. Drag the middle-right handle of either of the selected items to the 4-inch mark on the ruler.

15. Drag the middle-left handle of either of the selected items to the $3^{1}/_{2}$-inch mark on the ruler.

16. Select the Quantity label and control.

17. Resize the selected items so that the middle-right handles are at the $3^{3}/_{8}$-inch mark and the middle-left handles are at the $2^{5}/_{8}$-inch mark on the ruler.

18. Select the Fruit Type label and control and resize them so that the middle-right handles are at the $2^{1}/_{2}$-inch mark and the middle-left handles are at the $1^{5}/_{8}$-inch mark.

19. Select the Order Date label and control and drag the middle-right handles to the $1^{1}/_{2}$-inch mark and the middle-left handles to the $^{5}/_{8}$-inch mark.

Your screen should look something like the one in Figure 7-13.

20. Click the View toolbar button to change to Print Preview view.

You should now be able to see all of the header labels and data. None of the data or labels are cut off. You may notice, however, that the lines surrounding the headings no longer align with the text perfectly. You will fix this problem in the following section.

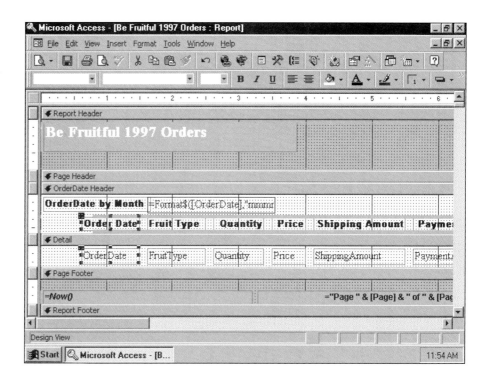

FIGURE 7-13
Resized labels and controls

RESIZING LINES IN DESIGN VIEW

Resizing lines in Design view is much like resizing labels and controls. You simply click the line to select it and drag the appropriate handle to size the line. If you hold down Shift while sizing a line, Access only allows the line to be changed either horizontally or vertically, but not both. This extra bit of control can help you to keep your lines perfectly straight.

HANDS ON

1. Click the View toolbar button to change to Design view.

2. Hold down Shift, click the drop-down arrow next to the Select Object box, and choose Line 21 from the list. Continue to hold down Shift.

   One of the lines above the headings is selected.

3. Place your mouse pointer over the first sizing handle so that the pointer takes the shape of a double-headed diagonal arrow. Then, drag it to the 5/8-inch mark. Continue to hold down Shift.

4. Scroll to the right and drag the last sizing handle for the line to the 7-inch mark on the ruler. Then release Shift.

5. Following Steps 2 through 4, resize Line 22, Line 23, and Line 24— one at a time—so that they extend from the 5/8-inch mark to the 7-inch mark on the ruler.

TIP   *If any of the lines appear at a slight angle instead of perfectly horizontal, you'll need to adjust their height. Double-click the line so that the Line dialog box appears. Select the All tab and change the Height box to 0". Then click the Close button to close the dialog box.*

6. Click the View toolbar button to change to Print Preview view.

The lines should now align with the headings.

ALIGNING HEADINGS

You may have noticed that the data in the Quantity and Price columns don't line up well with their headings. This problem can easily be fixed by changing their alignments.

1. Click the View toolbar button to change to Design view.

2. Click the Quantity control in the Detail section to select it.

3. Click the Center toolbar button.

The text is moved to the center of its box, indicating that the data in the Quantity column will now be centered within the column.

4. Select the Price label in the OrderDate Header section.

5. Click the Center toolbar button to center the heading.

As before, the text is moved to the center of the box. While the heading may look slightly out of alignment in Design view, once you switch to Print Preview view, you'll see how it looks in the actual report.

6. Click the View toolbar button to change to Print Preview view and view your changes.

If you view your report at 75%, it should look similar to the one in Figure 7-14.

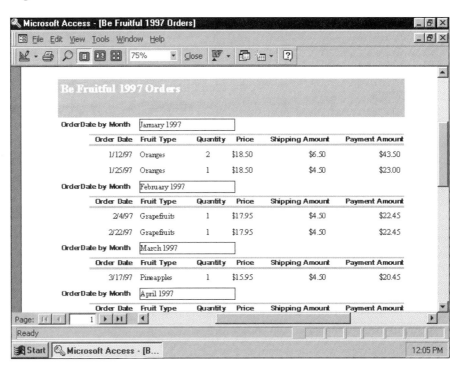

FIGURE 7-14

Print Preview view of final report

7. If you are happy with the appearance of your report, click the Print toolbar button to print it. Otherwise, make any necessary changes and then print your report.

8. Close the Print Preview window.

9. Click the Save toolbar button.

10. Click the File menu and choose Close.

You return to the Database window.

WORKING WITH MULTIPLE TABLES

You've already learned a few basics about working with multiple tables. Among other things, you found out how to create queries that draw data from more than one table, and you discovered how easy it is to create forms and reports based on those queries. Because working with multiple tables is a critical skill for managing databases well, you need to learn a little more.

In Lesson 4, you created some multi-table queries by establishing joins between two tables; these joins enable Access to recognize matching records in the tables. As you may remember, in some cases, Access can guess correctly which field is the join field; sometimes, you may need to establish the join manually by dragging from one common field to another.

At times, you'll want to establish permanent relationships between tables. This way, Access will always be certain which records match up and also will understand precisely the type of relationship the two tables have. Defining formal relationships between tables involves a few simple steps, as you'll soon learn. First, however, you need to know a bit more about the various types of relationships that can exist between tables.

IDENTIFYING RELATIONSHIPS BETWEEN TABLES

one-to-one relationship A relationship between two tables in which every record in each table can have either no matching records or only a single matching record in the other table.

one-to-many relationship A relationship between two tables in which each record in the primary table can have no records, one record, or many matching records in the related table, but every record in the related table has one—and only one—associated record in the primary table.

Any two tables can have one of several possible relationships. You will learn about the three types of relationships: one-to-one, one-to-many, and many-to-many.

If two tables have a **one-to-one relationship**, every record in a table can have either no matching records or only a single matching record in the other table. This situation might arise, for example, if you want to keep track of mailing addresses as well as regular addresses: You could include the mailing addresses in a separate table; each person would have at most one mailing address in this table, and many people would have none, because their mailing addresses would be the same as their regular addresses.

When you have a **one-to-many relationship**, one of the tables is called the primary table, while the other is called the related table. The **primary table** holds a primary key that is unique. In your BFCustomers table, the CustomerID field is the primary key. You ensured that the CustomerID field would be unique by defining it as an AutoNumber field. In that way, no two customer records have the same CustomerID.

primary table A table in a one-to-many relationship that can have zero, one, or many matching records in the related table; but every record in the related table has exactly one matching record in the primary table. You can think of a primary table as the "one" side in a one-to-many relationship.

related table A table in a one-to-many relationship in which every record has exactly one matching record in the primary table. Also known as a foreign table.

The second table in a one-to-many relationship is called the related table. The **related table** has a field that links it to the primary table. This field is called the **foreign key**. It need not be unique. In the BFOrders table, the foreign key is the CustomerID. This field was *not* defined as an AutoNumber field, because one customer can place many orders.

Two tables have a one-to-many relationship when each record in the primary table can have no records, one record, or many matching records in the other table, but every record in the related table has exactly one associated record in the primary table—no more and no less.

In a **many-to-many relationship**, a record in either table can relate to many records in the other table. While you will not create such a relationship in the Be Fruitful database, they are quite common. For example, BFOrders and BFFruits could have a many-to-many relationship—one order can relate to many different fruit types and each fruit type can be ordered many times.

OFFICE ASSISTANT

foreign key A field in a related table that has the same name and data type as the primary key in the primary table.

many-to-many relationship A relationship between tables in which each record in each table may have many matches in the other.

For examples of the different types of relationships, tables, and keys, ask the Office Assistant.

CREATING A ONE-TO-MANY RELATIONSHIP

You use the Relationships window to create the link between a primary and related table. Note that the primary table *must* have a unique primary key and the related table *must* have a foreign key that matches the field of the primary key. Otherwise, you will have to redefine the structure of the tables.

HANDS ON

1. Click the Tables object tab in the Be Fruitful Database window of your **Lessons** folder.

2. Click the Relationships button on the toolbar.

   The Show Table dialog box appears, which lets you choose the tables you want to relate.

3. Double-click BFCustomers.

   A Field list appears for the BFCustomers table in the Relationships window.

4. Double-click BFOrders.

5. Click the Close button of the Show Table dialog box.

   The BFOrders Field list is displayed to the right of the BFCustomers Field list in the Relationships window.

6. Drag and drop the CustomerID field from the BFCustomers Field list onto the CustomerID field on the BFOrders Field list.

   The Relationships dialog box appears, as shown in Figure 7-15.

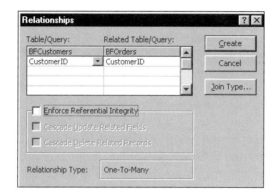

FIGURE 7-15

The Relationships dialog box

7. Click the Create button.

The dialog box closes and a line now appears between the CustomerID fields in the two tables.

8. Click the Close button of the Relationships window.

A warning box asks if you want to save this relationship.

9. Click Yes.

The relationship is saved and you return to the Database window.

UNDERSTANDING REFERENTIAL INTEGRITY

Tables that have been assigned relationships need to be protected. After all, if you were to delete a customer from the BFCustomers table, what would happen to the related orders in the BFOrders table? They would have no CustomerID field in the primary table. Such records are called **orphan records**. Fortunately, when you set up a relationship between tables, you can choose to include referential integrity. **Referential integrity** refers to certain rules that Access enforces to safeguard your data, ensuring that it makes sense and does not violate the relationship that you have defined for the tables. In terms of Be Fruitful's database, this means that every orders record must have an associated customer record but cannot have more than one related customer record.

orphan records Records in a related table with no associated record in the primary table.

referential integrity A set of rules that Access can enforce to preserve the defined relationship between tables.

If you choose referential integrity, Access will enforce these rules:

■ You cannot delete a record from the primary table that has a matching record or records in the related table. (For instance, you cannot delete a customer record if there are matching order records.)

■ You cannot add or change a record in the related table so that its foreign key no longer matches a record in the primary table. (For example, you cannot change the CustomerID field in the BFOrders table so that it no longer matches an existing customer ID in the BFCustomers table.)

■ You cannot change a primary key field in the primary table when the related table has associated records. (For instance, you cannot change the CustomerID field for a customer record that has matching orders; in BFCustomers, this isn't an issue, because you can't make changes to an AutoNumber field.)

By enforcing referential integrity, Access simply prevents you from making errors such as deleting customers for whom there are orders, or entering orders for nonexistent customers.

NOTE *If your existing tables violate the rules of referential integrity, you cannot establish formal relationships between them and choose the option to enforce referential integrity. For example, if you have order records with no matching customer record (which could easily occur if you had deleted a customer and forgot to also delete her orders), you would need to delete the associated order records and then try again to define a relationship and enforce referential integrity between the tables.*

EDITING A RELATIONSHIP

To have Access enforce referential integrity between the BFCustomers and BFOrders tables, you need to edit their relationship:

HANDS ON

1. Make sure you are in the Tables object tab of the Be Fruitful Database window.

2. Click the Relationships button on the toolbar.

You are brought directly to the Relationships window because you have previously established a relationship in this database.

NOTE *If you want to establish new relationships, click the Show Table toolbar button.*

3. Double-click the line that connects the two CustomerID fields.

The Relationships dialog box appears, as shown in Figure 7-16.

Click here to enforce referential integrity

Type of relationship

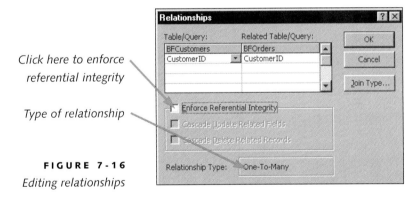

FIGURE 7-16
Editing relationships

4. Click the Enforce Referential Integrity check box so that a check mark appears in it.

5. Click OK.

Access changes the line that connects the fields. Note the 1 on the BFCustomers side and the ∞ on the BFOrders side, as shown in Figure 7-17. These marks indicate that referential integrity is enforced and describe the type of relationship defined. The 1 indicates the "one" side of the relationship, while the "∞" indicates the "many" side of the relationship. In other words, this relationship line shows that the BFCustomers table is the primary table and has only one record with a CustomerID that can match many of the same CustomerID in the related table, BFOrders.

Join line for one-to-many relationship with
referential integrity enforced

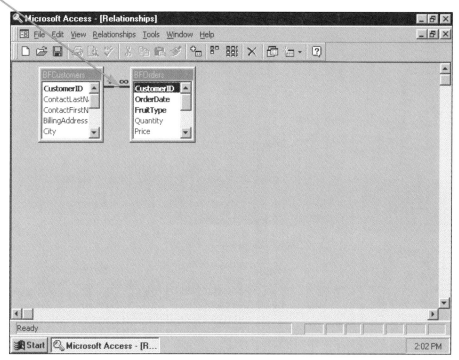

6. Click the Close button of the Relationships window.

Access automatically saves the changes to the relationship.

DELETING RECORDS UNDER REFERENTIAL INTEGRITY

To see the effect of adding referential integrity to a relationship, you can try to delete a record from the primary table:

HANDS ON

1. Open the BFCustomers table from the Database window.

The table appears in Datasheet view.

2. Click the record selector for Franklin Apfelbaum.

3. Press Delete.

Access displays the warning box shown in Figure 7-18. In this database, most customer records have associated order records—remember, deleting such records is forbidden by the rules of referential integrity.

4. Click OK.

5. Close the BFCustomers table.

NOTE   *A similar situation would occur if you tried to add a record to a related table that has no matching record in the primary table. A warning box would inform you of the situation and prevent you from adding the record.*

MAINTAINING REFERENTIAL INTEGRITY

Sometimes you may want Access to enforce referential integrity but not prevent you from deleting or modifying certain records or fields. There is a solution—actually, there are two solutions, called Cascading Deletes and Cascading Updates. If you turn on the **Cascading Deletes** feature, Access allows you to delete records from the primary table and automatically deletes any records with the same foreign key from the related table. (For example, if you deleted a customer's record, any orders for that customer would be deleted automatically.)

If you turn on the **Cascading Updates** feature, Access lets you modify the primary key field in a record in the primary table and then automatically updates the records in the related field to match. (If you could change the Customer ID field in Be Fruitful's database, this feature would enable you to enter a new customer ID in the BFCustomers table and have Access reflect that change automatically in the BFOrders table.)

Cascading Deletes A feature that causes Access to automatically delete any affiliated records from a related table when you delete a record from the primary table.

Cascading Updates A feature that causes Access to automatically update the associated field in any related table records when you modify the primary key field in a primary table record.

WARNING   *Because Cascading Deletes and Cascading Updates enable you to remove and modify many records at once, you could wind up deleting or altering more records than you intended. In other words, be sure to use these two options with care.*

TURNING ON THE CASCADING DELETES FEATURE

To delete related records while maintaining referential integrity, you must first turn on the Cascading Deletes feature:

 HANDS ON

1. Make sure the Database window for the Be Fruitful database is open.

2. Click the Relationships toolbar button.

Access displays the Relationships window showing the BFCustomers and BFOrders tables.

3. Double-click the *thin* part of the line that connects the two CustomerID fields.

Access displays the Relationships dialog box you saw earlier.

TIP   *You must click the thin part of the line; nothing happens if you click the thick parts of the line under the 1 and ∞ symbols.*

4. Click the Cascade Delete Related Records check box at the bottom of the dialog box to select it.

5. Click OK.

6. Close the Relationships window.

Access returns you to the Database window.

DELETING CASCADING RECORDS

Now you can delete a record from the primary table and all records with the same foreign key automatically.

HANDS ON

1. Double-click the BFOrders table to open it.

2. Count the number of orders for customer 1 and then close the table.

3. Open the BFCustomers table.

4. Select the record for Franklin Apfelbaum and press Delete.

Access displays the warning box shown in Figure 7-19 to confirm that you do indeed want to delete the record. Note that the warning box indicates that you will be deleting records from related tables.

FIGURE 7-19

Warning box when you delete a record from the primary table

![Microsoft Access warning dialog box. Relationships that specify cascading deletes are about to cause 1 record(s) in this table and in related tables to be deleted. Are you sure you want to delete these records? Buttons: Yes, No, Help.]

5. Click Yes.

6. Close the BFCustomers table.

7. Open the BFOrders table again.

You no longer see the order records for customer 1 at the top of the table. These were the related records for the record you deleted from the primary table.

8. Close the BFOrders table.

You are back at the Database window.

CREATING MAIN FORMS AND SUBFORMS

main form One form that includes another form, called the *subform*. The subform is linked to the main form. The main form has a one-to-many relationship with the subform.

subform A form within a form. The subform has a many-to-one relationship with the main form.

In Lesson 5, you created forms based on tables or queries, but you haven't actually created forms that in themselves draw on multiple tables. You'll do so here. Using the Form Wizard you can create one form, a main form, that includes another form, the subform, that is linked to the main form. The **main form** has a one-to-many relationship with the **subform**—that is, there is a single record in the main form and potentially many related records in the subform. This type of form is particularly useful for displaying one record from a primary table and all corresponding records from the related table. In Be Fruitful's database, for example, you could set up a main form and subform in which customer data is displayed in the main form and the matching orders data is displayed in the subform. This is what you'll do next.

In this exercise, you'll create a main form and a subform based on the BFCustomers and BFOrders tables that will enable you to view a customer's record along with all the associated orders.

1. Make sure the Tables object tab is selected in the Be Fruitful Database window and highlight the BFCustomers table.

The BFCustomers table will be the main form.

2. Click the Insert menu; then click Form.

The New Form dialog box appears.

3. Double-click Form Wizard.

You'll see the Form Wizard dialog box, which lets you choose the tables and fields to include in the form.

4. From the BFCustomers table, add CustomerID, ContactLastName, ContactFirstName, BillingAddress, City, StateOrProvince, and ZIPCode to the Selected Fields list.

These fields will make up the main form.

5. Click the Tables/Queries drop-down arrow and select Table: BFOrders.

The fields from the BFOrders table now appear in the Available Fields list box.

6. Add OrderDate, FruitType, Quantity, PaymentDate, and PaymentAmount to the Selected Fields list.

The fields from both the primary and related tables are selected.

7. Click the Next button.

A new dialog box appears. This dialog box asks how you would like to view the data. The Form with Subform(s) option button is selected by default.

8. Leave the Form with Subform(s) option selected and click Next.

The next dialog box asks you to choose the layout.

9. Click the Tabular option button and click Next.

10. Choose the Flax style in the dialog box that appears and click Next.

11. Accept the form and subform names suggested by Access by clicking the Finish button.

Access names your forms and displays the first record from the primary table as the main form and the related records in the subform, as in Figure 7-20.

You will notice a vertical scroll bar on the right side of the subform—to see all the orders for this customer, just scroll through them!

As you scroll through the forms, you will also notice two sets of navigation buttons—one set to choose the customer and another to choose the order for that customer.

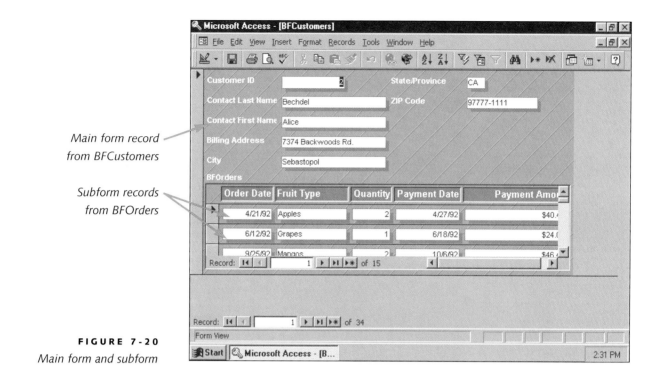

*Main form record
from BFCustomers*

*Subform records
from BFOrders*

FIGURE 7-20
Main form and subform

OFFICE ASSISTANT   *Access doesn't restrict you to creating a main form and a subform at the same time. Use the Office Assistant to learn how to create a subform and add it to an existing form or to change an existing form into a subform.*

12. Click the Print toolbar button.

A hard copy of your form is printed.

13. Close the form.

You return to the Database window.

14. Close the **Be Fruitful** database and exit Access.

LESSON SUMMARY AND EXERCISES

After you complete this lesson, you should know how to do the following:

MODIFYING FORMS IN DESIGN VIEW

- To view a form in Design view, select the form in the Database window and click the Design button.

- To change the length of a section, drag the bottom line of dots in the section.

- To add text to a Form Header, click the Label toolbox button, click and drag to create a box for the text, and type the text.

- To change the width of a control, select the control and drag a sizing handle.

- To change the appearance of a control, select the control and change the font characteristics from the Formatting toolbar.

- To change the position of an individual control, select the control and drag the move handle to the new position.

- To change the position of linked controls, select either control and drag the border to the new position.

- To change the sequence in which ⟨Tab⟩ moves the insertion point from one field to another in a form, click the View menu and choose Tab Order. Drag and drop field names to change their order in the list box.

MODIFYING REPORTS IN DESIGN VIEW

- To view a report in Design view, select the report in the Database window and click the Design button.

- To change the appearance of the Report Header, select the header and use the Formatting toolbar buttons.

- To change the report margins, click the File menu and choose Page Setup. Click the Margins tab and enter new values for the margins.

- To adjust control widths, choose the control from the Select Object drop-down list box. Drag the handles left or right.

WORKING WITH MULTIPLE TABLES

- To create a relationship between two tables, click the Relationships toolbar button. In the Show Table dialog box, select the tables you wish to relate. To establish the relationship, drag the primary key from one table to the foreign key in the related table. Then click the Create button.

- To edit a relationship, double-click the thin line that connects the primary and foreign keys.

- To enforce referential integrity, edit the relationship and select the Enforce Referential Integrity check box.

- To enable deletion of records from the primary table and the related table automatically, edit the relationship and select the Cascade Delete Related Records check box.

CREATING MAIN FORMS AND SUBFORMS

■ To create a form within a form, click the Insert menu and choose Form. Double-click the Form Wizard option, and then add the fields from both the primary and related tables. Click the Forms with Subform(s) option button in the Form Wizard dialog box.

NEW TERMS TO REMEMBER

After you complete this lesson, you should know the meaning of the following terms:

Cascading Deletes	many-to-many	primary table
Cascading Updates	relationship	referential integrity
controls	move handles	related table
foreign key	one-to-many	sections
grid lines	relationship	sizing handles
handles	one-to-one	Snap to Grid
main form	relationship	subform
	orphan records	tab order

MATCHING EXERCISE

Match the terms on the left with the definitions on the right:

TERMS

1. move handle

2. controls

3. subform

4. tab order

5. Cascading Deletes

6. Detail section

7. referential integrity

8. related table

9. primary table

10. foreign key

DEFINITIONS

a. Manner in which Access moves from field to field in Form view when you press Tab

b. Area of form in Design view that contains data that will be repeated for each record

c. In a one-to-many relationship, the table that contains the primary key

d. Handle on a control that lets you reposition that control individually

e. In a one-to-many relationship, the table that contains the foreign key

f. A form within another form

g. Common field in related table that matches a primary key in the primary table

h. Deletions in a primary table that are automatically reflected in the related table

i. Set of rules that Access enforces to ensure that your data makes sense

j. Elements of form that you can select and modify

COMPLETION EXERCISE

Fill in the missing word or phrase for each of the following:

1. The horizontal and vertical lines in Design view that allow you to precisely align your data are called the _____.

2. When you want to move two linked controls together in Design view, you must drag the controls' _____.

3. A(n) _____ is a box on a selected item used to change the size, shape, or position of the item.

4. The Label button used to create text boxes can be found on a special set of buttons called the _____.

5. Information that appears at the top of every page in a report appears in the _____ section of the Design window.

6. A(n) _____ relationship has one primary record connected to one, many, or no records in the related table.

7. To have Access automatically change records in the related table when you change the record in the primary table, turn on the _____ option.

8. To have Access automatically delete records from the related table when you delete the record from the primary table, turn on the _____ option.

9. If referential integrity is not enforced, a related table may contain _____ records which are not associated to a record in the primary table.

10. Use the _____ button on the _____ toolbar to change the background color of a section.

SHORT-ANSWER QUESTIONS

Write a brief answer to each of the following questions:

1. List at least two things Access prohibits when you enforce referential integrity.

2. What is the foreign key in a one-to-many relationship, and why can it *not* be a unique field?

3. Briefly describe tab order and when you would be likely to change the tab order for a form.

4. Mention one advantage and one potential disadvantage of activating the Cascading Deletes feature when you enforce referential integrity.

5. Name the toolbar you use to change the color of text in Design view. Explain how to display this toolbar if it's not already in view.

6. Mention three ways you could make a label stand out in a form.

7. Explain the difference between a one-to-one and a one-to-many relationship.

8. Describe how you would add Enforce Referential Integrity and Cascading Deletes to a relationship you had already created and saved.

9. List two ways to select a control in Design view. How could you select more than one control at a time?

10. Describe how you could remove a relationship between two tables. (Hint: The answer is not found directly in the lesson.) What Access feature can you use to find the answer if you cannot guess it yourself?

APPLICATION PROJECTS

Perform the following actions to complete these projects:

1. Modify the Joined After 1995 Tabular Form in the **Be Fruitful** database of the **Lessons** folder in your Student Data Disk. Rearrange the fields so that the Contact Last Name field appears before the Contact First Name field. Don't forget to move both the labels and controls. Save the revised form as **Joined After 1995 New**. Print one page of the form.

2. Open the Customer Names and Addresses report in Design view. Resize and rearrange the controls so that you can see more records at once on a page. Preview the report to see if you notice any problems. If any fields spill over to the next page, or if any text is cut off, correct the problems. As you preview the report, note whether more than three records print per page. If not, try to figure out how to decrease the space between records and print more than three records per page. Save the revised report as **Customer Names and Addresses New**. Print the report.

3. With the **Be Fruitful** database active, open the Relationships window and add the BFFruit table. Drag from the FruitType field in the BFFruit table to the FruitType field in the BFOrders table to establish a relationship between these two tables. In the Relationships dialog box that appears, click the Create button without selecting the Enforce Referential Integrity check box. (Access will insert a line to join the two fields but will not include the symbols that indicate which is the "one" and which the "many" table.) Close the Relationships window and save the changes. Delete the Apples record from the BFFruit table and print the BFOrders table to see that apple orders are still present. On a separate piece of paper, explain why Access did not delete the records in the BFOrders table that contain orders for apples.

4. Open the **Music** database in the **Projects** folder of your Student Data Disk. Create a one-to-many relationship between the Recordings and Recording Artists tables. Note that Recording Artists must be the primary table, because it contains the primary key. Select Enforce Referential Integrity and the Cascade Delete Related Records options. Save the relationship. Delete the record for Eric Clapton in the Recording Artists table and print both the Recording Artists and Recordings tables. (Note: In order to complete this project, you must have created the database and table in the Application Projects in Lessons 2 and 3.)

5. In the **Music** database, ensure that you have created a one-to-many relationship between the Recording Artists and Recordings tables. Then, create a main form and subform using the Recordings and Recording Artists tables. Select a layout of your choice and include the fields you feel are appropriate. Select the Standard style. Name the form **Artists and Their Albums** and name the subform **Artists and Their Albums Subform**. Change at least one border color, border style, and text color. Change the font size of one field in the main form. Preview the form and make any necessary adjustments. Print the form. (Note: In order to complete this project, you must have created the database and table in the Applications Projects in Lessons 2 and 3.)

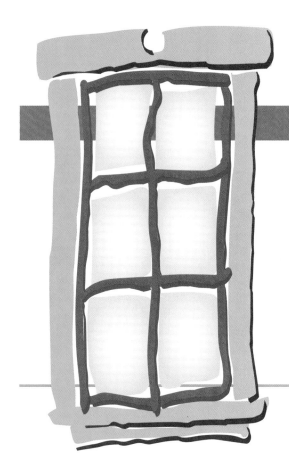

EXPLORING

HYPERLINKS

AND THE WEB

OBJECTIVES

After you complete this lesson, you will be able to do the following:

- *Display and understand the Web toolbar.*
- *Create a hyperlink to another object.*
- *Create a hyperlink to another database.*
- *Create a hyperlink to a Web site.*
- *Use the Go menu to visit a Web site.*
- *Access the Search Page and perform a search.*
- *Set and return to favorite places.*
- *Create a Web page.*
- *Publish your Web page.*

CONTENTS

Exploring the Web Toolbar

Creating Hyperlinks

Navigating on the Web

Creating Your Own Web Page

Publishing Your Web Page

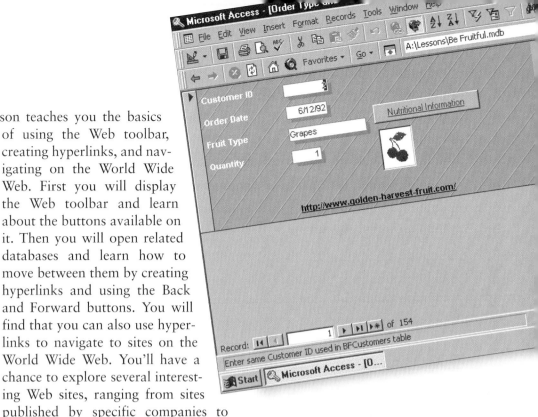

This lesson teaches you the basics of using the Web toolbar, creating hyperlinks, and navigating on the World Wide Web. First you will display the Web toolbar and learn about the buttons available on it. Then you will open related databases and learn how to move between them by creating hyperlinks and using the Back and Forward buttons. You will find that you can also use hyperlinks to navigate to sites on the World Wide Web. You'll have a chance to explore several interesting Web sites, ranging from sites published by specific companies to sites created by individuals who provide recipes. Since the Web contains so much information, this lesson will show you how to use a search engine to find specific information that you need. Lastly, you'll create your own Web page and learn how to publish it on the Internet.

EXPLORING THE WEB TOOLBAR

While in Design or Datasheet view, you may have noticed two buttons on the toolbar that you haven't yet explored—the Insert Hyperlink and Web Toolbar buttons. Using these and other toolbar buttons, Access allows you to link to other documents as well as to move to sites on the **World Wide Web** (or the **Web**), the most widely used system to navigate the Internet. The Web toolbar, which you'll learn to open in the following steps, includes other helpful tools.

World Wide Web (or **Web**)
A widely used tool to navigate the Internet.

N O T E   *Since you will be working with several databases and related files in Lesson 8, make sure all of the following files are contained on your current Student Data Disk before you begin the Lesson 8 activities:*

- *Be Fruitful database*

- *Shipping Charges database*

- *Fruit Information database*

- *Cherries.bmp*

HANDS ON

1. Open the **Be Fruitful** database in the **Lessons** folder on your Student Data Disk.

2. Click the Queries tab and open the California Phone Numbers query.

3. On the toolbar, click the Web Toolbar button.

The Web toolbar appears as shown in Figure 8-1. It contains the most frequently used Web commands.

N O T E   *Depending on various factors, the Web toolbar may appear above or below the other toolbar(s) currently displayed.*

Web toolbar ⟶

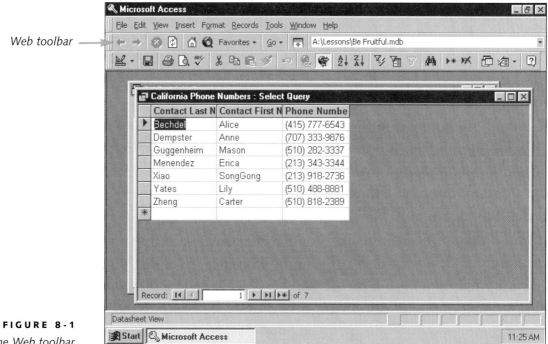

F I G U R E 8 - 1

The Web toolbar

Table 8-1 shows the buttons and menus that are available on the Web toolbar.

TABLE 8-1: WEB TOOLBAR BUTTONS AND MENUS

TOOLBAR BUTTONS		DESCRIPTION
Back	⇐	Displays the previous file or site that you visited (up to 10 sites).
Forward	⇒	Displays the next file or site that you visited (up to 10 sites).
Stop Current Jump	⊗	Stops the connection in progress.
Refresh Current Page	⊡	Reloads the current page.
Start Page	⌂	Loads the Microsoft Start Page or the Web page that you have specified as your Start Page.
Search the Web	◉	Loads the Microsoft Search Page or the Web page that you have specified as your Search Page.
Favorites menu	Favorites ▾	Allows you to add and access databases and Web sites that you frequently use.

Go menu	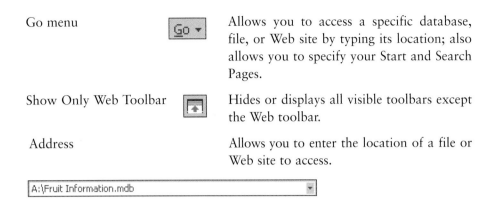	Allows you to access a specific database, file, or Web site by typing its location; also allows you to specify your Start and Search Pages.
Show Only Web Toolbar		Hides or displays all visible toolbars except the Web toolbar.
Address		Allows you to enter the location of a file or Web site to access.

> A:\Fruit Information.mdb

CREATING HYPERLINKS

hyperlink A shortcut, or jump, that links you directly to another object, document, or Web site.

A **hyperlink** is a shortcut, or jump, that links you to another object, document, or Web site with the click of your mouse. The text in objects that contain hyperlinks is shown in color, usually blue, and is underlined. After you select a hyperlink, the hyperlink changes in color (usually to purple) to indicate that you previously selected the hyperlink. In Access, hyperlinks can be added to tables, forms, and reports.

LINKING TO ANOTHER OBJECT

While working in a database, you can always return to the Database window to open another object within the database. Often, two or more objects are related and you'll find yourself switching back and forth between them to access information from each. In cases such as these, you can use a hyperlink to jump quickly from one object to another. For instance, while viewing and analyzing customer information in the BFCustomers table, you may want to link to another table or query that contains specific information about a group of customers. To do this, you can link the two objects with a hyperlink.

In the following steps, you'll create a new query and then create a hyperlink field in the BFCustomers table that links to a few queries in the Be Fruitful database.

CREATING A NEW QUERY

HANDS ON

1. Click the View toolbar button to see the California Phone Numbers query in Design view.

2. Select the text "CA" in the Criteria row of the StateOrProvince field and replace it with **"RI"**

Changing the criteria to RI will find all of the phone numbers for Rhode Island customers instead of those for California.

3. Click the File menu and choose Save As/Export. In the Save As dialog box, name the new query **Rhode Island Phone Numbers** and click OK.

4. Click the Close button to return to the Database window.

CREATING THE FIRST HYPERLINK

HANDS ON

1. Open the BFCustomers table and maximize the window.

2. Click the ZIP Code field selector to highlight the entire column.

3. Click the Insert menu and choose Hyperlink Column.

A new column appears between the State/Province and ZIP Code fields and the insertion point moves to the first record within that column, as shown in Figure 8-2. Since the state for this record is California, you are going to create a hyperlink to jump to the query that displays the phone numbers for all of the customers in California.

New hyperlink column

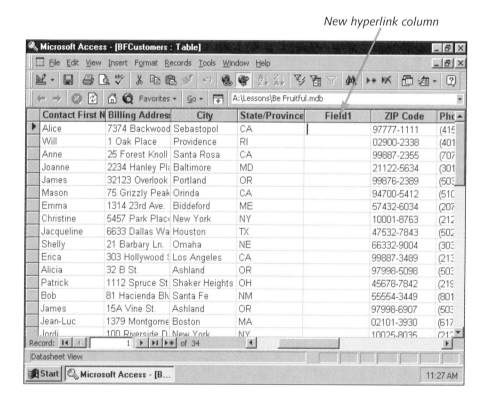

FIGURE 8-2
Hyperlink column added

NOTE   *You can designate an existing field as a hyperlink field by changing its Data Type in Design view.*

4. Click the Insert Hyperlink toolbar button.

The Insert Hyperlink dialog box appears.

5. Click the Browse button next to the Link to File or URL box.

The Link to File dialog box appears.

6. Using the Link to File dialog box, locate the **Be Fruitful** database in the **Lessons** folder on your Student Data Disk. Select the database and click OK.

Access inserts the name of the database in the dialog box.

When you are linking to an object within the current database, filling in this box is optional. If you leave it blank, Access assumes that you want to link to an object within the active database.

7. Click the Browse button next to the Named Location in File box.

The Select Location dialog box appears.

8. Click the Queries tab and then select the California Phone Numbers query.

9. Click OK.

Access returns to the completed Insert Hyperlink dialog box, as shown in Figure 8-3.

Database to link to

Object within database to link to

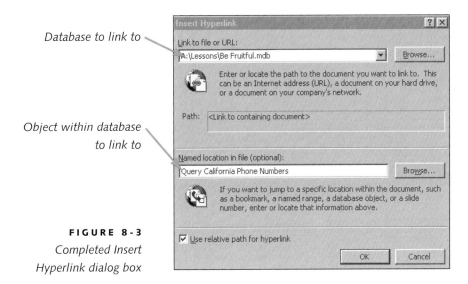

FIGURE 8-3
Completed Insert Hyperlink dialog box

10. Click OK to return to the BFCustomers table.

Press ⬇ to move the cursor to the next record. Note that the hyperlink is now visible in the column labeled Field1. The text, which displays the name of the object to which it will link, appears in blue and is underlined to indicate that a hyperlink exists.

11. Point to the hyperlink.

Notice that the mouse pointer changes from the shape of an I-beam to the shape of a hand.

12. Click the hyperlink.

Access opens and jumps to the California Phone Numbers query. As shown in Figure 8-4, this query displays the phone numbers of all of the customers who live in California.

13. Click the Back button on the Web toolbar to return to the BFCustomers table.

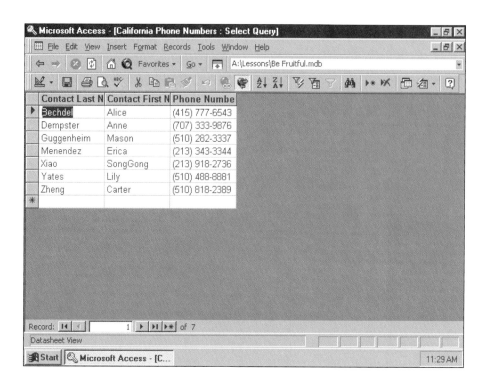

FIGURE 8-4

*Access links to the
specified query*

TIP   *To return to the previously viewed object, you can click the Back button on the Web toolbar or you can choose the object's name from the Window menu.*

OFFICE ASSISTANT   *To find out how to modify a hyperlink stored in a table, ask the Office Assistant.*

CREATING MORE HYPERLINKS

HANDS ON

1. Move to the second record and place the insertion point in the Field1 hyperlink column.

2. Click the Insert Hyperlink toolbar button.

The Insert Hyperlink dialog box appears.

3. Leave the Link to File or URL box blank and click the Browse button next to the Named Location in File box.

The Select Location dialog box appears.

NOTE   *Remember, when linking to an object within the active database, you can leave the Link to File or URL box blank.*

4. Click the Queries tab if it is not already selected and then select the Rhode Island Phone Numbers query.

5. Click OK.

Access returns to the completed Insert Hyperlink dialog box.

6. Click OK to return to the BFCustomers table.

Notice that the hyperlink that jumps to the California Phone Numbers query is purple in color while the new hyperlink is blue. Purple indicates that a hyperlink has been previously selected. Blue indicates that a hyperlink has not yet been selected.

7. Move the insertion point to Field1 for the third record.

You can also type the name of an object in the active database to create a hyperlink. This method will only work if the field (column) has already been designated as a hyperlink field.

8. Type **California Phone Numbers** and press ⌈Enter⌋.

9. Click the Rhode Island Phone Numbers hyperlink.

Access opens and jumps to the Rhode Island Phone Numbers query. As shown in Figure 8-5, this query points out that the current record contains information for the only customer who lives in Rhode Island.

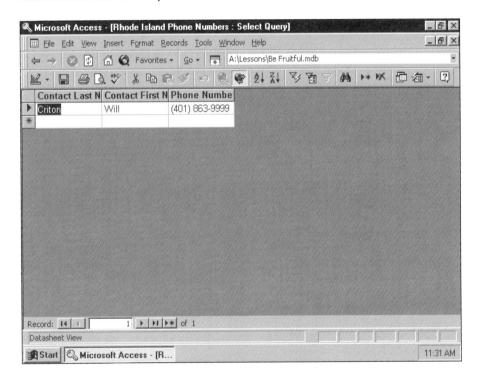

FIGURE 8-5

Access links to the specific query

10. Return to the BFCustomers table and try out your third hyperlink.

NOTE *If you create a hyperlink field within a table and then create a form that contains the hyperlink field, you can jump from that form to the linked object.*

11. Close the California Phone Numbers and Rhode Island Phone Numbers queries and then close the BFCustomers table.

Access returns you to the Database window.

NOTE *If you close the table containing the hyperlinks before closing the queries, you may get an error message and your new field may be repositioned.*

LINKING TO ANOTHER DATABASE

Access not only allows you to link from one object to another in the same database but also to link to another database. If the database to which you are linking is not open, Access automatically opens the document for you. In forms, you can create hyperlinks that appear as text, pictures, buttons, and other shapes. You'll learn how to create various hyperlinks in this section.

CREATING A TEXT HYPERLINK

In the following steps, you will create an AutoForm from the BFOrders table. Then, while using the form to enter an additional record, you'll create a link to a database that contains shipping prices.

1. In the Database window, click the Tables tab and select the BFOrders table.

2. Click the arrow next to the New Object toolbar button and select AutoForm.

Access generates an AutoForm with the fields and records from the BFOrders table as shown in Figure 8-6.

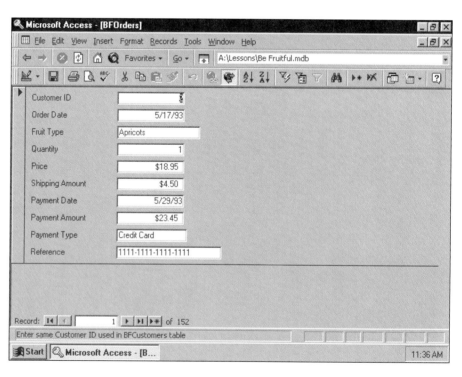

FIGURE 8-6

BFOrders AutoForm

3. Maximize the AutoForm window if it is not already maximized.

4. Click the New Record toolbar button.

5. Enter the following information into the new record on the form.

Customer ID:	**4**
Order Date:	**7/9/98**
Fruit Type:	**Apricots**
Quantity:	**2**
Price:	**18.95**

Now you need to find the shipping amount charged to a customer who orders two items. To do so, you can create a hyperlink to another database which contains shipping charges.

 6. If the Web toolbar is not displayed, click the Web Toolbar button on the toolbar.

 7. Click the View toolbar button to view the AutoForm in Design view.

N O T E   *You must display a form in Design view before creating a hyperlink.*

 8. Click the Insert Hyperlink toolbar button.

The Insert Hyperlink dialog box appears.

N O T E   *You can also choose Hyperlink from the Insert menu to create a hyperlink.*

9. Click the Browse button next to the Link to File or URL box.

10. Locate the database named Shipping Charges on your Student Data Disk. Select it and then click OK to return to the Insert Hyperlink dialog box.

11. Click the Browse button next to the Named Location in File box.

12. Click the Tables tab, select the Shipping Charges table, and click OK.

Your Insert Hyperlink dialog box will resemble the one shown in Figure 8-7.

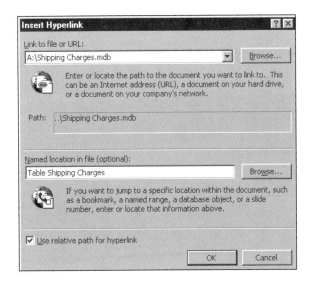

FIGURE 8-7

Insert Hyperlink dialog box

13. Click OK.

A hyperlink appears at the top of the Detail section. Like most hyperlinks, the text is shown in blue and underlined. When you create a hyperlink in a form, the text shows the path and file name of the file to which it links. However, you can change this text.

14. With the hyperlink selected, as you can tell by the presence of selection handles, click the Properties toolbar button.

NOTE   *You can also right-click the hyperlink and choose Properties from the shortcut menu that appears.*

15. If it is not already selected, click the Format tab in the Label dialog box that appears.

The Label box contains information specific to the hyperlink or control selected. Information displayed includes the name of the hyperlink, its color and text style, and other information.

16. If it is not already selected, highlight the text in the Caption box.

17. Type **Customer Shipping Charges** so that this text replaces the current text.

The Label dialog box should resemble Figure 8-8.

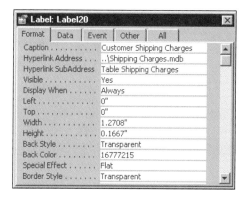

FIGURE 8-8

The Label dialog box

18. Click the Close button in the top-right corner of the Label dialog box.

The text for the hyperlink changes to Customer Shipping Charges.

19. Place the mouse pointer over a border of the hyperlink and drag it so that the hyperlink appears to the right of the Shipping Amount label and control.

The hyperlink will look like the one shown in Figure 8-9.

20. Resize the hyperlink field if necessary so that all of the text is readable.

21. Click the View toolbar button to return to Form view.

The new hyperlink appears next to the Shipping Amount field. Now you're ready to finish entering data for the new record.

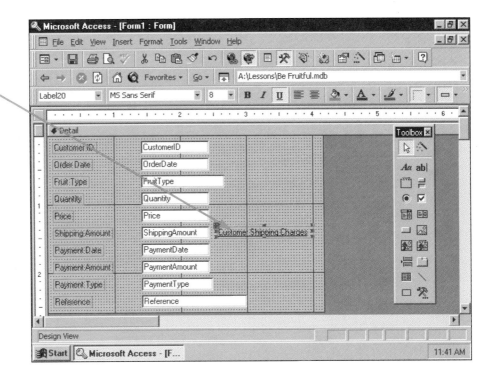

Place new hyperlink here

FIGURE 8-9
Placement of the new hyperlink

22. Click the Last Record navigation button to return to the last record.

23. To find the shipping charges for two items purchased, click the Customer Shipping Charges hyperlink.

N O T E *To jump to the file linked to the hyperlink, you must be in Form view. Clicking a hyperlink in Design view will simply select it.*

The Shipping Charges table in the Shipping Charges database opens and you can see that the charge to send two items is $6.50.

24. Click the Back button or click the first Access taskbar button to return to the BFOrders AutoForm. Enter **6.50** in the Shipping Amount field.

N O T E *When you link to an object in another database, a second occurrence of Access is opened to display that object. To switch between the databases, you can click the taskbar buttons at the bottom of the screen.*

25. Complete the record by entering the following information:

Payment Date: 7/20/98
Payment Amount: 44.40
Payment Type: Credit Card
Reference: 2222-2222-2222

26. Enter another new record with the following information:

Customer ID: 17
Order Date: 7/23/98
Fruit Type: **Mangos**
Quantity: 4
Price: 19.95
Payment Date: 8/1/98
Payment Type: **Check**
Reference: **#987**

27. Use the Forward button on the Web toolbar or the Customer Shipping Charges hyperlink to return to the Shipping Charges table to find the appropriate shipping amount. Enter the shipping amount in the field.

TIP   *You can use the Forward and Back toolbar buttons to move between the two documents.*

28. Calculate the Payment Amount and enter it in the appropriate field.

TIP   *The price ($19.95) is for the quantity of one. Remember to multiply the price by the quantity and add the shipping charges to determine the Payment Amount.*

29. Close the Shipping Charges table and database. Then, close the BFOrders AutoForm. When asked if you want to save the form, answer Yes and name the form **BFOrders AutoForm with Shipping Hyperlink**.

CREATING A COMMAND BUTTON HYPERLINK

In the following steps, you'll create a hyperlink that appears on a form in the shape of a button.

HANDS ON

1. Open the Order Type and Quantity form in the Be Fruitful database.

A database appears that lists the customer ID, date, quantity, and fruit type for each order placed. The customer service representatives at Be Fruitful can access this information while speaking to customers on the telephone. While talking to customers, they are often asked questions related to the season and the nutritional value of various fruits. Rather than closing this database and opening another one to access that information, you can create hyperlinks to the databases that contain the needed information.

2. Click the View toolbar button to switch to Design view.

3. If the toolbox is not displayed on screen, click the Toolbox toolbar button.

4. Click the Command Button button in the toolbox.

As you move the mouse pointer, it changes from the shape of an arrow to the shape of a button.

5. Click to the right of the FruitType control.

A command button appears, similar to the one shown in Figure 8-10.

N O T E *If the Command Button Wizard dialog box appears, simply press Cancel to close it.*

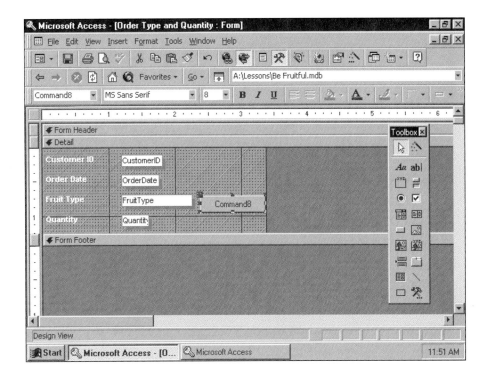

FIGURE 8-10

*Creating a
command button*

6. With the command button selected, click the Properties toolbar button.

The Command Button dialog box appears.

7. In the Format tab of the Command Button dialog box, change the Caption text to **Nutritional Information**

8. Press Tab several times to move to the Hyperlink Address box.

9. Click the box to the far right of the Hyperlink Address box.

The Insert Hyperlink dialog box appears.

10. Click the Browse button next to the Link to File or URL box, find and select the Fruit Information database on the Student Data Disk, and click OK.

11. Click the Browse button next to the Named Location in File box, select the Nutritional Information table, and click OK.

12. Click OK to return to the Command Button dialog box which should look similar to the one in Figure 8-11.

13. Click the Close button to close the Command Button dialog box.

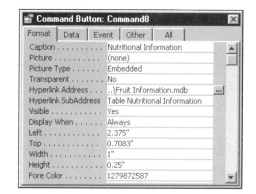

FIGURE 8-11

*Completed Command
Button dialog box*

14. If necessary, resize the command button so that you can see all of the text and move it so that it appears in a location similar to the one shown in Figure 8-12.

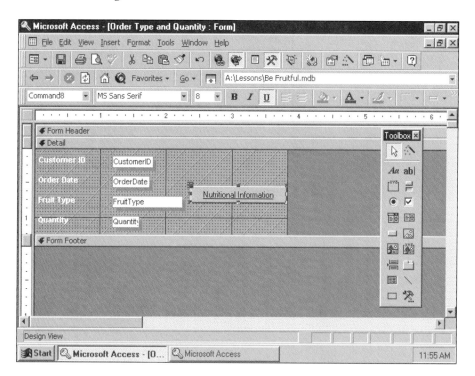

FIGURE 8-12

*Command button
hyperlink*

 15. Click the Image button on the toolbox.

16. Move the mouse pointer, which now takes the shape of a square picture, directly below the Nutritional Information command button hyperlink and click the mouse button to place an image.

The Insert Picture dialog box appears.

17. Locate and select the Cherries.bmp file on the Student Data Disk. Click OK.

A picture of two cherries appears. To change the picture to a hyperlink, you'll need to change its properties.

18. With the picture selected, click the Properties toolbar button.

19. In the Format tab of the Image dialog box that appears, click in the Hyperlink Address box.

20. Click the button that appears to the right of the Hyperlink Address box.

The Insert Hyperlink dialog box appears.

21. Use the Browse buttons to place the Fruit Information database in the Link to File or URL box and the Fruit Characteristics table in the Named Location in File box.

The Insert Hyperlink dialog box should look like the one in Figure 8-13.

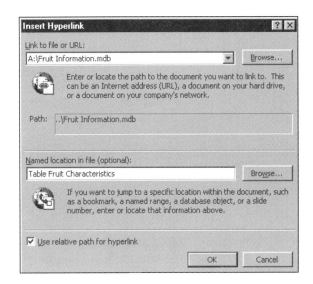

FIGURE 8-13

The Insert Hyperlink dialog box

22. Click OK.

23. Click the Close box to close the Image dialog box.

You've now created two new hyperlinks. You'll need to switch to Form view to test them out.

24. Click the View toolbar button to switch to Form view.

N O T E   *You can also follow these steps to create a hyperlink in a report. However, you can't activate the hyperlink directly from the report in Design view or in Print Preview view. Instead, you must output the report to Microsoft Word, Excel, or an HTML format.*

25. Navigate to the record for customer number 2 with an order date of 11/3/97.

This customer wants to know how many calories are in a pomegranate.

26. Click the Nutritional Information command button.

The hyperlink opens the Nutritional Information table of the Fruit Information database. As you can see by scrolling to the Pomegranates fruit type, each fruit contains 104 calories.

NOTE   *Each time you click a hyperlink, another occurrence of Access is opened to display the new file or object. You will see an Access taskbar button at the bottom of the screen for each database that is opened.*

27. Navigate back to the Order Type and Quantity form by clicking the first Microsoft Access taskbar button.

The customer would also like to know when pomegranates are in season and what ripe pomegranates should look like.

28. Click the image of the cherries to link to the Fruit Characteristics table.

Scroll down to find the needed information for pomegranates.

29. Close the Fruit Characteristics and Nutritional Information tables and then close the **Fruit Information** database. Close the occurrence of Access that contained this database.

TIP   *To avoid clutter on your Windows taskbar at the bottom of the screen, you may close the other open Access programs. To close a program directly from the taskbar, right-click its taskbar button and choose Close from the shortcut menu that appears.*

NOTE   *You can use these same steps to create hyperlinks to other types of documents, such as Microsoft Word or PowerPoint files.*

LINKING TO A WEB SITE

You can also insert a hyperlink to a Web site instead of to another Access document. Web sites on just about any topic imaginable are available on the Internet. The process for creating a Web hyperlink is very similar to that of creating a hyperlink for a file.

In the following steps, you'll create a hyperlink to a Web site published by a potential competitor of Be Fruitful.

HANDS ON

1. Make sure that you are in Design view of the Order Type and Quantity form, and click the Insert Hyperlink toolbar button.

The Insert Hyperlink dialog box appears.

2. In the Link to File or URL box, type **http://www.golden-harvest-fruit.com** and click OK.

NOTE   *Verify that you typed the URL correctly before you click OK.*

3. Drag the new hyperlink to the bottom-center of the form.

NOTE   *If the hyperlink is difficult to see because it blends in with the background color of the form, click the arrow next to the Fill/Back Color icon and select a different color for your hyperlink command button.*

TIP   *To remove a hyperlink from a cell, right-click the hyperlink while in Design view and choose Hyperlink, Edit Hyperlink from the shortcut menu. Then select Remove Link.*

4. Click the View toolbar button to switch to Form view.

The label *http://www.golden-harvest-fruit.com* becomes a hyperlink as shown in Figure 8-14. When you click the hyperlink, Access will jump to the site located at the specified URL. A **URL** (Uniform Resource Locator) is the "address" of a Web site. A URL can be made up of letters, numbers, and special symbols that are understood by the Internet.

URL The address used to identify a Web site. Stands for *Uniform Resource Locator.*

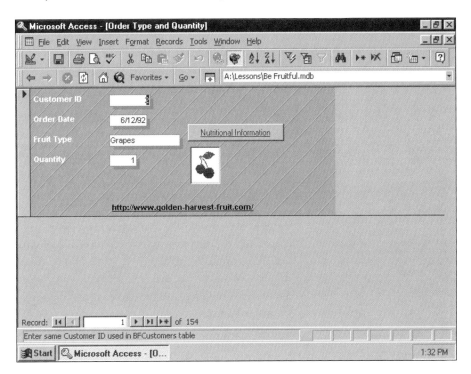

FIGURE 8-14

The Web address becomes a hyperlink

5. Click your new hyperlink to test it.

W A R N I N G

If your connection to the Internet is already active, Access will jump directly to the Golden Harvest Fruit Company Web site. If your connection to the Internet is not active, either the Sign In or Connect To dialog box will appear so that you can connect to the Internet or you will receive an error message telling you that no connection is established. Sign in or connect to your Internet service provider, if necessary, to continue.

Be patient! Many factors affect the speed of the connection to the Internet and Web sites; sometimes you'll connect instantly and other times it will take several minutes. Some of the factors that affect the connection time include the speed of your modem, the Internet service provider you are using, and the number of other people using the Internet at the moment.

6. When the Web page for the Golden Harvest Fruit Company appears, click the option to find out what kind of products the company offers. (It may be under a link called Products & Schedules.)

Keep in mind that Web pages use both text and graphics as hyperlinks to other pages. You will know when you are pointing to a hyperlink because your mouse pointer changes to the shape of a hand.

NOTE   *Web page owners update their pages constantly, so don't be surprised if you look at the same Web page tomorrow and the links have changed or the page looks different.*

7. Click the Back button to return to the previous page.

8. Click the option to find out about the fund-raising tips that Golden Harvest offers to users.

NOTE   *You may click the Access button in the Windows taskbar to return to the Access document at any time.*

9. Disconnect from the Internet unless your instructor tells you to remain connected.

NOTE   *Ask your instructor for assistance in disconnecting from the Internet, if necessary.*

10. Return to Access.

NAVIGATING ON THE WEB

Sometimes you'll want to visit a Web site just once while you are working in Access. Other times you'll find Web sites that you will visit often, so you'll want to be able to return to them. Regardless, these sites may not be directly related to a specific database. For that reason, Access allows you to access any Web site without creating a hyperlink. You can even add the Web sites to a list of personal favorites so that you can return to them quickly and easily.

VISITING A WEB SITE

If you want to visit a Web site without creating a hyperlink in your database, you can use the Go menu available on the Web toolbar.

In the next set of instructions, you'll visit a Web site that provides information about a credit card. Be Fruitful is thinking about starting to accept this credit card as payment from customers, but they would like to learn more about it first.

HANDS ON

1. Click the Go menu on the Web toolbar and choose Open.

The Open Internet Address dialog box appears.

2. In the Address box, type **http://www.novusnet.com** as shown in Figure 8-15.

FIGURE 8-15
The Open Internet Address box

3. Click OK.

If your connection to the Internet is already active, Access will jump directly to the Novus Web site. If your connection is not active, sign in or connect to your Internet service provider to continue.

The Novus credit card Web page appears. Novus offers several popular credit cards including the Discover Card. Be Fruitful currently accepts Visa and MasterCard as payment and is trying to learn more about the benefits of accepting the Discover Card as well. You'll use this Web page to explore those benefits.

4. Follow the links on the Novus Web page to learn about becoming a Novus merchant. See if you can learn about the services offered by Novus. Then see if you can find a list of other merchants who accept Novus credit cards.

TIP *If a connection to a Web site is taking too long or if you need to cancel it for any other reason, click the Stop Current Jump button on the Web toolbar.*

5. When you are finished exploring the site, disconnect from the Internet (unless your instructor tells you to remain connected).

6. Return to Access by clicking on its taskbar button.

NOTE *Ask your instructor for assistance in disconnecting from the Internet, if necessary.*

ACCESSING THE SEARCH PAGE

As in the previous example, you may learn of specific URLs to which you can connect. However, often you'll want to use the Internet to find information on a specific topic, but you don't know the address of a specific site. In these cases, you will want to use the Search Page.

In the following steps, you'll search for a Web site that provides recipes that use fruit as a main ingredient.

1. Click the Search the Web button on the Web toolbar.

WARNING

browser A software program that allows you to navigate the World Wide Web and to access information on the Internet. Popular browsers are Netscape and Microsoft Internet Explorer.

If your connection to the Internet is already active, Access will jump directly to the page specified as your Search Page. If your connection is not active, sign in or connect to your Internet service provider to continue.

Access connects you to your Internet service provider and the page that is specified as your Search Page appears. If you are using The Microsoft Network, your Search Page may resemble the one shown in Figure 8-16.

NOTE *If you are using the Netscape **browser**, you'll notice that although the appearance of your Search Page differs from Figure 8-16, the content is similar.*

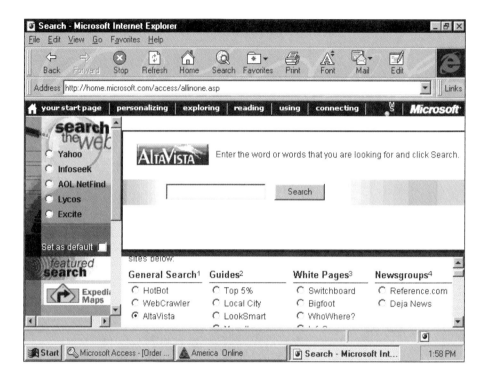

FIGURE 8-16
The Microsoft Search Page

OFFICE ASSISTANT

If you wish, ask your instructor for help changing your Search Page, or type **Set Search Page** *in the Office Assistant dialog box to get help.*

2. Type **recipes** in the Search text box.

In hopes of increasing the amount of business from current customers, Be Fruitful is starting a service that will provide fruit recipes to its customers. Using the World Wide Web, you should be able to find several appropriate recipes.

3. Select a search engine, if necessary, and process your search request.

4. When the results of your search appear, scroll down to see the numerous sites to which you can connect.

keyword Word or phrase used to define and narrow a search.

Most Search Pages allow you to type **keywords** to perform a search. Keywords are words that define your search. The results that you get from typing the keyword *recipes* will vary depending on the search engine you use, but they may resemble those in Figure 8-17.

NOTE

Most **search engines** *allow you to view the results of a search by titles or Web sites and with or without a summary of the Web page.*

search engine An Internet tool that allows you to search for information on a particular topic.

As you can see, the results will lead you to a variety of topics including recipes of all sorts using many types of foods and for many different meals. The top of the page will probably tell you how many results were found. For a search as general as this one, you are likely to find thousands of results. To narrow a search, you can use several keywords.

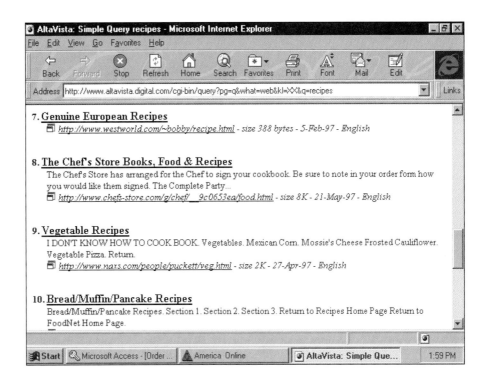

FIGURE 8-17

Initial search results

Screen content within figure:

AltaVista: Simple Query recipes - Microsoft Internet Explorer

File Edit View Go Favorites Help

Back Forward Stop Refresh Home Search Favorites Print Font Mail Edit

Address http://www.altavista.digital.com/cgi-bin/query?pg=q&what=web&kl=XX&q=recipes   Links

7. **Genuine European Recipes**
   http://www.westworld.com/~bobby/recipe.html - size 388 bytes - 5-Feb-97 - English

8. **The Chef's Store Books, Food & Recipes**
   The Chef's Store has arranged for the Chef to sign your cookbook. Be sure to note in your order form how you would like them signed. The Complete Party...
   http://www.chefs-store.com/g/chef/__9c0653ea/food.html - size 8K - 21-May-97 - English

9. **Vegetable Recipes**
   I DON'T KNOW HOW TO COOK BOOK. Vegetables. Mexican Corn. Mossie's Cheese Frosted Cauliflower. Vegetable Pizza. Return.
   http://www.naxs.com/people/puckett/veg.html - size 2K - 27-Apr-97 - English

10. **Bread/Muffin/Pancake Recipes**
    Bread/Muffin/Pancake Recipes. Section 1. Section 2. Section 3. Return to Recipes Home Page Return to FoodNet Home Page.

Start   Microsoft Access - [Order...   America Online   AltaVista: Simple Que...   1:59 PM

5. Return to the top of the Search Page (clicking the Back button if necessary) and type the keywords **"fresh fruit" recipes** in the Search text box.

NOTE *If you contain two or more words in quotation marks, most search engines will look for pages that contain those two words together in the order specified.*

6. Choose a search engine, if necessary, and process your search request.

When the results appear, scroll down to see them. The results you find may resemble those found in Figure 8-18. As you can see, the results using several keywords usually suggest sites that are more targeted to the information you are seeking.

7. From your results, choose a site that contains a recipe which sounds appealing to you. Click the hyperlink and explore the site.

NOTE *If the site does not provide the information that you thought it would, click the Back button and choose another site.*

8. Navigate back to the search results and choose a second recipe. Explore the site.

NOTE *You can print the contents of a page by clicking the Print button on the toolbar.*

9. After you have found a few recipes that use fruit as a main ingredient, disconnect from the Internet (unless your instructor tells you to remain connected).

10. Return to Access.

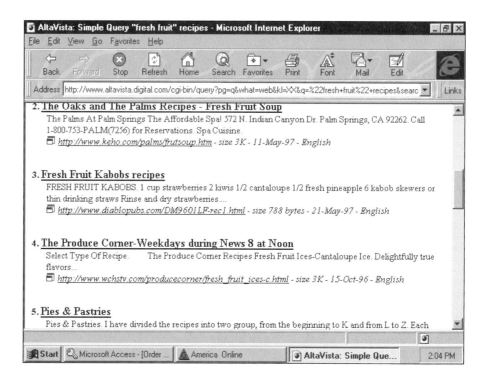

FIGURE 8-18
Second search results

NOTE

Access also allows you to choose a Start Page. Like the Search Page, this page provides a good starting point for exploring the Web. Instead of allowing you to type keywords to search for a specific topic, the Start Page provides links to dozens of interesting sites. Most Start Pages, such as Microsoft's Internet Start, change daily to provide variety for its users.

REVISITING FAVORITE PLACES

favorites or **bookmarks** Tools used to provide a shortcut to the location of a specific Web site or document so that you can return to it later without typing its address.

As you may be starting to realize, hundreds of thousands of Web sites are available at the click of your mouse. With so many sites available, you may have difficulty keeping track of the ones that you'll use most often. Access provides an easy way to do just that. You can keep a list of **favorites** or **bookmarks** to which you can return quickly.

In the following steps, you'll add a site to your list of favorites and return to it using the Favorites menu on the Web toolbar.

1. Click the Go menu on the Web toolbar and choose Open.

The Open Internet Address dialog box appears.

2. In the Address box, type **http://www.fedex.com** and click OK.

WARNING

If your connection to the Internet is already active, Access will jump directly to the Federal Express site. If your connection is not active, sign in or connect to your Internet service provider to continue.

In a moment, the Federal Express home page will appear on your screen. Be Fruitful sometimes uses this delivery service for rush deliveries.

3. Take a few minutes to explore the links on this page. See if you can find out how much it would cost to mail a 10-pound package valued at $50.00 from the city in which you live to ZIP Code 44117. Assume that you would use a FedEx box and schedule a FedEx courier to pick up the package.

4. Return to the Federal Express home page.

T I P *You can return to a home page by using the Back button or by typing its address in the Address box near the top of the screen. Some Web pages offer a hyperlink that you can click to return to the home page.*

5. Add this site to your list of favorite places.

The steps you take to do this will vary depending on the browser software you are using. Most browsers show a Favorites or Bookmarks menu from which you can select an option such as Add to Favorites or Add Bookmark.

T I P *If you are unsure how to add this site to your list of favorite places, access the Help menu on your browser software.*

6. Return to Access and make sure the Order Type and Quantity form is active.

Access allows you to add other documents to your list of favorites. You can use this feature to open documents quickly that you frequently use.

7. Click the Favorites menu on the Web toolbar and choose Add to Favorites as shown in Figure 8-19.

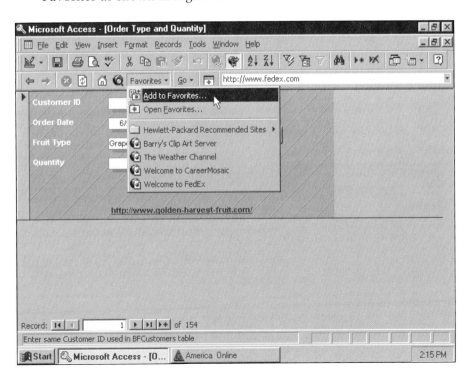

FIGURE 8-19

Favorites menu on the Web toolbar

8. When the Add To Favorites dialog box appears, make sure that Be Fruitful.mdb.url appears in the File Name box and click Add.

9. Close the Order Type and Quantity form and then close the Be Fruitful Database window. If asked if you want to save changes, click Yes.

Now you can return easily to the sites that you've designated as favorites or bookmarks.

10. To return to the Be Fruitful database, click the Favorites menu on the Web toolbar and choose Be Fruitful.mdb.

Access remembers where the database is stored and automatically retrieves the file. The Database window appears on the screen.

11. If you are using Microsoft Internet Explorer as your browser, click the Favorites menu on the Web toolbar and choose Welcome to FedEx.

NOTE

If you are using the Netscape browser, click the browser button on the Windows taskbar or click Start Page on the Web toolbar in Access. Then access your Bookmarks menu and choose Welcome to FedEx.

The Federal Express home page appears on the screen. Notice that you did not type the address to return to this Web page.

12. Disconnect from the Internet and return to Access.

13. Close all of the open databases.

CREATING YOUR OWN WEB PAGE

Hypertext Markup Language
A system for tagging a document so that it can be published and viewed by others on the Web.

Once you create a database, you may want to share it with others. You can share it with millions of people by publishing your page on the Web. Before you can publish your page, you must save it in a format that is readable by the Web. This format, called **Hypertext Markup Language** (HTML), is a system for tagging a document so that you can publish the document and allow others on the Web to view it.

In the following steps, you will save a database report as a Web page.

HANDS ON

1. Open the **Fruit Information** database on the Student Data Disk.

2. Create a tabular report that contains all of the fields and records from the Nutritional Information table. Choose any style you desire. Name the report **Nutritional Information Tabular Report**.

3. Change the text color, if desired.

4. Enlarge the size of the text and adjust the column widths if necessary.

OFFICE ASSISTANT

If you've forgotten how to change the font size, the text color, or the column widths, ask the Office Assistant for help.

Your report should resemble the one shown in Figure 8-20.

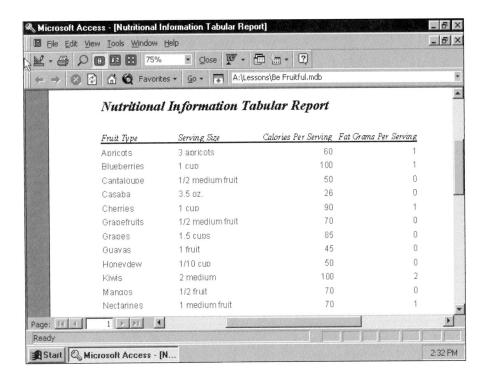

FIGURE 8-20
Nutritional Information Tabular Report

NOTE

Before you save an object as a Web page, enlarge the font size of the text. When published on the Web, large text is much easier to read. Also, variations of fonts and colors will catch the user's eye, so consider adding these enhancements to any object that you will publish as a Web page.

5. Click the Save toolbar button to save the report.

6. Click the File menu and choose Save As HTML.

The Publish to the Web Wizard appears. This wizard will guide you through the process of creating a Web page from a form, report, table, or query.

OFFICE ASSISTANT

If the Save as HTML option is not available on the File menu, you will need to run the Setup program to add the Web Page Authoring component. Ask your instructor or the Office Assistant for help.

7. Read the message in the first Publish to the Web Wizard dialog box and then click Next.

The second Publish to the Web Wizard dialog box appears.

8. Click the Reports tab and then select Nutritional Information Tabular Report by clicking the Select button. A check mark will appear in the check box, as shown in Figure 8-21.

9. Click Next to continue.

The third Publish to the Web Wizard dialog box appears.

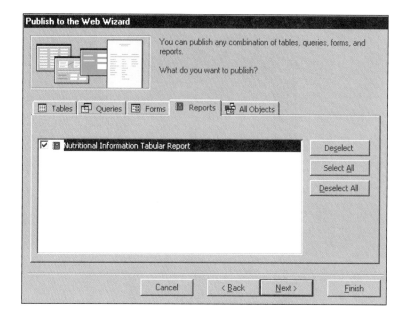

FIGURE 8-21

The second Publish to the Web Wizard dialog box

10. Make sure the box where you can insert the name of a template is blank and click Next.

The fourth Publish to the Web Wizard dialog box appears, as shown in Figure 8-22.

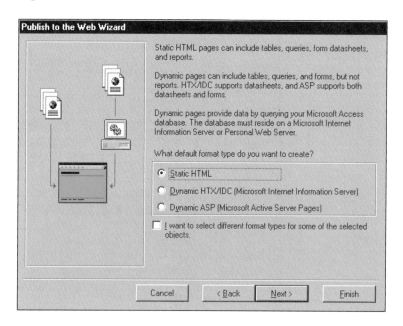

FIGURE 8-22

The fourth Publish to the Web Wizard dialog box

11. Make sure Static HTML is selected and click Next.

OFFICE ASSISTANT   *To learn the differences between static and dynamic HTML pages, ask the Office Assistant.*

12. In the fifth Publish to the Web Wizard dialog box, select the correct drive and folder in which to save your HTML page, as shown in Figure 8-23. Use the drive and folder to which you have been saving files. If the wrong location is shown in the dialog box, use the Browse button to change it.

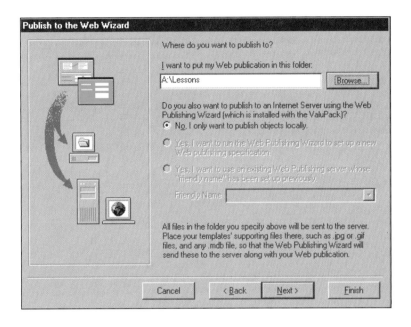

FIGURE 8-23

The fifth Publish to the Web Wizard dialog box

13. Click Next.

14. In the next dialog box, make sure that the Yes, I Want to Create a Home Page box is *not* selected, and click Next.

NOTE *You may wish to create a home page when you publish more than one object. A home page can be a starting point to connect all of the objects.*

15. In the final Publish to the Web Wizard dialog box, make sure that Yes, I Want to Save Wizard Answers to a Web Publication Profile is *not* selected and click Finish.

Access saves your Web page and returns you to the report you created. Although you cannot open and view the Web page in Access, you can open it in Microsoft Excel or Word. If one of these programs is available to you, start the program and click the Open toolbar button. When the Open dialog box appears, choose HTML Document(s) in the Files of Type box, find your newly created HTML document, and double-click it to open it. This particular report will probably look best when viewed in Excel.

16. Close your report and then close the Database window.

17. Exit Access.

PUBLISHING YOUR WEB PAGE

Now that you've created a Web page, you may want to share it with other Web users. To make your work accessible to others, you can publish it on your intranet or the World Wide Web. To add your work to an intranet or a network, contact your network administrator or your instructor. The process will vary depending on the type of system on which you are working.

To publish your work on the World Wide Web, you'll need to contact your local Internet service provider. Each service provider has unique requirements and will likely charge a fee for the space you use. Ask your instructor for additional details on publishing your Web page on the World Wide Web.

LESSON SUMMARY AND EXERCISES

After you complete this lesson, you should know how to do the following:

EXPLORING THE WEB TOOLBAR

- Open the Web toolbar by clicking the Web Toolbar button on the Standard toolbar.

- Understand the purpose of each of the buttons on the Web toolbar.

CREATING HYPERLINKS

- Use the Insert Hyperlink toolbar button to create a hyperlink to another object within the same database.

- Use the Insert Hyperlink toolbar button to create a hyperlink to another database.

- Use the Insert Hyperlink toolbar button to create a hyperlink to a Web site.

NAVIGATING ON THE WEB

- Navigate to a Web site by selecting the Go, Open command on the Web toolbar and then typing the URL of the site.

- Access the Search Page by clicking the Search the Web button on the Web toolbar and perform a search to find specific information.

- Set an Access document or a Web site as a favorite place or bookmark.

- Return to a favorite place using the Favorites menu on the Web toolbar.

CREATING YOUR OWN WEB PAGE

- Appropriately format a document before saving it as a Web page.

- Convert an Access document to a Web page by choosing File, Save as HTML from the menu bar.

PUBLISHING YOUR WEB PAGE

- Publish your Web page on the World Wide Web or your organization's intranet.

NEW TERMS TO REMEMBER

After you complete this lesson, you should know the meaning of these terms:

bookmarks	keyword
browser	search engine
favorites	URL
hyperlink	Web
Hypertext Markup Language	World Wide Web

MATCHING EXERCISE

Match each of the terms with the definitions on the right:

TERMS	DEFINITIONS
1. World Wide Web	**a.** Word(s) used to describe the topic for which you are searching
2. Stop Current Jump	**b.** A tool used to travel around the Internet
3. URL	**c.** Menu used to return to specified documents and Web sites
4. Search Page	
5. Start Page	**d.** Web page that offers various links to interesting topics
6. keyword	
7. hyperlink	**e.** The address of a Web site
8. navigate	**f.** The term used to describe moving around on the Internet
9. Go menu	
10. Favorites menu	**g.** Button used to cancel the current connection
	h. Identified by blue, underlined text
	i. Menu on the Web toolbar that allows you to type the address of a Web site
	j. Web page that lets you type keywords to find sites on a specific topic

COMPLETION EXERCISE

Fill in the missing word or phrase for each of the following statements:

1. When you point to a hyperlink in Form view, the mouse pointer changes to the shape of a(n) _____.

2. You can use the _____ and _____ buttons to navigate among active documents.

3. Setting favorite places or bookmarks allows you to _____ quickly to specific Web sites and documents.

4. The format used for tagging a document so that you can publish the document on the Web is called _____.

5. The _____ Wizard appears when you select File, Save As HTML from the menu bar.

6. To assign a hyperlink address to a command button, click the _____ toolbar button.

7. To remove a hyperlink from an object, right-click the hyperlink and choose _____ from the shortcut menu.

8. Use the _____ button to remove from your screen all toolbars except for the Web toolbar.

9. The address of a Web site is called the _____.

10. Hyperlinks allow you to jump instantly to a(n) _____, _____, or _____.

SHORT-ANSWER QUESTIONS

Write a brief answer to each of the following questions:

1. In what instances would you use the Stop Current Jump button?

2. If you create a hyperlink that links to another object within the same database, what should you type in the Link to File or URL box in the Insert Hyperlink dialog box?

3. Name at least three factors that might affect how quickly you can connect to a Web site.

4. List at least five keywords you could use on the Search Page to find information about a major league baseball team. Contrast the results you think you would get if you used one keyword versus five keywords.

5. How might you reformat an object before saving it as a Web page? Explain the purpose of reformatting an object.

6. How can you return to an Access database from a Web site?

7. What happens if you click a hyperlink in Design view? In Form view? In Report view?

8. List two ways to create a hyperlink in a form.

9. How can you jump to a Web site from Access without creating a hyperlink?

10. Describe the purpose of bookmarks or favorite places.

APPLICATION PROJECTS

Perform the following actions to complete these projects:

1. Open the **Be Fruitful** database in the **Lessons** folder on your Student Data Disk. Display the Web toolbar. Then, open the BFOrders AutoForm with Shipping Hyperlink form and add a text hyperlink that jumps to the BFFruit table. Move the hyperlink to the right of the Price control and change the caption to read Fruit Prices. Create a new record containing the following information:

Customer ID:	**28**
Order Date:	8/7/98
Fruit Type:	**Plums**
Quantity:	3
Payment Date:	8/16/98
Payment Type:	**Check**
Reference:	**#508**

Use the Fruit Prices and Customer Shipping Charges hyperlinks to find the correct values for the Price and Shipping Amount fields. Calculate the Payment Amount. Close the form and save the changes. Close the database.

2. Open the **Fruit Information** database on your Student Data Disk and then create an AutoForm that contains all of the fields and records in the Fruit Characteristics table. Create a command button hyperlink that jumps to the BFFruit table of the Be Fruitful database. Change the text in the command button to read Fruit Prices and Shipping Units. Place the command button in an appropriate spot on the form and resize it if necessary. Test your hyperlink to make sure it jumps to the correct database. Save the form as **Fruit Characteristics AutoForm**. Close both of the databases.

3. Create a new database called **Job Search** and save it in the **Projects** folder on your Student Data Disk. Within the database, create a table called **Employers** that includes the following fields: Position Available,

Company Name, Address, City, State, ZIP Code, Fax Number, Contact Name, Internet Address, and Notes. Assign appropriate data types to all fields, making the Internet Address field a hyperlink field. Use the Search the Web toolbar button to navigate to the Search Page. Type a few keywords related to a career in which you are interested. Find at least four companies that offer opportunities in your selected career and print the Web pages or write down the appropriate information. Enter the information that you found into your new table. Test your hyperlinks to make sure that they jump to the correct sites.

4. Use the Go menu on the Web toolbar to go to the E.span site *(http://www.espan.com)*. Search this site for potential employers who offer positions in your career choice from the previous project. From this information, add at least two employers to the **Job Search** database that you created in Application Project 8-3. Add the E.span home page to your list of bookmarks or favorites.

5. Use the Go menu on the Web toolbar to go to the America's Job Bank site *(http://www.ajb.dni.us)*. Search this site for more potential employers who offer positions in your career choice. Find at least two additional employers and add them to your **Job Search** database. Add the America's Job Bank site to your list of bookmarks or favorites. Write a brief paragraph comparing the E.span site to the America's Job Bank site. Which site did you find more useful? Explain your answer.

6. Return to the E.span site using your list of favorites or bookmarks. Navigate through this site to find tips on resume writing. Then see if you can find any self-assessment tools that might help you in a career search. Print the pages that provide helpful information or take notes as you navigate through the page.

7. Open your **Job Search** database in the **Projects** folder of your Student Data Disk. Create an AutoForm that contains the records and fields in the table containing potential employers. Name the form **Employers AutoForm** and save it. Then save it as a Web page. If Microsoft Excel or Word is available, use it to view your Web page.

FEATURE	MOUSE ACTION	KEYBOARD ACTION	ICON
BASIC SKILLS			
Start Access	Click the Start button, move to Programs, click Microsoft Access		Start
Open a menu	Click menu name on menu bar	Press Alt in combination with underlined letter in menu name	
Close a menu	Click menu name on menu bar or anywhere outside of menu	Esc, Esc	
Open a database	Click File, Open Database	Ctrl+O	
Create a new database	Click File, New Database	Ctrl+N	
Close a dialog box	Click on Cancel or Close	Esc	
Close any window	Click on window's Close button	Ctrl+F4	
Exit Access	Click File, Exit or click Access's Close button	Alt+F4	
Undo previous action	Click Edit, Undo	Ctrl+Z	
GETTING HELP			
Display Help topics	Click Help, Contents and Index, click Contents tab	Alt+H, C	
Use Office Assistant	Click Help, Microsoft Access Help	F1	
Display Screen Tips	Click Help, What's This?	Shift+F1	
Search for Help topics	Click Help, Contents and Index, click Index tab	Alt+H, C	
Exit Help system	Click Close button	Esc	

FEATURE	MOUSE ACTION	KEYBOARD ACTION	ICON
DATABASES AND TABLES			
Create a new database	Click File, New Database	Ctrl+N	
Open a database	Click File, Open Database	Ctrl+O	
Create a new table	Click New button in Table tab of Database window	Alt+I, T	
Display table objects	Click Table tab in Database window	Alt+V, J, T	
Open a table	Select table name, click Open button in Database window	Select table name in Database window, Alt+O	
WORKING IN TABLE DESIGN VIEW			
Modify the table design	Select table name, click Design button in Database window	Select table name in Database window, Alt+D	
Move to next column	Click in desired column	Tab	
Move to previous column	Click in desired column	Shift+Tab	
Switch to and from Field Properties area	Click in desired area of Table Design window	F6	
Select field (row)	Click field selector		
Set primary key	Select field or fields, click Edit, Primary Key	Alt+E, K	
Save table design	Click File, Save	Ctrl+S	
Save table design under new name	Click File, Save As	F12	
Insert row (field)	Click Insert, Rows	Alt+I, R	
Delete row (field)	Click Edit, Delete Rows	Del	
WORKING IN THE DATASHEET			
Move to next field	Click in column	Tab or Enter	
Move to previous field	Click in column	Shift+Tab	
Move to first field in current record	Click in column	Home	
Move to last field in current record	Click in column	End	

FEATURE	MOUSE ACTION	KEYBOARD ACTION	ICON
Move to first field in first record	Click in column	Ctrl+Home	
Move to last field in last record	Click in column	Ctrl+End	
Move to first record	Click Edit, Go To, First	Ctrl+↑	⏮
Move to last record	Click Edit, Go To, Last	Ctrl+↓	⏭
Move to previous record	Click Edit, Go To, Previous	↑	◀
Move to next record	Click Edit, Go To, Next	↓	▶
Move to specific record	Double-click on current record number, enter new record number, and press Enter	F5, enter new record number, and press Enter	
Select all records	Click Edit, Select All Records	Ctrl+A	
Copy data to Clipboard	Click Edit, Copy	Ctrl+C	📋
"Paste append" records from Clipboard into open table	Click Edit, Paste Append	Alt+E, N	
Switch between navigating and editing		F2	
Select record	Click on record selector	Shift+Spacebar (toggle)	
Select column	Click on column selector	Ctrl+Spacebar (toggle)	
Add new record	Click Edit, Go To, New Record	Alt+E, G, W	▶*
Delete record	Click Edit, Delete Record	Select record, Del	✖
Delete character to right of insertion point		Del	
Delete character to left of insertion point		Backspace	
Undo changes to current field	Click Edit, Undo	Esc	↩
Undo changes to current record	Click Edit, Undo	Esc	↩
Undo most recent change	Click Edit, Undo	Ctrl+Z	↩

FEATURE	MOUSE ACTION	KEYBOARD ACTION	ICON
Display Zoom window for adding or editing text		Shift+F2	
Duplicate value in current field from previous record		Ctrl+'	
Open Find dialog box	Click Edit, Find	Ctrl+F	🔍
Open Replace dialog box	Click Edit, Replace	Ctrl+H	
Narrow or widen column	Drag column's left border or choose Format, Column Width	Alt+O, C	
Increase or decrease row height	Drag any border between record selectors or choose Format, Row Height	Alt+O, R	
Move one or more columns	Select column(s). Drag column selector		
Hide columns	Click Format, Hide Columns	Alt+O, H	
Open Unhide Columns dialog box	Click Format, Unhide Columns	Alt+O, U	
Freeze columns	Click Format, Freeze Columns	Alt+O, Z	
Unfreeze columns	Click Format, Unfreeze All Columns	Alt+O, A	

SORTING AND SELECTING RECORDS

FEATURE	MOUSE ACTION	KEYBOARD ACTION	ICON
Sort selected fields in ascending order	Click Records, Sort, Sort Ascending	Alt+R, S, A	A↓Z
Sort selected fields in descending order	Click Records, Sort, Sort Descending	Alt+R, S, C	Z↓A
Open Filter By Form window	Click Records, Filter, Filter By Form	Alt+R, F, F	🗃
Open Advanced Filter/Sort	Click Records, Filter, Advanced Filter/Sort	Alt+R, F, A	

FEATURE	MOUSE ACTION	KEYBOARD ACTION	ICON
Apply filter	Click Records, Apply Filter/Sort	Alt+R, Y	
Remove filter	Click Records, Remove Filter/Sort	Alt+R, R	
Clear selection criteria	Click Edit, Clear Grid	Alt+E, A	
Initiate new query	Click Insert, Query	Alt+I, Q	
Run query	Click Query, Run	Alt+Q, R	
Add tables to existing query	Click Query, Show Table	Alt+Q, T	
Join tables	Drag common field from one Field List to the other		
Delete join	Click join line and press Del		
Switch to Query Design view	Click View, Design view	Alt+V, D	
Switch to Datasheet view	Click View, Datasheet view	Alt+V, S	
Save query	Click File, Save	Ctrl+S	
Save query under new name	Click File, Save As/Export	F12	

BUILDING FORMS

FEATURE	MOUSE ACTION	KEYBOARD ACTION	ICON
Create AutoForm	Click Insert, AutoForm	Alt+I, O	
Move to first record	Click Edit, Go To, First	Ctrl+Home	
Move to last record	Click Edit, Go To, Last	Ctrl+End	
Move to previous record	Click Edit, Go To, Previous	Ctrl+Page Up	
Move to next record	Click Edit, Go To, Next	Ctrl+Page Down	
Move to specific record	Highlight current record number, enter new record number, and press Enter	F5, enter new record number, and press Enter	
Switch to Datasheet view	Click View, Datasheet view	Alt+V, S	

FEATURE	MOUSE ACTION	KEYBOARD ACTION	ICON
Switch to Form view	Click View, Form view	Alt +V, F	
Switch to Design view	Click View, Design View	Alt +V, D	
Save form	Click File, Save	Ctrl +S	
Add new record to form	Click Edit, Go To, New Record	Alt +E, G, W	
Preview form	Click File, Print Preview	Alt +F, V	
Close Print Preview	Click View, Form View	Alt +V, F	Close
Print form	Click File, Print	Ctrl +P	

CREATING REPORTS

FEATURE	MOUSE ACTION	KEYBOARD ACTION	ICON
Create AutoReport	Click Insert, AutoReport	Alt +I, E	
Move to specific page	Double-click current page number, enter new page number, and press Enter	F5 , enter new page number, and press Enter	
Zoom display in or out	Click on report	Alt +V, Z	
Save report	Click File, Save	Ctrl +S	
View report in Print Preview	Click View, Print Preview	Alt +V, V	
View report in Design view	Click View, Design View	Alt +V, D	
Print report	Click File, Print	Ctrl +P	
Close report in Print Preview	Click Close button	Ctrl + F4	Close

WORKING IN FORM OR REPORT DESIGN VIEW

FEATURE	MOUSE ACTION	KEYBOARD ACTION	ICON
Select control	Click control		
Select multiple controls	Shift + click controls		
Select all controls	Click Edit, Select All	Ctrl +A	
Deselect single control	Shift + click control or click away from the control		

FEATURE	MOUSE ACTION	KEYBOARD ACTION	ICON
Deselect all controls	Click away from all controls		
Display or hide toolbox	Click View, Toolbox	Alt+V, O	🛠
Display or hide rulers	Click View, Ruler	Alt+V, R	
Display or hide grid	Click View, Grid	Alt+V, G	
Turn on Snap to Grid feature	Click Format, Snap to Grid	Alt+O, N	
Display Tab Order dialog box for a form	Click View, Tab Order	Alt+V, B	
Display list of available fonts	Click the Font drop-down list arrow in toolbar		
Display list of available font sizes	Click the Font Size drop-down list arrow in toolbar		
Boldface text in selected control			**B**
Italicize text in selected control			*I*

ESTABLISH TABLE RELATIONSHIPS

FEATURE	MOUSE ACTION	KEYBOARD ACTION	ICON
Set up table relationships	Click Tools, Relationships	Alt+T, R	🔗
Edit table relationships	Double-click the join line	Alt+T, R	

WORKING WITH HYPERLINKS AND THE WEB

FEATURE	MOUSE ACTION	KEYBOARD ACTION	ICON
Display Web toolbar	Click View, Toolbars, Web	Alt+V, T, select Web	🌐
Create hyperlink	Click Insert, Hyperlink	Alt+I, I	🌐
Go to a Web site	On the Web toolbar, click Go, Open	Alt+G, O	
Go to the Search Page	On the Web toolbar, click Go, Search the Web	Alt+G, W	🔍
Go to the Start Page	On the Web toolbar, click Go, Start Page	Alt+G, S	🏠

FEATURE	MOUSE ACTION	KEYBOARD ACTION	ICON
Set a bookmark or favorite place	On the Web toolbar, click Favorites, Add to Favorites		
Go to a bookmark or favorite place	On the Web toolbar, click Favorites, click name of favorite place or bookmark from drop-down list		
Create your own Web page	Click File, Save As HTML	Alt +F, H	
Stop current connection			

GLOSSARY

action An instruction or command that you can combine with other instructions in a macro to automate a task.

ascending sort A sort that arranges letters from A to Z, numbers from smallest to largest, and dates from earliest to most recent.

AutoForm A form that Access builds for you automatically; the AutoForm gathers the information it needs by examining the selected table or query.

AutoReport A report that Access builds for you automatically, based on the selected table or query.

bookmarks Tools used to provide a shortcut to the location of a specific Web site or document so that you can return to it later without typing its address. Also called *favorites*.

browser A software program that allows you to navigate the World Wide Web and access information on the Internet. Popular browsers are Netscape and Microsoft Internet Explorer.

captions Words or phrases used to abbreviate or clarify field names. Captions are used as labels in forms and tables.

Cascading Deletes A feature that causes Access to automatically delete any affiliated records from a related table when you delete a record from the primary table.

Cascading Updates A feature that causes Access to automatically update the associated field in any related table records when you modify the primary key field in a primary table record.

click A mouse action in which you move the mouse until the mouse pointer is located over the desired option or item and then press and quickly release the left mouse button.

Clipboard A temporary storage area in your computer's memory.

columnar form A form that displays each field on a separate line with field labels or captions to their left as identifiers.

columnar report A report that displays all fields in a single column with field labels or captions to their left as identifiers.

common field A field that has the same name and data type as a field in one or more other tables. You need to set up common fields in preparation for sharing data between tables. The common field is what lets Access find matching data in different tables.

comparison operator A symbol that is used to compare a value or text in the table to characters that you enter.

continuous The process that feeds into a printer pages of paper attached to each other, as in the paper used by most dot-matrix printers.

controls Form or report elements that display data, perform actions, or decorate the form or report. You can manipulate controls in Design view.

current record The record that is active. In Datasheet view, the current record is the row that contains a triangle or pencil icon in the record selector.

data type A designation that determines the type of data that can be entered into a field, such as text, numbers, and dates.

database An organized collection of information about similar entities. In Access, database also means a collection of objects—such as reports, forms, tables, and queries—associated with a particular topic.

Database window A window that lets you gain access to all the objects (tables, forms, reports, queries, and so on) in a particular database.

datasheet A tabular layout of rows and columns that allows you to add, edit, and view your data immediately.

DBMS (database management system) A system for storing and manipulating the data in a database.

default value A field property that uses the specified value for new records.

descending sort   A sort that arranges letters from Z to A, numbers from largest to smallest, and dates from most recent to the earliest.

Design view   A view that permits you to set up and modify the structure and appearance of tables, queries, forms, reports, macros, and modules.

dialog box   A special type of window that requests further information needed before a command can be executed.

ditto key   The Ctrl+' key combination, which repeats the value from the same field in the previous record.

double-click   A mouse action in which you press and quickly release the left mouse button twice in rapid succession with the mouse pointer over your selection.

expression   A combination of field names, values, and comparison operators that can be evaluated as criteria for most types of filters.

favorites   Tools used to provide a shortcut to the location of a specific Web site or document so that you can return to it later without typing its address. Also called *bookmarks*.

Field list   A small window that lists all of the fields in a table or query. You can select fields to include in a filter or query from the Field list.

field properties   Field settings that control the way a field looks and behaves.

fields   Columns in a table that contain categories of data.

filter   A way of displaying your data to see only a selected portion of it.

footer   Text that appears at the bottom of every printed page in a report.

foreign key   A field in a related table that has the same name and data type as the primary key in the primary table.

forms   Screens that present a custom layout for your data, enabling you to view, edit, and enter the data from your tables.

freeze   An option that lets you make columns permanently visible on the screen.

glossary term   An underlined word or phrase in the Help system that shows you the definition of the word or phrase when you click it.

grid lines   A set of lines in Design view that lets you precisely align the data in your form or report.

groups   Categories of information from the table or query that you can use to arrange records and show subtotals in a report.

handles   A set of boxes that encloses a control in a form or report when you're in Design view to indicate that the control is selected. These handles enable you to change the control's size and location.

header   Text information that is repeated at the top of every page in a report.

hot key   Underlined letter in menu or option names that you use to select that option. Press the hot key in combination with Alt to open a menu; then press the hot key by itself to choose an option within a menu.

hyperlink   A shortcut, or jump, that links you directly to another object, document, or Web site.

Hypertext Markup Language   A system for tagging a document so that it can be published and viewed by others on the Web.

import   The operation in which data from outside of the database is brought into the database.

insertion point   A vertical line in a text box that lets you see where characters will be inserted when you type them from the keyboard.

join   A method of notifying Access how to match up records from one table with the appropriate records from any other tables.

jump   An icon that enables you to "jump" to another related Help window.

keyboard shortcuts   A way of using the keyboard to execute a command without going through the menu system. Usually a combination of Ctrl plus one letter keystroke.

keyword   Word or phrase used to define and narrow a search.

landscape orientation   A method of printing a report across the length of the page or horizontally.

macro   A set of one or more actions that you can use to automate a task.

mailing labels   Sets of names and addresses or other information that you can gather from tables or queries and print for mass mailings and the like.

main form   One form that includes another form, called the subform. The subform is linked to the main form. The main form has a one-to-many relationship with the subform.

many-to-many relationship   A relationship between tables in which each record in each table may have many matches in the other.

menu bar   Bar below the title bar that lists the names of the available menus.

module   A set of programmed statements that are stored together as a unit; a module is used to automate a task.

move handles   Handles that are used to drag a control to another location in Design view.

objects   The major components of Access, including tables, queries, forms, reports, macros, and modules.

Object tabs   A set of tabs across the top of the Database window that represents the types of objects available in Access.

Office Assistant   An animated character that can answer specific questions, offer tips, and provide Help for Access features.

one-to-many relationship   A relationship between two tables in which each record in the primary table can have no records, one record, or many matching records in the related table, but every record in the related table has one—and only one—associated record in the primary table.

one-to-one relationship   A relationship between two tables in which every record in each table can have either no matching records or only a single matching record in the other table.

online   The status of a printer when it is ready to accept output from your computer.

orphan records   Records in a related table with no associated record in the primary table.

portrait orientation   A method of printing a report across the width of the page or vertically.

primary key   A field or set of fields that uniquely identifies each record in the table.

primary table   A table in a one-to-many relationship that can have zero, one, or many matching records in the related table; but every record in the related table has exactly one matching record in the primary table. You can think of a primary table as the "one" side in a one-to-many relationship.

properties   The characteristics of a particular field, table, or database.

query   A question to the database, asking for a set of records from one or more tables or other queries that meets specific criteria.

query design grid   The grid in the Query Design view window that you use to make decisions about how to sort and select your data and which fields to include in the Recordset.

records   Rows in a table that contain the set of fields for one particular entity.

record selector   The box to the left of a record that you can click to select the entire record.

Recordset   A subset of your data sorted and selected as specified by a query. Recordsets change to reflect modifications to the data in your tables, and you can often make changes to Recordsets that are reflected in the underlying table(s).

referential integrity   A set of rules that Access can enforce to preserve the defined relationship between tables.

related table   A table in a one-to-many relationship in which every record has exactly one matching record in the primary table. Also known as a *foreign table*.

relational databases   Database programs that let you link two or more tables in order to share data between them.

reports   Database objects that permit you to produce polished printed output of the data from tables or queries. Some Access reports automatically generate totals and grand totals of the values in particular fields.

reverse video   White text against a dark background.

right-click   A mouse action in which you press and quickly release the right mouse button.

root folder   The main folder in a disk. Every folder and file is located within the root folder.

row selector   A small box to the left of a field (in Table Design view) that you can click to select the entire field.

save   To take information from your computer's memory and store it on a more permanent medium —usually a floppy disk or a hard drive.

ScreenTips   Text boxes that appear on the screen showing the name and description of various elements on the Access screen.

scroll bars   Shaded bars along the bottom and right side of a window used to view hidden portions of a document.

search engine   An Internet tool that allows you to search for information on a particular topic.

sections   Areas of a report or form. Can be a Report or Form Header, Report or Form Footer, Page Header, Page Footer, Group Header, Group Footer, or Detail section.

select   To choose an item to indicate to Access that you want to operate on that particular item. Alternatively, select can mean to extract specified subsets of data based on criteria that you define.

select queries   Queries that you can use to sort, select, and view records from one or more tables.

selection criteria   Instructions that tell Access exactly which records you want to extract from the database.

sheet feed   The process that feeds paper into a printer one sheet at a time, such as with inkjet and laser printers.

sizing handles   Handles that are used to enlarge or reduce the size of a control in Design view.

Snap to Grid   An option in Design view that limits the freedom of dragging to predefined intervals.

sort   To rearrange records into alphabetical, numerical, or chronological order.

subform   A form within a form. The subform has a many-to-one relationship with the main form.

tab order   The order in which Access moves from field to field when you press Tab.

tables   Receptacles for data organized into a series of columns (fields) and rows (records).

tabular form   A form that displays all of the fields for a single record in one row, field names or captions as column headings, and data in the table or query as a tabular arrangement of rows and columns.

tabular report   A report that displays the fields for a single record in one row, field names or captions as column headings, and all data in the table or query as a tabular arrangement of rows and columns.

toggle key   A key that turns on a function when you press it and turns off the function when you press it again. Examples include Num Lock and Caps Lock.

toolbar   A row of graphical buttons for executing common commands quickly.

ToolTip   The name of a toolbar button displayed immediately below the toolbar when the mouse pointer is placed over the button.

URL   The address used to identify a Web site. Stands for *Uniform Resource Locator*.

wildcard character   A character used in searches and filters to find a variable string of characters. For instance, *we** would find all words that start with *we,* such as *weather, well,* and *weekday.*

Wizard   An Access tool that guides you through the process of creating tables, queries, forms, or reports. A Wizard prompts you with questions about the object you are creating and builds the object based on the answers you supply.

World Wide Web   A widely used tool to navigate the Internet. Also known as the *Web.*

WYSIWYG   On-screen view or preview that closely resembles the final printed output. WYSIWYG is computer jargon for "what you see is what you get."

A

Access
    exiting, 32
    initial dialog box, 7
    learning your way around, 8-14
    menus, 9
    quitting, 31
    screen, 8
    starting, 5
    startup window, 7
accessing the Search Page, 247
action, 23, 270
adding
    and deleting fields from query design view, 126
    and editing data by use of forms, 150-152
    and removing fields, 62
    captions to fields, 61
    data to a table, 71-76
    data using a form, 150
    information with the ditto key, 88
    record(s), 73-75
    totals and subtotals to a report, 178
adjusting header widths and Detail controls, 210
Advanced Filter/Sort method, using the, 117
aligning headings, 213
Apply Filter toolbar button, 112
arranging fields on mailing labels, 182
ascending sort, 106, 270
AutoForm, 140, 270
    creating an, 140-143
    exploring an, 140
AutoNumber fields, 53
AutoReport, 163, 270
    creating an, 163-167
    exploring an, 164

B

Back toolbar button, 230
blank data, querying for, 132
Bold toolbar button, 200
bookmarks, 250, 270
browser, 247, 270
building a multi-table query, 129
Byte number type, 55

C

canceling changes to the datasheet layout, 97
Caption field property, 57
captions, 61, 270
Cascading Deletes, 219, 270
Cascading Updates, 219, 270
Center toolbar button, 213
changing
    appearance of a label, 199
    column widths, 92
    datasheet display, 91-97
    detail controls in Design view, 201
    field properties, 57
    margins for a report, 209
    order of fields, 94

    Page Footer, 209
    Report Header, 209
    row heights, 93
    tab order, 204
choosing a primary key, 58
Clear Grid toolbar button, 113
click, 5, 270
Clipboard, 78, 270
column widths, changing the, 92
columnar form, 143, 270
    creating with the Form Wizard, 143
columnar report, 168, 270
    creating with the Report Wizard, 168
columns
    displaying hidden (unhiding), 95
    hiding, 95
Command Button dialog box, 242
command button hyperlink, creating, 240
commands, summary of, 262-269
common field, 42, 270
comparison operator(s), 118, 270
    table of, 118
Contents tab, using the, 26-28
continuous, 181, 270
controls, 199, 270
copying
    data from another table, 77
    tables from another database, 80-81
creating
    AutoForm, 140-143
    AutoReport, 163-167
    columnar form with the Form Wizard, 143
    columnar report with the Report Wizard, 168
    command button hyperlink, 240
    database, 42-43
    hyperlinks, 231-246
    main forms and subforms, 220-222
    tables, 44-52
    tabular form(s) with the Form Wizard, 148
    tabular reports, 172
    text hyperlink, 236
    totals in reports, 176-179
    Web page, 252-255
Currency fields, 53
current record, 72, 270

D

data
    adding to a table, 71-76
    copying from another table, 77
    pasting into a table, 78
    retrieving from another table, 76-80
database, 3, 270
    copying tables from another, 80-81
    creating a, 42
    linking to another, 236
    opening, 15
    planning a, 39-42
    table, 16
Database window, 16, 270

datasheet, 71, 270
    display, changing the, 91-97
    editing and viewing records in the, 81-88
Datasheet view, switching from Form to, 147
data type, 52, 270
Date/Time fields, 53
DBMS, 3, 270
Decimal Places field property, 56
Default Value field property, 57
Delete Record toolbar button, 86
deleting records under referential integrity, 218
descending sort, 106, 271
Design view, 18, 271
    changing detail controls in, 201
    modifying forms in, 193-208
    modifying reports in, 208-214
    resizing controls in, 201
    resizing lines in, 212
    sections in, 193
    viewing a report in, 208
    working in, 195
designing basic queries, 121-129
Detail section, 194
    modifying the appearance of the, 205
dialog box, 11, 271
    Command Button, 242
    common features, 11
    Insert Hyperlink, 233
    Insert Picture, 242
    Label, 238
    Open Internet Address, 246
    Open, 10
    Relationships, 216
    Save As, 60
    Tab Order, 205
displaying hidden columns (unhiding), 95
ditto key, 88, 271
Double number type, 56
double-click, 6, 271
duplicate information using the ditto key, 88

E

editing
    and viewing records in the datasheet, 81-88
    in the Zoom window, 87
    records using a form, 151
    records, 84
    relationship(s), 217
exiting Access, 32
exploring
    an Autoform, 140
    the Web toolbar, 229-231
expression, 117, 271

F

favorite places, revisiting on the Web, 250
favorites, 250, 271
Favorites menu toolbar button, 230
Field list, 118, 271
field properties, 56, 271
    changing, 57
fields, 4, 271
    adding and removing, 62
    moving, 63
field sizes, picking, 55

File menu, 9
Fill/Back Color toolbar button, 207
Filter By Form method, using the, 111
Filter By Form toolbar button, 111
Filter By Selection method, using the, 109
Filter By Selection toolbar button, 109
Filter For Input method, using the, 116
filter, 105, 271
filtering
    data, 109-121
    for records that meet multiple criteria, 115
    for records that meet one of several values, 113
    records within a range, 120
Find tab, using the, 29-30
Find toolbar button, 88
finding values in a table, 88
First Record navigation button, 83
Font Size toolbar button, 200
Font toolbar button, 200
Font/Fore Color toolbar button, 200
footer, 163, 271
foreign key, 215, 271
Form Footer, 194
Form Header, 194
Form view, switching to Datasheet view from, 147
Form Wizard
    creating a columnar form with, 143
    creating a tabular form with, 148
form(s), 20, 271
    adding data using a, 150
    editing records using a, 151
    generating a printout of a, 156
    previewing and printing, 156-157
    selecting records through a, 154
    sorting records through a, 153
    when and why to use, 139
Format field property, 56
Formatting toolbar, 200
Forward toolbar button, 230
freeze, 96, 271
freezing columns, 96

G

generating
    a printout of a form, 156
    mailing labels, 180-184
glossary term, 27, 271
Go menu, 246
Go menu toolbar button, 230
grid lines, 195, 271
Group Footer, 194
Group Header, 194
Grouping Intervals dialog box, 177
Grouping Options button, 177
grouping records in a tabular report, 173
groups, 173, 271

H

handles, 199, 271
header, 163, 271
headings, aligning, 213
Help system, 24-31
    Contents and Index, using the, 26-30
    Office Assistant, using the, 24-26
hiding columns, 95

hot key, 8, 271
Hyperlink fields, 53
hyperlink(s), 231, 271
    creating, 231-246
    creating a command button, 240
    creating a text, 236
Hypertext Markup Language, 252, 271

I

identifying relationships between tables, 214
Image toolbar button, 242
import, 80, 271
importing a table, 80
Index tab, using the, 28-29
Input Mask field property, 57
Insert Hyperlink
    dialog box, 233
    toolbar button, 232
Insert Picture dialog box, 242
insertion point, 50, 271
Integer number type, 55
introducing databases, 3-4
italic toolbar button, 209

J

join, 129, 271
join line
    when building a multi-table query, 130
    when editing a relationship, 217
jump, 27, 271

K

keyboard shortcuts, 10, 271
keyword, 248, 271

L

label box, creating a, 198
Label button, 197
Label dialog box, 238
Label Wizard, 180
landscape orientation, 170, 272
Last Record navigation button, 82
learning your way around Access, 8-14
Line/Border Color toolbar button, 206
Line/Border Width toolbar button, 206
linking
    to another database, 236
    to another object, 231
    to a Web site, 244
Long Integer number type, 55
Lookup Wizard fields, 53

M

macro, 23, 272
mailing labels, 22, 272
    arranging fields on, 182
    orms and appearance, selecting, 180
    generating, 180-184
    printing, 184-185
    sorting, 183
main form, 220, 272
main forms and subforms, creating, 220-222
maintaining referential integrity, 219
many-to-many relationship, 215, 272

margins, changing for a report, 209
Memo fields, 52
menu bar, 8, 272
menus
    issuing commands by using the, 8
    table of, 9
Microsoft Windows 95 desktop, 5
modifying
    and saving a query, 125
    appearance of the Detail section, 205
    forms in Design view, 193-208
    reports in Design view, 208-214
    table design, 60-64
module, 23, 272
mouse actions
    click, 5
    double-click, 6
    right-click, 6
move handles, 199, 272
moving
    a field, 63
    from field to field, 83
    from record to record, 82
Multiple Pages toolbar button, 157
multiple tables
    querying, 129-133
    working with, 214-220
multi-table query, building a, 129

N

navigating on the Web, 246-252
navigation buttons, 82
New Object toolbar button, 129
Next Record navigation button, 83
Number fields, 52, 55
number types, 55-56

O

Object tabs, 16, 272
objects, 16, 272
Office Assistant, 24-26, 272
OLE Object fields, 53
one-to-many relationship, 214, 272
    creating a, 215
one-to-one relationship, 214, 272
online, 23, 272
Open dialog box, 10, 12
Open Internet Address dialog box, 246
opening
    a database, 15-16
    a saved query, 128
    a table, 71
order of fields, changing the, 94
orphan records, 216, 272

P

Page Footer, 194
    changing the, 209
Page Header, 194
pasting data into a table, 78
planning a database, 39-42
    categories of information, determining the, 40
    how tables work together, determining, 41
    number of tables needed, determining the, 40

purpose of a database, determining the, 39
portrait orientation, 170, 272
previewing and printing forms, 156-157
Previous Record navigation button, 83
primary key, 42, 272
    choosing a, 58
    setting the, 58
primary table, 214-215, 272
Print Preview toolbar button, 156
Print toolbar button, 157
printing
    an Access report, 23
    reports and mailing labels, 184-185
Properties toolbar button, 238
properties, 52, 272
Publish to the Web Wizard, 253
publishing your Web page, 256

Q

queries, designing basic, 121-129
query design grid, 122, 272
query design view, adding and deleting fields from, 126
query, 19, 272
    building a multi-table, 129
    modifying and saving a, 125
    opening a saved, 128
    setting up a simple, 122
querying
    for blank data, 132
    multiple tables, 129-133
quitting Access, 31-32

R

record(s), 4, 272
    adding, 73-75
    searching for, based on their contents, 88-91
record selector, 72, 272
Recordset, 122, 272
referential integrity, 216, 272
    deleting records under, 218
    maintaining, 219
    understanding, 216
Refresh Current Page toolbar button, 230
related table, 215, 272
relational databases, 4, 272
Relationships dialog box, 216
Relationships toolbar button, 215
relationship(s)
    editing, 217
    identifying between tables, 214
Remove Filter toolbar button, 110
repeat information using the ditto key, 88
replacing values in a table, 90
Replication ID number type, 56
Report Footer, 194
Report Header, 194
    changing the, 209
Report Wizard
    creating a columnar report with, 168
    using the, 168-176
report(s), 22, 272
    adding totals and subtotals to a, 178
    creating totals in a, 176-179
    printing, 184-185

viewing pages in a, 166
    when and why to use, 163
Required field property, 57
resizing
    controls in Design view, 201
    lines in Design view, 212
retrieving data from another table, 76-80
reverse video, 84, 273
revisiting favorite places on the Web, 250
right-click, 6, 273
root folder, 12, 273
row heights, changing the, 93
row selector, 58, 273
Run toolbar button, 124

S

save, 59, 273
Save As dialog box, 60
Save As HTML option, 253
saving the table design, 59-60
ScreenTips, 30, 273
    using the, 30-31
scroll bars, 17, 273
search (find) and replace records, 88-91
search engine, 248, 273
Search Page, accessing the, 247
Search the Web toolbar button, 230
searching for records based on their contents, 88-91
sections, 194, 273
sections in Design view, 193
select, 84, 105, 273
select queries, 122, 273
selecting
    data types, 52-55
    form controls, 199
    mailing label forms and appearance, 180
    records through a form, 154
selection criteria, 111, 273
setting
    field properties, 56-57
    primary key, 58
setting up a simple query, 122
sheet feed, 181, 273
Show Only Web Toolbar button, 231
Show Table toolbar button, 130
Single number type, 56
sizing handles, 199, 273
Snap to Grid, 195, 273
sort, 105, 273
Sort Ascending toolbar button, 107
Sort commands, using the, 106-108
Sort Descending toolbar button, 108
sorting
    and selecting data with forms, 153-155
    and selecting data, 105
    mailing labels, 183
    records through a form, 153
Special Effects toolbar button, 206
Start Page toolbar button, 230
starting Microsoft Access, 5-7
Stop Current Jump toolbar button, 230
subform, 220, 273
Summary Options button, 178
switching from Form to Datasheet view, 147

T

Tab Order dialog box, 205
tab order, 204, 273
    changing the, 204
table design
    modifying the, 60-64
    saving the, 59-60
Table Wizard, using the, 44-49
table(s), 4, 273
    adding to a, 71-76
    copying data from another, 77
    copying from another database, 80-81
    creating, 44-52
    importing, 80
    opening a, 71
    pasting data into a, 78
    querying multiple, 129-133
    retrieving data from another, 76-80
    sorting your, 106
tabular form, 148, 273
    creating with the Form Wizard, 148
tabular report, 172, 273
    creating, 172
    grouping records in a, 173
Text fields, 52
text hyperlink, creating, 236
toggle key, 8, 273
toolbar, 12, 273
    buttons, table of, 13
    command shortcuts for mouse users, 12
    standard, for Access, 13
    using the, 14
toolbox, using the, 197
Toolbox toolbar button, 197
ToolTip, 13, 273
totals in reports, creating, 176-179
Two Pages toolbar button, 157

U

Undo toolbar button, 85
undoing
    changes to a saved record, 86
    editing mistakes, 85
unhiding (displaying hidden) columns, 95
Uniform Resource Locator, 245
URL, 245, 273
using the Report Wizard, 168-176

V

View toolbar button, 125
viewing
    pages in a report, 166
    report in Design view, 208
visiting a Web site, 246

W

Web page
    creating your own, 252-255
    publishing your, 256
Web site
    linking to a, 244
    visiting, 246
Web toolbar, exploring the, 229-231
Web Toolbar toolbar button, 229
Web, 229
    navigating on the, 246-252
wildcard character, 116
Windows 95 Programs menu, 6
Wizard, 44, 273
World Wide Web, 229, 273
WYSIWYG, 22, 273

Y

Yes/No fields, 53

Z

Zoom toolbar button, 164
Zoom window, editing in the, 87